Robert Frost
Among His Poems

To Julia R. Berkley,
who has shown

That life is only life forevermore
Together wing to wing and oar to oar

Robert Frost Among His Poems

A Literary Companion to the Poet's Own Biographical Contexts and Associations

by JEFFREY S. CRAMER

McFarland & Company, Inc., Publishers
Jefferson, North Carolina, and London

The present work is a reprint of the library bound edition of Robert Frost Among His Poems: A Literary Companion to the Poet's Own Biographical Contexts and Associations, *first published in 1996 by McFarland.*

LIBRARY OF CONGRESS CATALOGUING-IN-PUBLICATION DATA

Cramer, Jefffrey, S., 1955–
Robert Frost among his poems : a literary companion to the poet's own biographical contexts and associations / by Jeffrey S. Cramer.
p. cm.
Includes bibliographical references and index.

ISBN-13: 978-0-7864-3090-1
softcover : 50# alkaline paper ∞

1. Frost, Robert, 1874–1963. 2. Poets, American — 20th century — Biography. 3. Frost, Robert, 1874–1963 — Bibliography. 4. Autobiography in literature. 5. Self in literature. I. Title.
PS3511.R94Z6115 2007
811'.52 — dc20
[B] 95-39536

British Library cataloguing data are available

Manufactured in the United States of America

McFarland & Company, Inc., Publishers
Box 611, Jefferson, North Carolina 28640
www.mcfarlandpub.com

CONTENTS

The thing is to get among the poems...

—Robert Frost, "The Prerequisites"

ACKNOWLEDGMENTS

Many people and institutions contributed knowingly and unknowingly to this book.

I gratefully acknowledge the assistance of the following individuals, who have given help in a variety of ways: Andrew J. Angyal; Philip Cronenwett of the Dartmouth College Library; Alfred Kazin; Edward Connery Lathem; Dan Lombardo of the Jones Library, Amherst; Earl Wilcox.

I would also like to thank my colleagues and friends who have offered their assistance: Bill Grealish and Nancy R. Browne of the Boston Public Library; Joseph A. Horn for his help with Greek and Latin sources; Dennis Lien and Terry A. Garey; Stephen L. Glass; Michael P. Palmer, Claremont, California; Thomas Jenkins; Austin Meredith and the "Stack of the Artist of Kouroo" Project.

I am grateful to the following people and institutions for providing me with photocopies of material: the Derry (New Hampshire) Public Library; the Robert Frost Memorial Library, Amherst College; the Huntington Library; Mugar Library, Boston University; the New Hampshire State Library; the Inter-Library Loan Department of the Boston Public Library; Olive M. Abbott, alumni historian, Pinkerton Academy; June Payne of the John Fitzgerald Kennedy Library; Cynthia T. Richmond of the McCain Library, Agnes Scott College; James McCarthy of Harvard University Archives.

A great debt is owed to William O'Donnell, of the University of Massachusetts, Amherst, who first introduced me to a Frost beyond "The Road Not Taken."

I must also pay my debt to the many scholars and researchers who have come before me and provided information that was useful in annotating the poems and identifying sources. Their work truly laid the foundation for this book.

To the Boston Public Library I am grateful for permitting me a certain flexibility in my schedule which allowed me to reach my deadline.

Finally, I thank my wife, Julia Berkley, and our two daughters, Kazia and Zoë Berkley-Cramer, for allowing me to steal away moments destined for them but devoted to Frost.

Grateful acknowledgment is made to the following:

State University of New York Press for permission to quote from (1) Robert Newdick's *Newdick's Season of Frost: An Interrupted Biography of Robert Frost*, © 1976 State University of New York; (2) Lesley Frost's *New Hampshire's Child: The Derry Journals of Lesley Frost*, © 1969 State University of New York; and (3) Arnold Grade's *Family Letters of Robert and Elinor Frost*, © 1972 State University of New York.

Earl Wilcox and *The Robert Frost Review* for permission to reprint part two of this book, a revision of what originally appeared as "Forgotten Frost: A Study of the Uncollected and Unpublished Poetry of Robert Frost" in *The Robert Frost Review* (1992 and 1993).

CNA Associates for permission to quote from *The Pilgrim Spirit: A Pageant in Celebration of the Tercentenary of the Landing of the Pilgrims at Plymouth, Massachusetts, December 21, 1620*, written and produced by George P. Baker for the Pilgrim Tercentenary Commission of Massachusetts (Boston: Marshall Jones Co., 1921).

The University of Oklahoma Press for permission to quote from Louis Mertin's *Robert Frost: Life and Talks-Walking*, © 1965 by the University of Oklahoma Press.

The University of Massachusetts Press for permission to quote from *Frost: A Time To Talk: Conversations & Indiscretions* recorded by Robert Francis (Amherst: University of Massachusetts Press, 1972), © 1972 by Robert Francis.

The University Press of New England for permission to quote (1) Robert Francis's "Apple Peeler," reprinted from *The Orb Weaver*, © 1960 by Robert Francis, Wesleyan University Press, by permission of University Press of New England; and (2) from William R. Evans's *Robert Frost and Sidney Cox: Forty Years of Friendship*, © 1981 by the Trustees of Dartmouth College.

Yale University Press for permission to quote the sestet beginning, "A man is as tall as his height..." used to advertise Thomas Hornsby Ferril's *Westering* (New Haven, Conn., Yale University Press, 1934).

Barbara Holden Yeomans and Dartmouth College for permission to quote from "Reminiscences of Robert Frost."

INTRODUCTION

Robert Frost Among His Poems is intended to provide information crucial to an understanding of a body of work often misunderstood. As Frost expressed it in "The Fear of Man":

> May I in my brief bolt across the scene
> Not be misunderstood in what I mean.

Yet despite this fear, and his annoyance at critics who would "outrage" his poems, Frost was not always helpful. Often he was playfully misleading, like the guide in "Directive" who "only has at heart your getting lost." Biographers and critics would sometimes give conflicting stories about the origin of a particular poem while claiming Frost as their ultimate source.

While often expressing his aversion to footnotes and annotations, Frost never really forbad anyone entrance to the hidden world behind his poems. As he wrote in "Kitty Hawk":

> Have no hallowing fears
>   Anything's forbidden
> Just because it's hidden.

For Frost, the poet's meaning is the poem's meaning. Other interpretations were simply not as valid. "I once made a resolve," Frost said, "never to put any book to any use it wasn't intended for by its author" [58:30]. And again, "You can't trust these fellows who write what made a poet write what he wrote. We all of us read our pet theories into a poem" [103:81-82].

Although he wrote that "It would be hard to gather biography from poems of mine except as they were all written by the same person, out of the same general region north of Boston, and out of the same books, a few Greek and Latin, practically no others in any other tongue than our own" [66:500], Frost admitted that his poems "were built on incidents and are therefore autobiographical. [...] It is all fact—no fancy, but lots of teasing. [...] Some of the poems combine many incidents, many people and places, but all are real" [103:72].

In some cases Frost's poems were answers to an unfinished argument or a response to another poet's poem. As Frost said during an interview, "I could probably name twenty or thirty poems that were just answers to somebody that had [...] left me unsatisfied with the last thing he said in an argument" [51:174].

In Part One, this commentary attempts to identify Frost's intentions by placing each poem into the biographical, historical and geographical context of his life and time; by identifying conscious and unconscious points of association; by annotating words and phrases; and by dating, where possible, the composition of each poem and giving the place of first publication. Part One follows the arrangement of the poems as published in *The Poetry of Robert Frost* (1969).

Part Two consists of an annotated bibliography of those poems which Frost had published in his lifetime which remained uncollected at the time of his death, along with those poems which were published posthumously or have remained unpublished.

When *The Poetry of Robert Frost* was published in 1969, it was the intention of the publisher, Holt, Rinehart and Winston, to publish only those poems which Frost had included in his previous volumes. It was not their intention to include any of the poems that Frost had left either uncollected or unpublished at the time of his death. Yet beyond the 345 poems in the collected edition, there is a corpus of over 100 relatively unknown poems—a quarter of Robert Frost's entire poetic output—which has been ignored.

Since Frost's death in 1963, more than 60 poems have been posthumously published. There still remain, however, more than 30 unknown poems; poems which, because they have remained unpublished, are, in effect, ignored as an area of study. In his essay, "The Prerequisites," Frost wrote, "We read A the better to read B (we have to start somewhere; we may get very little out of A). We read B the better to read C, C the better to read D, D the better to go back and get something more out of A. Progress is not the aim, but circulation. The thing is to get among the poems [...]." With Frost's poetry such circulation is impossible given the unavailability of such a large portion of his work.

If one could get among all the poems, one would find that an image in "The Offer" was reworked in "The Wind and the Rain"; or that "Immigrants" from *West-Running Brook* was originally published as part of his 1920 poem "Return of the Pilgrim"; or that "Winter Ownership" contains language which anticipates "The Gift Outright."

No attempt has been made to offer a definitive bibliography of those poems which, at the time of his death, Frost had left unpublished. Fragments, inscriptions, occasional poems and manuscripts will continue to turn up until all Frost items in private collections find their way into public and university libraries. Yet there is a wealth of material already available to the student and scholar in many sources (most no longer in print)—scattered in periodicals, Frost collections in various libraries, biographies, collections of letters—which, brought together, would serve the student well for the many years it will take before a truly definitive edition of the poetry could reasonably be made available.

For the uncollected and posthumously published poetry, this study will provide either a brief description of each poem or the poem itself, including its date of composition and publication history. For the unpublished poetry, a brief description of the subject matter of each poem will be provided, along with its length and rhyme scheme, probable date of composition, the collection in which it is housed, and, if available, its catalog number.

For the sake of consistency, the following terminology has been employed: "published" for poems published during Frost's lifetime; "printed" for posthumously published works; and "reprinted" for subsequent printings. The arrangement in Part Two will be chronological by date of composition if it can be determined or by date of publication.

When it comes to dating Frost's poems, the poet himself often gave conflicting dates. This sometimes stemmed from his confusing the date of composition with the date of publication in either periodical or book form, or his choosing one time the date of a poem's inception and another time its completion, or simply from the fact that the poet was attempting to date a poem thirty years after he wrote it. Where conflicting dates have been found every possible means has been used to determine the correct one. Otherwise, all dates are given with their respective sources.

Frost's prose, both written and oral, has been quoted where it offers insight on particular poems. For the reason of limitations of space and so that this work may remain as close as possible to Frost's own word on his poetry, critical commentary herein has been minimized.

All editorial deletions from printed texts have been indicated by bracketed ellipses; nonbracketed ellipses are from the quoted text. The correction of typographical errors and, in the interest of consistency of treatment throughout this volume (where the many sources quoted were prepared under quite variant editorial policies), the necessary restyling of punctuation has been effected without special indication. In any circumstance where such a correction could cause a different interpretation, the original punctuation or spelling was retained.

References will be found incorporated into the body of the text using bracketed numerical citations referring to items listed in the bibliography at the end of this book. Volume numbers will follow a period; page numbers will follow a colon.

CHRONOLOGY

1874 Robert Lee Frost born in San Francisco, California, March 26

1876 Frost's sister, Jeanie Florence Frost, born in Lawrence, Massachusetts

1885 Frost's father dies of tuberculosis in May; Frost with his mother and sister move to Lawrence and in September to Salem, New Hampshire

1888 Begins high school at Lawrence High School, commuting from Salem

1890 Publishes his first poem, "La Noche Triste," in the *Lawrence High School Bulletin*

1892 Graduates Lawrence High School, sharing valedictory honors with Elinor Miriam White; chosen Class Poet; enters Dartmouth College, which he leaves before his first semester is completed

1893 Teaches eighth-grade in Methuen, Massachusetts; in summer, works as light-trimmer in the Arlington Mill in Lawrence

1894 In winter, works as gate-tender at the Arlington Mill; in spring teaches in a district school in Salem; *Twilight* privately printed; publishes "My Butterfly" in *The Independent* (New York) November 8; in winter, works briefly as a reporter for local newspapers

1895 In spring, teaches at private school owned by his mother; marries Elinor Miriam White in Lawrence on December 19

1896 First child, Elliott, born on September 25

1897 Enters Harvard College as special student

1899 Withdraws from Harvard College; returns to Lawrence; second child, Lesley, born on April 28

1900 Elliott Frost dies of cholera on July 8; in October, moves to Derry, New Hampshire; begins poultry farming; mother dies of cancer on November 2

1902 Third child, son Carol, born on May 27

1903 First of 11 prose pieces on poultry farming published in two regional poultry periodicals over the next three years; fourth child, Irma, born on June 27

1905 Fifth child, Marjorie, born on March 29

1906 Begins teaching at Pinkerton Academy in Derry

1907 Sixth child, Elinor Bettina, born on June 18, but dies within two days of birth

1911 Resigns from Pinkerton Academy; moves to Plymouth, New Hampshire; begins teaching at the New Hampshire State Normal School; sells Derry farm, which he had inherited from his paternal grandfather

1912 Moves to Beaconsfield, Buckinghamshire, England

1913 *A Boy's Will* published in London

1914 Moves to London briefly, then to Gloucestershire; *North of Boston* published in London

1915 Returns to America; *A Boy's Will* and *North of Boston* published in New York; purchases farm in Franconia, New Hampshire

1916 *Mountain Interval* published

1917 Begins teaching at Amherst College

1920 Resigns from Amherst College; returns to Franconia; moves to South Shaftsbury, Vermont

1921 Appointed as Poet in Residence at the University of Michigan

1922 Reappointed for second year at the University of Michigan as Fellow in Creative Arts

1923 First of several editions of *Selected Poems* published; son Carol marries Lillian LaBatt on November 3; *New Hampshire* published; returns to Amherst College

1924 Pulitzer Prize for *New Hampshire*; first grandchild, William Prescott Frost, born on October 15

1925 Leaves Amherst College; honored at "Fiftieth Birthday Dinner" in New York City; returns to the University of Michigan as Fellow in Creative Arts

1926 Resigns from the University of Michigan; returns to Amherst College

1928 Travels abroad (France, England, and Ireland); *West-Running Brook* published

1929 Sister Jeanie dies on September 7

1930 First of several editions of *Collected Poems* published

1931 Pulitzer Prize for *Collected Poems*; receives Russell Loines Poetry Prize from the National Institute of Arts and Letters

1933 Daughter Marjorie marries Willard E. Fraser on June 3

1934 Daughter Marjorie dies on May 2 from child-bed fever

1936 Serves as Charles Eliot Norton Professor of Poetry at Harvard University; *A Further Range* published

1938 Elinor Frost dies of a heart attack in Gainesville, Florida, on March 21; resigns from Amherst College; sells Amherst home; returns to South Shaftsbury but then moves to an apartment in Boston

1939 Enlarged edition of *Collected Poems* published; appointed Ralph Waldo Emerson Fellow in Poetry at Harvard University; purchases Homer Noble Farm in Ripton,Vermont

1940 Purchases property in South Miami, Florida, for winter home; son Carol commits suicide on October 9

1941 Awarded Gold Medal by Poetry Society of America; purchases home in Cambridge, Massachusetts

1942 *A Witness Tree* published

1943 Pulitzer Prize for *A Witness Tree*; terminates Harvard University assignment; becomes George Ticknor Fellow in the Humanities at Dartmouth College; hospitalized with pneumonia in December

1945 *A Masque of Reason* published

1947 *Steeple Bush* and *A Masque of Mercy* published

1949 *Complete Poems* 1949 published; accepts life appointment as Simpson Lecturer in Literature at Amherst College

1953 Receives award from the American Academy of Poets

1954 *Aforesaid* published in limited edition for Frost's eightieth birthday; sent by the U.S. Department of State as delegate to the World Congress of Writers in São Paulo, Brazil

1955 "Robert Frost Mountain" in Ripton, Vermont, so designated by a state legislative act

1957 Sent on "goodwill mission" by the U.S. Department of State to Britain and Ireland

1958 Named to term as Consultant in Poetry at the Library of Congress; receives awards from the Poetry Society of America, the American Academy of Arts and Sciences, and the Huntington Hartford Foundation, among others

1960 Receives Congressional Gold Medal

1961 Participates in John F. Kennedy's presidential inauguration for which he writes "For John F. Kennedy His Inauguration"; visits Israel and Greece; designated by state legislature as Poet Laureate of Vermont

1962 Briefly hospitalized for pneumonia; receives Congressional Gold Medal; *In the Clearing* published; sent on "goodwill mission" by the U.S. Department of State to Russia; enters Peter Bent Brigham Hospital in Boston for tests on December 3; prostate operation on December 10

1963 Dies on January 29 at Peter Bent Brigham Hospital in Boston and cremated; ashes interred at the cemetery of the First Congressional Church in Old Bennington,Vermont, on June 16; is survived by daughters Lesley and Irma and five grandchildren

1969 *The Poetry of Robert Frost* is published

PART ONE

A COMPANION TO THE COLLECTED POETRY

The Pasture

This poem was first published as a prologue to *North of Boston* (1914). "The Pasture" was moved to its current place as prologue to collected and selected editions of Frost's beginning with the 1930 edition of Frost's *Collected Poems* and all subsequent editions. According to Frost, this poem was written in 1910 [3:98]. He considered it to be "a poem about love that's new in treatment and effect. You won't find anything in the whole range of English poetry just like that" [117:20]. In 1940, as recorded by Daniel Smythe, Frost said of this poem:

> About "[The] Pasture" I usually say this, in this style: "I will lead off with one that is taken more often by the anthologists than any other. It is one somebody used years ago to express something I have been talking about lately—how we have talked on the subject of 'Confusion.' [...] This was one used long ago, when I was young, to express the opposite of confusion. The first stanza is called unclouded [...]."
>
> I have always had an interest in that word, "confusion." I don't think I really thought of it in this poem, but it could be thought of in connection with it. I wrote it a long time ago. I never had a greater pleasure than on coming on a neglected spring in a pasture in the woods. We clean out the leaves, then wait by to watch the uncloudiness displace the cloudiness. That is always a pleasure to me; it might be taken as a figure of speech. It is my place to see clarity come out of talk and confusion. You didn't need to know that was in the poem [136:56–57].

Title *The Pasture*: to the west of the Frost farm in Derry, New Hampshire, and visible from the large bay window at the front of the house, were two small pastures.

ℓ 1. *pasture spring*: Frost's west-running brook (see "West-Running Brook") was fed by this pasture spring.

A Boy's Will

Frost's first book of poetry (excluding the privately printed *Twilight*) was published in London by David Nutt in 1913. An American edition was published in New York by Henry Holt and Company in 1915 simultaneously with the American publication of Frost's second book, *North of Boston*. The book was dedicated "To E.M.F." The initials were for Frost's wife, Elinor Miriam Frost. The title was taken from the refrain of Henry Wadsworth Longfellow's poem "My Lost Youth": "A boy's will is the wind's will / And the thoughts of youth are long, long thoughts" [1.1:406]. The book was originally divided into three numbered sections and each poem, with the exception of "Going for Water" and "Reluctance," was glossed in the table of contents:

PART I

INTO MY OWN The youth is persuaded that he will be rather more than less himself for having forsworn the world.
GHOST HOUSE He is happy in society of his choosing.
MY NOVEMBER GUEST He is in love with being misunderstood.
LOVE AND A QUESTION He is in doubt whether to admit real trouble to a place beside the hearth with love.
A LATE WALK He courts the autumnal mood.
STARS There is no oversight of human affairs.
STORM FEAR He is afraid of his own isolation.
WIND AND WINDOW FLOWER Out of the winter things he fashions a story of modern love.
TO THE THAWING WIND He calls on change through the violence of the elements.
A PRAYER IN SPRING He discovers that the greatness of love lies not in forward-looking thoughts;
FLOWER GATHERING nor yet in any spur it may be to ambition.
ROSE POGONIAS He is no dissenter from the ritualism of nature;
ASKING FOR ROSES nor from the ritualism of youth which is make-believe.
WAITING—AFIELD AT DUSK He arrives at the turn of the year.
IN A VALE Out of old longings he fashions a story.
A DREAM PANG He is shown by a dream how really well it is with him.
IN NEGLECT He is scornful of folk his scorn cannot reach.
THE VANTAGE POINT And again scornful, but there is no one hurt.
MOWING He takes up life simply with the small tasks.
GOING FOR WATER

PART II

REVELATION He resolves to become intelligible, at least to himself, since there is no help else;
THE TRIAL BY EXISTENCE and to know definitely what he thinks about the soul;
IN EQUAL SACRIFICE about love;
THE TUFT OF FLOWERS about fellowship;
SPOILS OF THE DEAD about death;
PAN WITH US about art (his own);
THE DEMIURGE'S LAUGH about science.

PART III

NOW CLOSE THE WINDOWS It is time to make an end of speaking.
A LINE-STORM SONG It is the autumnal mood with a difference.
OCTOBER He sees days slipping from him that were the best for what they were.
MY BUTTERFLY There are things that can never be the same.
RELUCTANCE

On the glosses which he supplied for *A Boy's Will,* Frost has commented that he wrote them to give the poems a more connected look than they may have had [3:107]. As he explained to Louis Mertins:

> As I sat there [arranging the poems] I even made some marginal notes, setting forth what each poem stood for. It seemed to me, though, that there was too personal a note in them—too much of Robert Frost in these marginal identifications. Timidity caused me to shrink back from this, false modesty. [...] So, I rewrote the marginal notes, taking the capital "I"out, and stressing the third person, transferring them thus over to an imaginary individual. You can never tell which person I am writing under. "I" sometimes means "he," while "he," as in this case ["Storm Fear"], means "I." We'll leave "we" out of the consideration [103:106–107].

In 1942 Frost reiterated that the poems for *A Boy's Will* were selected "looking backward over the accumulation of years to see how many poems I could find towards some one meaning it might seem absurd to have had in advance, but it would be all right to accept from fate after the fact" [140:277].

That Frost may have had a more concrete plan in mind than he later admitted regarding the creation of the particular type of book *A Boy's Will* represents is made apparent when one looks at the poems which were written or begun prior to the publication of his first book. Following is a list of poems from each of Frost's books from his second to his last which could possibly have been included in *A Boy's Will:*

From *North of Boston*: "The Death of the Hired Man," "The Black Cottage," "The Housekeeper," "Good Hours"
From *Mountain Interval*: "Bond and Free," "An Old Man's Winter Night," "The Telephone," "Meeting and Passing," "Hyla Brook," "The Oven Bird," "Pea Brush," "Putting in the Seed," "An Encounter," "Range-Finding," "Loneliness," "House Fear," "The Last Word of a Bluebird," "The Line-Gang"
From *New Hampshire*: "The Axe-Helve," "I Will Sing You One-O," "Dust of Snow," "Misgiving," "The Need of Being Versed in Country Things"
From *West-Running Brook*: "On Going Unnoticed," "Bereft," "Hannibal," "The Flower Boat"
From *A Further Range*: "Design"
From *A Witness Tree*: "The Subverted Flower," "The Quest of the Purple-Fringed," "To a Moth Seen in Winter"
From *Steeple Bush*: "A Rogers Group"
From *In the Clearing*: "[We Vainly Wrestle...]"

In Frost's *Collected Poems* (1930) three poems, "Asking for Roses," "In Equal Sacrifice," and "Spoils of the Dead," were omitted, and one poem, "In Hardwood Groves," was added. In the 1934 edition of *A Boy's Will*, "Asking for Roses" was included but "In Equal Sacrifice," "Spoils of the Dead," and "In Hardwood Groves," were not. *Collected Poems* (1939 and all subsequent editions) followed the contents of the 1930 edition. For the texts of the three poems omitted from *A Boy's Will*, see pages 227–230.

Frost wrote to Susan Hayes Ward about *A Boy's Will* on May 13, 1913, from England, calling it "a good book in spots." He went on to say that such poems as "Into My Own," "My November Guest," "A Dream Pang," "Mowing," and "Reluctance" were "the unforced expression of a life I was forced to live" [66:73]. In 1920 Frost wrote to G.R. Elliott that he still liked some of the lyric poems from his first book, naming, in particular, "My November Guest," "To the Thawing Wind," "Mowing," "Going for Water," "October," and "Reluctance" [66:248].

Although Frost wrote that very little of what he had been writing in England went into *A Boy's Will* [66:60], a statement confirmed by his later saying that all the poems in it were written in New Hampshire and Massachusetts [3:107], he did imply that at least one or two poems written in England were used [66:60].

Into My Own

First published as "Into Mine Own" in *New England Magazine*, May 1909, the poem was begun, according to Newdick, between April and June 1894 while Frost was teaching in Salem, New Hampshire [110:43]. According to Frost in 1930, the poem was written in 1901 [3:98]. Frost wrote to

John Bartlett that in this poem he "went away from people (and college) [...]" [2:37].

l. 4. *edge of doom*: echo of Shakespeare's "Sonnet 116" (*ll.* 11–12): "Love alters not with his brief hours and weeks, / But bears it out even to the edge of doom" [134:1770].

l. 6. *steal away*: possible echo of the black American spiritual also referred to in "Build Soil," *l.* 278.

ll. 13–14. *They would not ... true*: during a 1959 interview with John Ciardi, Frost said: "Those lines are really about loyalty, aren't they? I know more about loyalty now than I did when I wrote them. But the situation of loyalty is always the same" [18:54].

Ghost House

First published in *The Youth's Companion*, March 15, 1906, according to Frost in 1930 the poem was written in 1901 [3:98] and may have been inspired by an old cellar hole with a tall chimney standing in it, all that remained of a house which had burned down years earlier, near the Derry farm, halfway between Klein's Hill and the house of their neighbor, Napoleon Guay [142:300]. The house, which had burned down in 1867, had belonged to Marshall Merriam, who owned almost all of the land which became the Frost farm [40:I,19,4–5 NOTES].

My November Guest

First published in *The Forum*, November 1912, according to Frost in 1930 the poem was written in 1903 [3:98]. Frost referred to "My November Guest" in 1955 as "a pleasant reminder of the days when the clouds were just beginning to break. It was published here [in America] behind me after I had gone to England for a change" [97:11]. In a letter to Thomas B. Mosher in 1912, Frost admitted that the poem was not "a new force in literature" but more simply "a beginning—that is all [...]" [66:47].

l. 1. *My Sorrow*: Frost's wife, Elinor. A few days after Elinor underwent surgery for cancer in 1937, Frost wrote to Louis Untermeyer that she had been "the unspoken half of everything I ever wrote, and both halves of many a thing from 'My November Guest' down to the last stanzas of 'Two Tramps in Mud Time' [...]" [66:450]. In 1939, a year after Elinor died, upon finding a letter which Elinor had written to their daughter Lesley in 1917, Frost wrote to Lesley:

> My, my, what sorrow runs through all she wrote to you children. No wonder something of it overcasts my poetry if read aright. No matter how humorous I am I am sad. I am a jester about sorrow. She colored my thinking from the first just as at the last she troubled my politics. It was no loss but a gain of course. She was not as original as I in thought but she dominated my art with the power of her character and nature [48:209–210].

Love and a Question

First published in *A Boy's Will.* The inspiration for this poem had been provided, according to Lawrance Thompson, by a tramp who, stopping at the Frost farm in Derry, asked permission to sleep in the barn. Frost, fearing that if he refused the man might burn down his barn, gave the man food that night, a bed of blankets and rugs by the kitchen stove, and breakfast in the morning. After the man departed, Frost questioned the rights of the property owner and the rights of a man such as this who makes a claim on the pity or, in this case, the fear of the property owner [142:377].

ll. 23–24. *And wished her ... pin*: echo of the anonymous Scottish ballad, "Waly, Waly" (*ll.* 35–36): "I'd lock'd my heart in a case o' goud, / And pinn'd it wi' a siller pin" [4:42].

A Late Walk

First published in *The Pinkerton Critic* (October 1909), according to Frost in 1930 the poem was written in 1897 [3:98]. It was originally written as a love poem for Elinor [142:360].

l. 4. *sadder than any words*: each autumn Frost was stricken with a recurring mood of regret [142:360].

Stars

First published in *A Boy's Will*, according to Frost the poem was written in Lawrence [3:107]. Lawrance Thompson places the writing of this poem in 1900, between the death of Elliott Frost on July 8 and the move to the Derry, New Hampshire, farm around October 1. It may have been started in Lawrence, Massachusetts, before the Frosts moved to Methuen in 1899 [142:546–547].

Following the death of Elliott, Elinor Frost was inconsolable. She suffered in silence for many days while Frost blamed himself for not calling the doctor soon enough to save their son. Frost kept saying that this was God's punishment for his neglect which was, in his own estimation, tantamount to murder. When Elinor could finally speak, she reproved Frost for his belief that this was God's punishment. She thought Frost was being unreasoning and self-centered for his belief in his punishment without seeing the injustice of the idea that the child's life had also been taken from the child and from her. She told Frost that there was no God, that there could not be. The world was completely evil and she hated all life that was left in it, including her own. At the time, Frost was inclined to agree, and his bitterness provided the notion that "there is no oversight of human affairs," which provided the ending to the poem that may have been started a year or two earlier [142:258].

ℓ 11. *Minerva*: the Roman goddess of wisdom and artisans.

Storm Fear

First published in *A Boy's Will*, according to two references by Frost the poem was written in 1911 in Plymouth, New Hampshire [3:98, 104]. Frost once referred to the poem as having been written on the Derry farm, but he may have been confused by the locale in the poem [3:107]. The internal evidence in the poem (*ℓ* 10, "Two and a child"), which refers to Frost, Elinor and their daughter Lesley, places the date of the poem sometime between the move to Derry in October 1900 and the birth of Carol in May 1902, although, according to what Frost told Louis Mertins regarding *A Boy's Will*, "'Storm Fear' was the youngest of the lot, the last finished before publication" in 1912 [103:106]. The most likely scenario for the writing of this poem is that it was, except for a little revision performed in England in 1912, written in 1911 in Plymouth, possibly worked up from fragments dating from the early Derry days.

Regarding the pronouns in this poem, Frost said,

> You can never tell which person I am writing under. "I" sometimes means "he," while "he," as in this case, means "I." We'll leave "we" out of the consideration [103:107].

Although Frost had many imagined fears, he had a real basis for the fright he felt during a New England winter storm. Gentle snowfalls could build to blizzard-like violence. On such nights, Frost would be afraid to go to bed, believing the house might be torn apart. If he did go to bed, he could not sleep [142:280]. In her journal, eight-year-old Lesley describes a December 1907 storm on the Derry farm:

> Last night there was a great snow storm outside, but inside it was nice and cosy. It was my bedtime, but I didn't want to go to bed because you could here [sic] the wind outside whistling around the corner of the house and coming in every crack in the windows and the fine sharp flakes banging against the window pane, and then I was such a bad dreamer that I was afraid I might dream that thousands of little men were breaking in to carry me off, but I was tired and I didn't think much about it. After I got to bed I stayed awake and thought a little about how deep it might be in the morning [40:V.300–331].

In a letter written to his daughter Lesley in February 1920, Frost's own "storm fear" is apparent:

> I write this snowed in by the greatest snow-storm of all time with very little hope of ever mailing it. We are running short of food fuel and water. How long we can last we are not experienced enough in rationing to calculate. (We could last longer of course if Marjorie would eat less.) Rescuing parties have been by with teams of six and eight horses, but they are merely local and neighborly; they are satisfied if they push the snow a little from our doors: they are not intended to establish communication with the outside world. Everybody is frightened but Margerie [sic] [and Carol {and Irma (and Mama)}]* who doesn't know enough, isn't, I fear, tall enough, to appreciate the seriousness of snow actually half way up our windows [48:75; *multiple bracketing is by Frost].

As of 1925, Frost felt he had never written a "tighter" poem [3:112]. He referred to it as being almost lyrical [66:248].

l. **10.** *Two and a child*: the two were Frost and Elinor, the child was Lesley. Their son Elliott had died shortly before the Frosts moved to the Derry farm. This would put the date of the subject of the poem sometime between the move to Derry in October 1900 and the birth of Carol in May 1902.

Wind and Window Flower

First published in *A Boy's Will*, according to Frost in 1930 the poem may have been written circa 1905 [3:98] although he also once referred to the poem as having been written in Lawrence, which would date the poem in the 1890s [3:107].

To the Thawing Wind

First published in *A Boy's Will*, this poem was sent to Susan Hayes Ward at Christmas 1911 with the title "To the Loud Southwester" [142:549]. Frost told an audience at Bread Loaf, "This is what we waited for in the spring in the days when we were shut in on the farm" [25:133]. As Frost said during a 1921 interview:

> You know, I somehow have always written more about just that period when the backbone of winter breaks and the thaw starts. Somehow that part of spring seems to appeal to me more. No, I will not say that it appeals to me more, but I just seem to have written about it more [51:33].

A Prayer in Spring

First published in *A Boy's Will*, according to Frost in 1930 the poem was written in 1903 [3:98].

ll. 9–12. *the darting bird ... still*: hummingbird.

Flower Gathering

First published in *A Boy's Will*, this poem was written during the summer of 1896 in Allenstown, N.H. [142:530, 3:108]. During the Frosts' stay at their cottage in Allenstown, on their delayed honeymoon, Frost, with or without Elinor, would walk the neighboring areas botanizing. Being seven months pregnant, Elinor became less and less inclined to accompany Frost, insisting, however, that he continue his explorations. Sometimes Frost got so involved in what he was seeing and was away so long that Elinor would begin to worry that he was stuck in a swamp. Her anger showed itself in reticence or silence. On one such occasion Frost wrote her this poetic apology [142:219].

Rose Pogonias

First published in *A Boy's Will*, the poem was written on the Derry farm in 1901 [3:99, 108]. Robert Newdick refers to Frost's confirmation of a story by a Mrs. Pettee that the origin of this poem took place during a walk which Frost took with Mr. Pettee, a forger, after the latter's release from prison [110:261]. No date is given for this walk nor has further identification of the Pettees been found.

ll. 17–24. *We raised a ... flowers*: for a similar wish that the flowers may be given a chance, see "The Last Mowing."

Waiting
Afield at Dusk

First published in *A Boy's Will*, this poem was written before 1895, in Lawrence, Massachusetts [3:103], or possibly in Salem, New Hampshire [3:108]. Although rarely read by Frost at his readings, he did read it at least once, prefacing it by calling it a "gentle" and "personal" poem which did not lend itself to reading to an audience [165:MS Frost 219].

l. 23. *the worn book of old-golden song*: Francis Turner Palgrave's *The Golden Treasury*, which Frost discovered in 1892 and which remained a favorite of his for the rest of his life.

l. 26. *one absent*: Elinor Miriam White, who, from 1892 to 1895 attended St. Lawrence University, before marrying Frost in 1895.

In a Vale

First published in *A Boy's Will*. Lawrance Thompson wrote that Frost began "In a Vale" while he was still attending high school [142:303]. Frost dated the poem as between 1896 and 1901 [3:99, 103]. In a letter to Sidney Cox in 1915, Frost recalled: "A place I passed at night alone something like twenty years ago made 'In a Vale' then and there in my head and I wrote it down with few changes the next morning" [31:73].

l. 14. *fain to list*: during a 1957 interview Frost told Cecil Day Lewis, "You can see in some poems some lingering words like 'fain' and 'list' that I was getting rid of, that I was ashamed of to begin with. [...] I don't remember thinking much about style except that I was ashamed at 'thee' and 'thou' and 'thine' and such things as that" [78:27].

A Dream Pang

First published in *A Boy's Will*, the poem may have been written in 1902 [3:99], although Frost once placed the writing of the poem as at Lawrence, Massachusetts, which would date it in the late 1890s [3:108]. An early version of this poem was sent to Susan Hayes Ward on August 6, 1907, with the boast that in time he would be mastering the sonnet form [142:561].

l. 1. *I had withdrawn in forest*: during the years on the Derry farm, when the tensions of family life seemed too strong, Frost would sometimes find it necessary to get out of the house, away from Elinor and off the farm. He would often plunge into the woods behind the farm, walking until he was almost exhausted, at which point he would return to Elinor, repentant [142:310].

ll. 7–8. *I dare not ... wrong*: for a similar stalemate, see "The Thatch" (*ll.* 6–7).

In Neglect

First published in *A Boy's Will*, according to Frost the poem was written in 1905 on the Derry farm [3:99, 108]. In a 1915 letter to Sidney Cox, Frost included Ezra Pound's review of *A Boy's Will*, which contained the inaccurate story that Frost's grandfather and uncle had left him disinherited, this being the supposed inspiration for the poem. Frost crossed out certain lines from the review with a note to Cox, "I have scraped out some personalities (very private) which are not only in bad taste but also inaccurate" [31:56]. Pound could not be blamed for the inaccuracies of a story which had come from Frost himself. Apparently, Frost told the same story later in life to his biographer, Robert Newdick, who made this note to himself:

> And also true, Robert's granduncle Elihu W. Colcord, probably thought to punish him severely by ignoring him in his will and leaving all his money to build a dormitory for Sanborn Seminary at Kingston; but Robert showed his mettle and Elinor's by turning the intended rebuke into a poem! [110:74-75].

The poem, not specifically related to the incident of Frost's grandfather and uncle, deals with the years of neglect on the Derry farm when both Frost and Elinor felt Frost's poems were very good but not the fashion of the moment [110:268]. Elinor liked the isolation of their "wayside nook" and it was more her attitude than Frost's which had inspired his lines [142:350, 143:508]. Frost realized, however, that such an attitude was merely an attitude. In his 1939 "The Doctrine of Excursions" he admitted, "A writer can live by writing to himself alone for days and years. Sooner or later to go on he must be read" [8:xix]. In 1955 Frost expressed it this way:

> It's an old story. Courage and adventure. Courage for that kind of adventure. To write is not the horrible thing. The horrible thing is not having anybody want it for a long time [51:152].

The Vantage Point

First published in *A Boy's Will*, according to Frost in 1930 the poem was written in 1900 [3:99]. An early version of this poem was sent to Susan Hayes Ward in August 1907 as "Choice of Society" [133:60].

Mowing

First published in *A Boy's Will*. Frost's comment to Elizabeth Shepley Sergeant that this was the first "talk song" he was aware of and that it was written prior to "My November Guest" places this poem early in the Derry period [132:295]. Frost's dating this poem as 1900 on the Derry farm confirms the above statement [3:99, 108]. Commenting on his early poems in *A Boy's Will* in which he had used such dated phrases as "fain" and "list," he said of "Mowing," "Yes, now that's perfectly clear, straight goods—mine" [78:27]. Frost wrote to Sidney Cox in 1914 that it was the best poem in his first book [31:56].

l. 2. *my long scythe whispering to the ground*: this line was repeated in "The Tuft of Flowers," *l.* 32.

l. 8. *fay and elf*: Frost said during a reading that he had "no business" mentioning these words and had always felt sorry about using them. Poetry is "not getting up fanciful things" [25:123].

l. 13. *The fact is the sweetest dream that labor knows*: at a 1962 reading, Frost spoke of this line as "a definition of poetry" [25:189]. For similar comments, see 25:123, 133.

Going for Water

First published in *A Boy's Will*, according to Frost the poem was written in 1905 on the Derry farm [3:99, 108].

l. 4. *the brook if still it ran*: Hyla Brook, on the Derry farm, which dried up at the end of each summer; see "Hyla Brook."

Revelation

First published in *A Boy's Will.* Frost has dated the poem as having been written as early as prior to 1895 [3:103] and as late as 1898 [3:99].

ll. 1–2. *We make ourselves ... flout*: Frost said that you could say this about anything you write [25:136].

ll. 7–8. *We speak the ... friend*: at a 1959 reading Frost said that "we have to be so damn literal about it. This is the same question of why God came to send us a son down in this neighborhood" [25:136].

l. 12. *Must speak and ... are*: Frost told a 1959 audience that people want to be found out [25:136].

The Trial by Existence

First published in *The Independent*, October 11, 1906, this poem was begun in 1892 but not revised and completed until early 1906 [142:290]. Frost gave various dates for this poem, all placing it in the nineties [3:99, 103, 108]. He said he had tried to write this poem "while still in High School but failed with it" [120:191].

Frost wrote to his friend Louis Untermeyer in 1916 that

> the day I did "The Trial by Existence" (*Boy's Will*) says I to myself, this is the way of all flesh. I was not much over twenty, but I was wise for my years. I knew then that it was a race between me the poet and that in me that would be flirting with the entelechies or the coming on of that in me [66:202].

In a letter to Susan Hayes Ward written in December, 1906, he referred to this poem as "grafting Schopenhauer upon Christianity" [133:70]. Frost told Robert Newdick that Rossetti's "The Blessed Damozel" "is written all over '[The] Trial by Existence'" [110:298].

ll. 65–67. *'Tis of the essence ... clear*: cf. *The Masque of Reason, ll.* 62–63.

The Tuft of Flowers

First published in *The Derry Enterprise* March 9, 1906, the poem was written early enough to be used in his English A class at Harvard in 1897. According to Lawrance Thompson, the poem had been inspired by an experience which happened while Frost was haying for John Dinsmore, at Cobbett's Pond near Salem, New Hampshire [142:318].

Frost wrote to John Bartlett on February 26, 1913, that he came back to people and college in this poem [2:37]. Frost told an audience at Bread Loaf in 1955 that the subject was "togetherness" [25:84]. This poem, Frost said, was "one I always considered one of my best" [103:90]. In a 1937 letter, Frost linked "The Tuft of Flowers" with "Reluctance," "West-Running Brook" and the passage about home in "The Death of the Hired Man" as having the "same subject [...] my position [...] between socialism and individualism" [118:5].

ll. 1–2. *I went to ... sun*: during a 1955 reading, Frost described what mowing had been like when he was young:

> [...] in the old days we mowed by hand a great deal—more than we do now. We do some of that now. There was always a boy or somebody—some fellow around like me—to toss the grass, open it up, let the sun at it. The mowing was apt to be done in the dew of the morning for better mowing, but it left the grass wet and had to be scattered [to dry]. We called it—the word for it was "turning" the grass [25:85].

l. 8. *alone*: cf. "Home burial," *l.* 101.

l. 24. *scythe had bared*: following this line, the first publication through the *Collected Poems* (1946) version have this couplet:

> I left my place to know them by their name,
> Finding them butterfly weed when I came.

l. 26. *By leaving them to flourish*: in a reading at Bread Loaf in 1962, Frost spoke of this poem as containing a definition of poetry in that the poet writes his poem but leaves it to flourish with others [25:189].

l. 27. *Nor yet to ... him*: Frost reminded an audience that the mower did this just because he liked the flowers [25:180], without any self-consciousness [25:85].

l. 28. *from sheer morning gladness at the brim*: about this line, Frost said:

> My idea of poetry is in this poem where it says [quotes line 28]: That's the heart of the whole thing. That's the poem [103:78].

l. 32. *his long scythe whispering to the ground*: this line was repeated in "Mowing," *l.* 2.

Pan with Us

First published in *A Boy's Will*, according to Frost in 1930, the poem was written in 1902 [3:99].

Title *Pan*: the Greek god of shepherds and hunters.

l. 6. *pipes*: Pan was the traditional inventor of the panpipes.

The Demiurge's Laugh

First published in *A Boy's Will.* Frost wrote to Susan Hayes Ward towards the end of 1906 that he has been "ambitious" trying to get some of his "larger thoughts into shape" and then refers to "The Demiurge's Laugh" as one which "ought to be made into something" [133:72].

Title *Demiurge*: a Gnostic subordinate deity who is the creator of the material world.

Now Close the Windows

First published in *A Boy's Will*, this poem was written at Dartmouth in the fall of 1892 [142:539; 3:99]. Frost once dated the poem as having been written prior to 1895 [3:108], perhaps confirming the above date.

In Hardwood Groves

First published as "The Same Leaves" in *The Dearborn Independent*, December 18, 1926, this poem was not originally published in *A Boy's Will* but was added in *Collected Poems* (1930). It served as a substitute for "Spoils of the Dead," which was removed from *A Boy's Will* [142:559]. The poem was begun in 1905 but not completed until 1925 [3:99].

A Line-Storm Song

First published in *New England Magazine*, October 1907.

October

First published in *The Youth's Companion*, October 3, 1912, this poem was written on the Derry farm [142:570; 3:108] possibly in 1901 [3:99]. Frost referred to it in 1962 as a poem "innocent of everything I know of" [13:188].

l. 1. *O hushed October morning mild*: in a 1958 Bread Loaf reading, Frost admitted giving this poem a consciously prayerful sound [25:124].

l. 21. *For the grapes' sake along the wall*: near the Derry farm lived Nathaniel Head, on whose land, which had a downward slope, was built a substantial retaining wall. Along this wall, Mr. Head had planted Concord grapevines [40:I,36,2-3 NOTES].

My Butterfly

First published in *The Independent*, November 8, 1894, with the subtitle "An Elegy," this poem had also been privately published in 1894 in *Twilight*. To Louis Untermeyer in 1917, Frost wrote that he had read his first poem at age fifteen, written his first poem at sixteen, and had written his first published poem, "My Butterfly," at eighteen [151:61]. In 1925 he referred to this "ode" as his "first real poem" [3:111].

The poem was inspired by Frost's finding in the fall of 1892 at Dartmouth a butterfly wing among some dead leaves. It was written, or at least begun, in 1892 or 1893, in Lawrence, Massachusetts [3:99, 108], although it may not have been written, or at least finished, until the spring of 1894 [142:162; 57:210]. He told Elizabeth Shepley Sergeant that he wrote the poem "all in one go in the kitchen of our house in Tremont Street" [133:34]. For a variant of this poem, see 57:208.

ll. 8-17. *The gray grass ... dance*: Frost wrote in 1947 that of the poems printed in his privately printed *Twilight*, the only poem he liked enough to keep was "My Butterfly" for the eight lines beginning "The gray grass [...]" which he felt was when he "first struck the note that was to be mine" [66:526-527]. Frost said in 1915, "I still like as well as anything" the eight lines beginning "the gray grass [...]" [110:36].

Reluctance

First published in *The Youth's Companion*, November 7, 1912. "Except for one very important change (which wouldn't you like to know!)" [110:164], "Reluctance" was written in late 1894 after the Dismal Swamp episode, which took place in the fall of that year while Elinor White was attending St. Lawrence University, although Frost once dated the poem as late as 1908 [3:99].

Frost had put together a small privately printed book of poems entitled *Twilight* in an edition of two copies, one for himself and one for Elinor. He made a special trip to visit her at St. Lawrence University to present her with this token of his love. Because of both the unexpectedness of Frost's arrival and the rules of propriety (which did not allow for a man to visit a young woman except during certain prescribed hours), Frost was not as warmly received as he had hoped. Feeling deeply rejected, he destroyed his copy of *Twilight* and returned home. On November 6, 1894, Frost took the train to

Virginia thereupon to head for the Dismal Swamp, where he intended to commit suicide as a form of retaliation against Elinor's somewhat cold treatment of him. Many years later Frost wrote of the episode and his falling in with a group of men headed for Elizabeth City in Part One of "Kitty Hawk." After his return to Lawrence on November 30, Frost turned his apparent loss of Elinor's affection into the poem "Reluctance," eventually placed as the final poem to *A Boy's Will* [142:173–189].

In a letter to Thomas B. Mosher in 1912, Frost admitted that the poem was not "a new force in literature" but more simply "a beginning—that is all [...]" [66:47]. In a 1937 letter, Frost linked "Reluctance" with "The Tuft of Flowers," "West-Running Brook" and the passage about home in "The Death of the Hired Man," as having the "same subject [...] my position [...] between socialism and individualism" [118:5]. On the rhyme-scheme in the poem, Frost wrote,

> Does anyone believe I would have committed myself to the treason-reason-season rhyme-set in my "Reluctance" if I had been blasé enough to know that these three words about exhausted the possibilities? No rhyming dictionary for me to make me face the facts of rhyme [45:52].

ll. 19-24. *Ah, when to ... season?*: Frost, in his 1948 talk "Speaking of Loyalty," said:

> The loyalty I'm speaking of—I don't know whether I'm permitted to deal with it in written words of my own—I've written a great deal about it; once away back when I was very young in a stanza I'll venture to say to you [reads final stanza of "Reluctance"]. Even a season—that pain of the end of summer—is in it for me, the person, the place, friendship, parting is such sweet sorrow, and so on [57:410–411].

Compare "Brown's Descent," *l.* 60, in which Brown did bow "with a grace to natural law."

North of Boston

Originally published in London by David Nutt in 1914, there was an issuance of *North of Boston* in New York by Henry Holt and Company having a cancel title page dated 1914 and a binding distinct from the English one. This was followed in 1915 by Holt's own edition of *North of Boston*. The title *North of Boston* was taken from a Boston newspaper advertisement which Frost remembered while he was living in England. It mentioned properties for sale in a geographical area referred to simply as "north of Boston" [142:434]. The book was dedicated "To E.M.F. This Book of People." The initials E.M.F. were for Frost's wife, Elinor Miriam Frost. Regarding his "book of people" Frost said in 1937:

> I am often more or less tacitly on the defensive about what I call "my people." That doesn't mean Americans—I never defend America from foreigners. But when I speak of my people, I sort of mean a class, the ordinary folks I belong to. I have written about them entirely in one whole book: I called it *A Book of People*. But I found as I went around, seeing colleges more than anything else, that one and another spoke or implied something about my people that I didn't care for. I went a long way once to see one or two of my little things acted as if they were plays. They were very short plays, too short to act, but they have something of the dramatic in them. All the actors were cultivated people and they thought the way to represent my [...] people on the stage was to have them hop a little as if they were going over clods. And one of the actors who acted in the thing—I did not know what to say to him afterwards. I was full of too much to say, and I thought perhaps I would put it this way:
>
> "They are much the same as we are. As a matter of fact," I said—I didn't know just how to make him understand—"as a matter of fact, both of them had been to college."
>
> I don't think he would ever hop for them again. I was a little angry-threewith him, but that was what I had to say to him, because there are people who don't go to college and who don't hop clods [74:(9)].

Frost said *North of Boston* is "a book of people, not of poor people. They happen to be people of simplicity or simple truth miscalled simplicity" [151:305]. The page following the table of contents had the following statement: "'Mending Wall' takes up the theme where 'A [sic] Tuft of Flowers' in *A Boy's Will* laid it down." In the original editions of *North Of Boston* "The Pasture" was used as an introductory poem. Both it and the final poem, "Good Hours," were set in italics. In *Collected Poems* (1930 and all subsequent editions) "The Pasture" was removed from its place in *North of Boston* and used as the introductory poem to the collected editions.

Frost claimed that three poems, written on the farm in Derry, New Hampshire—"The Death of the Hired Man," "The Black Cottage," and "The Housekeeper"—were the beginning of *North of Boston*. The other poems were written in England "on an inspiration compounded of homesickness and the delight of new friendships. I wrote whole poems of two hundred lines at a sitting" [33:2]. Frost also said that three other poems—"The Mountain," "After Apple-Picking," and "The Wood-Pile"—were "largely written" before he went to England [133:119]. In a July 6, 1913, letter to the English poet F.S. Flint, Frost wrote about how he had

> tried to get variety in my material. I have the following poems in something like shape for my next book:
>
> 1 "The Death of the Hired Man"—an elegy
> 2 "The [sic] Hundred Collars"—a comedy
> 3 "The Black Cottage"—a monologue
> 4 "The Housekeeper"—a tragedy
> 5 "The Code—Heroics"—a yarn
> 6 "The Mountain"—a description
> 7 "Arrival Home"—an idyll
> 8 "Blueberries"—an eclogue
>
> [...] One thing I'd like to ask: Did I reach you with the poems, did I get them over, as the saying is? Did I give you a feeling of and for the independent-dependence of the kind of people I like to write about. I am no propagandist of equality. But I enjoy above all things the contemplation of equality where it happily exists [5:82–83].

Frost wrote to Louis Untermeyer on August 7, 1916, that seven of the *North of Boston* poems were almost humorous, and that four—"The Mountain," "A Hundred Collars," "The Code," and "The Generations of Men"—could almost be considered jokes [151:40]. At a talk in October 1937 at Haverford College, Frost said that when he wrote *North of Boston* "it was in innocence of heart—no implications" [74:(12)]. Frost told Louis Mertins that the theme of *North of Boston* was his "forgiving people for being people" [103:107]. Frost said that the poems selected for *North of Boston*, like those for *A Boy's Will*, were done so "looking backward over the accumulation of years to see how many poems I could find towards some one meaning it might seem absurd to have had in advance, but it would be all right to accept from fate after the fact" [140:277].

Mending Wall

First published in *North of Boston*. In a letter to Sydney Cox on June 25, 1915, Frost referred to the poem as "Building Wall" [31:93]. A note in the first edition of *North of Boston* (1914) states that "'Mending Wall' takes up the theme where 'A [sic] Tuft of Flowers' in *A Boy's Will* laid it down." The theme, as glossed in *A Boy's Will*, was "about fellowship."

At a talk at Wesleyan University in 1936, Frost said, "I wrote the poem 'Mending Wall' thinking of the old wall that I hadn't mended in several years and which must be in a terrible condition. I wrote that poem in England when I was very homesick for my old wall in New England" [142:432–433]. In a frank admission recorded in 1958 by Louis Mertins, Frost said:

> Somebody said, "what about walls—wouldn't you like to get rid of walls?" No, we always have walls—have always had them. While some are being torn down, others are being built up. Whether you want 'em or not you'll always have 'em [103:353].

At a reading in 1954 Frost referred to "Mending Wall" as a parable, warning that it contained "intimations" [25:55]. In Moscow, in 1962, he told his audience, "People are frequently misunderstanding it or misinterpreting it. The secret of what it means I keep" [144:316]. Frost put it simply in a 1944 interview when he said that there was "no rigid separation between right and wrong. 'Mending Wall' simply contrasts two types of people" [51:112]. "I played exactly fair in it," Frost said in 1945. "Twice I say 'Good fences' and twice 'Something there is—" [26:355].

ll. 5–9. *The work of ... dogs*: cf. "The Rabbit Hunter."

l. 7. *left not one stone on a stone*: echo of Matthew 24:2, Mark 13:2, and Luke 21:6 in which Jesus says that "there shall not be left here one stone upon another, that shall not be thrown down" [131:1032, 1063, 1105].

l. 12. *my neighbor*: Napolean Guay (sometimes Gay), a French-Canadian farmer who lived to the south of Frost on the Londonderry turnpike. A stone wall marked the boundary between the Frost apple orchard and Guay's rented property, a grove of white pines [142:284].

Guay is also mentioned in "New Hampshire" [*l.* 259] as "Gay of Atkinson" and is the woodchopper who inspired "The Axe-Helve."

l. 21. *Oh*: during the Charles Eliot Norton Lecture at Harvard University on March 25, 1936, Frost said he was proud of the "Oh" in this line [26:356].

l. 27. *"Good fences make good neighbors."*: Frost once said that you say this line differently from the way one would say it in *l.* 45 [25:136]. As he said during a 1961 interview, "It's the other fellow in the poem who says that, you know... I don't know. Maybe I was both fellows in the poem..." [51:257]. The phrase "Good fences make good neighbors" is proverbial and is found as early as 1850 when it appeared on page 13 of the 1850 edition of *Blum's Farmer's and Planter's Almanac* (Winston-Salem, North Carolina). It appeared again on page 11 of the 1861 issue.

l. 34. *And to whom ... offense*: in a 1923 letter to Sidney Cox, Frost wrote, "The worst we can do is give each other offense" [31:148].

l. 36. *I could say "Elves" to him*: in a story written for his children at the Derry farm in 1906-1907 entitled, "The Last Apple Fall," Frost wrote:

> They sat down in the grass together to try to understand. Their backs were to the wall so that when a stone fell off it they were taken by surprise. They hardly turned in time to see two little heads pop out of sight on the pasture side. Carol saw them better than Lesley. "Fairies!" he cried. Lesley said, "I can't believe it." "Fairies sure," said Carol [69:39].

l. 40. *old-stone savage*: during the Charles Eliot Norton Lecture at Harvard University on March 25, 1936, Frost said he was proud of the hyphen in "old-stone savage" [26:356].

The Death of the Hired Man

First published in *The New Republic*, February 6, 1915. This poem was written on the farm in Derry and was dated by Frost as 1905 [110:61; 3:99]. Frost claimed to have written the poem in two hours, without changing a word [51:25]. At a 1960 reading, Frost said that he had always desired to write something about the kind of American hired man that he had lived and worked with and had himself been [25:144]. Sydney Cox recalls:

> In "The Death of the Hired Man" he [Frost] spoke of the passage about "part of a moon" and the ... about a cloud, but he said that though they were more like older poetry he thought some of the less noticed things were more important (viz): The way in which the sentences suggest the tones in such passages as that in which she tries to get Warren to lower his voice; & the one in which Warren says he tells him (the hired man) "he'll have to then." And the neat colloquial sentences like the one about "Young Wilson's college boy's assurance piqued him [...]."
>
> He spoke of the latter [i.e. "The Death of the Hired Man"] as a little drama in which the gradual change in Warren is shown. It has four distinctly drawn characters. It has climax and surprise; and it perfectly observes all the old unities [31:89].

Frost wrote to Sydney Cox in 1932:

> The idea is the thing with me. It would seem soft for instance to look in my life for the sentiments in "The Death of the Hired Man." There's nothing to it believe me. I should fool you if you took me so. [...] To be too subjective with what an artist has managed to make objective is to come on him presumptuously and render ungraceful what he in pain of his life had faith he had made graceful [31:204].

When asked for a preface for "The Death of the Hired Man" for inclusion in Whit Burnett's *The World's Best* (New York: Dial Press, 1950), Frost wrote in 1945: "The employee here depicted is no longer numberous enough to be dealt with statistically by the Departments of Economics and Sociology. [...] In conclusion I beg to protest that it was with no such thoughts as these that the poem was written. By the way, it's in blank verse, not free verse" [120: 241].

After a 1915 dramatic production of this poem in which the characters of Warren and Mary were portrayed by talking crudely and walking clumsily, Frost was appalled that it was not clear to the actors that the characters were intelligent people. He told the actor who played Warren that both of the characters had been to college [26:359; 74:9; 143:60]. Referring to this poem as "one of the little plays," Frost said that "the danger, is that you shall make the man [Warren] too hard. That spoils it. That's the error the people made: they made the man too hard. And all our thinking turns on that" [74:12].

l. **1.** *Mary sat musing ... table*: during a 1960 reading, Frost admitted to the unconscious metrical error of this line having six feet instead of five [25:139].

l. **98.** *He hates to ... books*: in a 1960 interview, Frost said:

> But of course I'm not for the bookworm. Here's a word of caution you might want to note. In my "Death of the Hired Man," that I wrote years ago, there's this line: "He hates to see a boy the fool of books."
>
> It's interesting to see how country folks are sometimes wise without books [51:219].

l. **107.** *harplike morning-glory strings*: according to Newdick, "RF was shocked when he found he had repeated himself, e.g. the harp-like figure in 'A Lone Striker' [*l.* 29] and in 'The Death of the Hired Man.' He tries always for different tones, and of course to avoid any repetition" [110:334].

ll. **118–119.** *Home is the ... in*: according to Edgar Gilbert, Frost's friend from his days in the Lawrence mills (1893–1894), this part of the poem was inspired by the grudging reception given by Frost's paternal grandfather to Frost's mother and her two children after the death of Frost's father [110:246]. Whether this is Gilbert's own observation or was given to him by Frost is unknown.

In a 1937 letter, Frost linked this passage with "Reluctance," "The Tuft of Flowers," and "West-Running Brook" as having the "same subject [...] my position [...] between socialism and individualism" [118:5].

ll. 122–123. *Picked up a ... by*: according to Wade Van Dore, Frost was "habitually a breaker of sticks" [152:117].

The Mountain

First published in *North of Boston*. In a letter to Robert Newdick, Frost claimed that "The Mountain" "was all done in one sitting and stands today pretty exactly as I wrote it" [110:98]. Frost made the same claim of writing "with one stroke of the pen" to Elizabeth Shepley Sergeant [132:300]. Sydney Cox wrote how Frost

> alters combinations and puts names and places together differently as convenience suggests. For example in "The Mountain" the mountain's name comes from another place & the town was not Lunenburg but one in Vt. near Lake Willoughby. Mr. F. says "The M" is purely descriptive. (I had remarked that someone to whom I had read it wondered about "the meaning") [31:90].

As Frost confirmed:

> To a large extent the terrain of my poetry is the Derry landscape, the Derry farm. Poems growing out of this, though composite, were built on incidents and are therefore autobiographical. There was something about the experience at Derry which stayed in my mind, and was tapped for poetry in the years that came after. It is all fact—no fancy, but lots of teasing. I never invent for poetic expression. No poet really has to invent, only to record. Some of the poems combine many incidents, many people and places, but all are real. Take the mountain the man "worked around the foot of all his life." That wasn't one, but several mountains. But it was just as real for all its being composite. Those mountains surrounded the Derry farm, and stretched farther than the eye could see [103:72].

l. 19. *Lunenburg*: town in Massachusetts.

l. 91. *Hor*: mountain in the Lake Willoughby region of New Hampshire, but also the mountain in Exodus 20:22–29 on which Aaron died. In a high school essay, "Petra and Its Surroundings," Frost wrote of the biblical Mt. Hor:

> On the summit of Mt. Hor, nestles a shrine beneath which, the Arabians say, lie the bones of the priest, Aaron. It is a place of the wildest grandeur—one worthy the last resting place of the Israelitish orator, overlooking as it does the mountain fastnesses of the warlike sons of Esau, through whose country the Jews strove so long in vain to force a passage [121:Dec. 1881, p. 1].

l. 104. *But all the fun's in how you say a thing*: Frost made the claim during a reading at Bread Loaf that there was nothing he wouldn't dare say if the person was equal to understanding the tone in which he said it [25:108].

A Hundred Collars

First published in *Poetry and Drama*, December 1913.

l. 1. *Lancaster*: town in New Hampshire.

ll. 48–49. *Weekly News, Published in Bow*: weekly newspaper published in the town of Bow, New Hampshire.

l. 117. *Bill Taft*: William Howard Taft (1857–1930), 27th President of the United States (1909–1913).

Home Burial

First published in *North of Boston*. According to Frost, this poem was written in England. "I believe," he said, "I was not over two hours with 'Home Burial.' It stands in print as it was in the first draft" [33:2]. Sidney Cox recalls:

> The poem was too close to home, bringing back memories of the death at three and a half of his firstborn child, Elliott, at the Powder House Hill farm, some fifteen years before [1900]. "Home Burial" (the very title has a double meaning) evoked too strongly the differing ways Frost and his wife, Elinor, responded to Elliott's death. He covered his pain with talking, she with silence [31:76].

The poem was also in part inspired by the marital estrangement which overtook Elinor's sister and brother-in-law, Leona and Nathaniel Harvey, after the death of their firstborn child in Epping, New Hampshire, in 1895 [142:597]. Frost also once simply stated that the man in "Home Burial" was "more practical and matter-of-fact about death than the woman" [118:3]. Frost once admitted:

> This is a poem I never like to read in the afternoon. Then one of the girls [a student] asked me why I didn't like to read it in the afternoon—too much passion in it for afternoon reading? She wanted to know. I had never put it before that way. Just thought of it at the moment. But I said it then. Best time for passion's in the evening. Who can get all worked up at a matinee performance. Evening's the time for opera—the play. Afternoon's not the time for such [103:377-378].

l. **17.** *"Oh," and again, "Oh."*: in a 1916 interview Frost said:

> Take, for instance, the expression "oh." The American poets use it in practically one tone, that of grandeur: "Oh Soul!" "Oh Hills!"—"Oh Anything!" That's the way they go. But think of what "oh" is really capable: the "oh" of scorn, the "oh" of amusement, the "oh" of surprise, the "oh" of doubt—and there are many more. But these are disdained by the academic poets [51:13].

Robert Newdick's notes from a 1935 meeting with Frost mention as a topic of conversation: "On quantity in English verse: How long is oh? In pain the oh may be drawn out all night. Step on a person's foot and the oh may be second-short" [110:270].

l. **30.** *"Don't, don't, don't, don't"*: Sidney Cox remembers that according to Frost "the four 'don'ts' were the supreme thing in it" [31:89]. This is confirmed in a letter to John Cournos in which Frost stated that although they would also be good in prose, they "gain something from the way they are placed in the verse" [66:130]. In Frost's introduction to Edwin Arlington Robinson's *King Jasper* he wrote of

> the pleasure with which Pound and I laughed over the fourth "thought" in [*ll.* 27–28 of "Miniver Cheevey"] [...].
>
> Three "thoughts" would have been "adequate" as the critical praiseword then was. There would have been nothing to complain of, if it had been left at three. The fourth made the intolerable touch of poetry. With the fourth, the fun began [129:xi].

l. **101.** *One is alone ... alone*: cf. "The Tuft of Flowers," *l.* 8.

ll. **102–107.** *Friends make pretense ... won't*: on this point of how far one should carry sympathy, Frost wrote to Louis Untermeyer on April 12, 1920: "And I suppose I am a brute in that my nature refuses to carry sympathy to the point of going crazy just because someone else goes crazy, or of dying just because someone else dies" [151:103]. In August 1938, Frost wrote to J.J. Lankes: "God damn me when he gets around to it. I refused to be bowed down as much as she [Elinor] was by other deaths" [143:511]. Compare with "Out, Out—," *ll.* 33–34, and "Departmental," *l.* 40–41.

l. 106. *But the world's evil*: according to Frost, after the loss of their son, Elinor repeatedly said, "The world's evil" [142:597].

l. 114. *"If—you—do!"*: in a letter to John Cournos, Frost wrote of these three words: "I am not bothered by the question whether anyone will be able to hear or say those three words ("If—you—do!") as I mean them to be said or heard. I should say that they were suYciently self expressive" [66:130].

The Black Cottage

First published in *North of Boston*. Frost had written "two versions, in and around 1905-6, one in rhyme [see page 210] which I lost on purpose as a failure and the other that came down with some changes into *North of Boston*" [110:163]. Frost made the claim that the first eclogue—"really too much action in them for true eclogues"—was "The Black Cottage" [151:360]. This poem was the only one which Frost had persistently tried to get published in the seven years prior to its publication in *North of Boston* [33:2].

The inspiration for the poem came from the cottage which stood between the Frost farm and Derry Village. It was inhabited by Sarah J. Upton, the widow of George R. Upton, the first volunteer from Derry to enlist in the Grand Army of the Republic near the start of the Civil War. He was killed in action [142:592]. Frost was later to say that there was "nothing decadent in a soldier's widow dying poor in a house that hasn't been painted for years; nor in a soldier's widow dying in the belief that her soldier hadn't fought in vain" [118:3].

l. 31. *Gettysburg or Fredericksburg*: Gettysburg, Pennsylvania, is where, July 1–3, 1863, a battle was fought in which the Union Army won a decisive victory over the Confederate forces. Fredericksburg, Virginia, is the site of the Union Army's greatest defeat at the hands of the Confederates on December 12, 1862.

l. 52. *Garrison*: William Lloyd Garrison (1805–1879), American abolitionist.

l. 53. *Whittier*: John Greenleaf Whittier (1807–1892), American poet.

ll. 61–64. *That all men ... Jefferson*: Thomas Jefferson (1743–1826), 3rd President of the United States (1801–1809), who wrote in the Declaration of Independence that "all men are created equal."

l. **68.** *Welshman*: Jefferson.

l. **88.** *I would have changed the Creed*: referring to the Apostles' Creed, used in Roman Catholic and most Protestant services as the principal traditional affirmation of faith. The Anglican *Book of Common Prayer* version of the creed begins, "I believe in God the Father Almighty, Maker of Heaven and Earth; And in Jesus Christ his only Son [...]." Frost wrote to Sidney Cox in 1914, "Sometime we *must* discuss that minister and his creed. I make it a rule not to take any 'character's' side in anything I write. So I am not bound to defend the minister you understand" [31:53].

l. **94.** *'descended into Hades'*: one of the last additions to the Creed, this refers to Christ's descent into hell, based on I Peter 3:19–20 and 4:6.

ll. **101–103.** *But suppose she ... heartache*: this section may have been a later addition inspired by Frost's reflection in a notebook he kept in England, "She would have felt as sad for any omission in the creed as the child who remembers while in bed that he has forgotten to kiss his mother good night" [156:224].

ll. **109–110.** *Most of the ... favor*: Frost wrote to Charles Lowell Young in 1917: "Now I get my punishment [...] for letting myself believe even for the least division of an hour that there is any such thing as progress. *Mea culpa*" [143:116].

ll. **111–118.** *As I sit ... on*: according to Robert Newdick,

> If he wrote [in 1887], it was usually to add to an endless serial that he had begun in San Francisco—a story about a tribe of Indians who lived in a far-off mountain canyon secure from the outside world. Sometimes after he was a grown man Frost would put himself to sleep by dreaming of those same strange Indians off by themselves in their mountain fastness. A reminiscence of those dreams forms a part of the minister's philosophizing in "The Black Cottage." The speaker wishes for an isolated, uncoveted place where ideas could be held and not assailed by aggressive intruders [110:22–23].

Blueberries

First published in *North of Boston.* According to Frost, the poem was written in 1912 [3:99] and was probably inspired by Frost's reminiscences of his childhood. After the death of Frost's father, William Prescott Frost, Jr., in 1885, the Frosts moved back to New England, feeling like poor relations. That summer they spent some time in Amherst, New Hampshire, on the farm of the late William Frost's uncle and aunt, Benjamin S. and Sarah Frost

Messer. The Messers supplemented their meager farming income by picking wild blueberries and raspberries to sell to the storekeepers in the neighboring town of Milford. Frost and his sister, Jeanie, loved to hunt for the low- and high-bushed blueberries and, even more, they loved the ride to Milford on the wagon with Uncle Messer, stacks of crated blueberries behind them [142:52–53].

l. 29. *chewink*: common Finch.

l. 37. *democrat*: light farm wagon with two or more seats, usually drawn by two horses.

A Servant to Servants

First published in *North of Boston*. A note written by Frost in Edward Connery Lathem's copy of the first edition of *North of Boston* explains that the poem was "a composite of at least three farm wives [...]" [142:568]. One he met in San Francisco and had lost track of, one in New Hampshire and one in Vermont [118:4]. As Lawrance Thompson wrote of the Vermont one:

> Of all the casual acquaintances made by Frost that summer [1909] among visiting botanists and year-round residents [on the northern shore of Willoughby Lake, Vermont], only one of them touched him deeply enough to inspire a poem. In his repeated visits to the Connolley farmhouse to buy milk and eggs, he sometimes lingered to talk with the farmer's wife. Haggard and careworn from her daily rounds of cooking for her husband and his hired men, Mrs. Connolley feared that she could not keep up the pace demanded of her. Frost was touched by her fears more than by her predicament. She admitted that insanity ran in her family, that her father's brother "wasn't right," and she herself had been "put away" for a short time. Recently, she had begun to fear that the same thing might happen again [142:352].

Of Mrs. Connolley, Frost wrote, "One to my reproach went insane. I never should have written her into a poem if I had realized her destiny" [118:4].

The New Hampshire one was the wife of Loren Bailey of Salem, New Hampshire, on whose farm Frost worked the summer of 1889. His experiences on the farm also provided inspiration for his poem, "The Grindstone." Frost called Mrs. Bailey the "hardest worked and frailest of all. [...] She was very kind to me about my working hours. She lent me Jane Porter's *Scottish Chiefs*, one of the first books I ever read through" [118:4].

l. 164. *a long rain*: while the Frosts camped at Willoughby Lake in 1909, their stay was marred by a long period of rainy weather [142:353].

After Apple-Picking

First published in *North of Boston*, the poem was "written in Beaconsfield" [142:432]. Frost's claim to have "played certain poems through without fumbling a sentence" included this poem [9:471]. At a 1958 reading Frost called it an "observing" poem [25:127]. As he was to inscribe in a copy of *Selected Poems* (1923) after this poem, "Imagery and after-imagery are all there is to poetry" [3:111]. In reference to the poems in *North of Boston*, Frost wrote to John Cournos in 1914 that "After Apple-Picking" is the only poem in the volume that will intone [66:129–130].

l. 40. *woodchuck*: the comparison of man and woodchuck comes out of Emerson's essay "Nature," from *Essays: Second Series,* in which he admonishes, "let us be men instead of woodchucks [...]" [30:548].

l. 41. *Long sleep*: from Emerson's essay "Fate," from *The Conduct of Life,* in which he writes, "When hybernation was observed, it was found, that, whilst some animals became torpid in winter, others were torpid in summer: hybernation then was a false name. The *long sleep* [Emerson's italics] is not an effect of cold, but is regulated by the supply of proper food to the animal" [30:961].

The Code

First published as "The Code—Heroics" in *Poetry*, February 1914. In a 1913 letter to John Bartlett it was referred to as "The Code (of Farm Service)" [66:89].

The Generations of Men

First published in *North of Boston*. In a 1913 letter to John Bartlett, Frost called it "The Cellar Hole" and referred to it as a "love affair" and "the least successful of all" [66:89]. Despite this last comment, Frost included this poem in the selections he made for *The Poems of Robert Frost* (New York: Modern Library, 1946) and his *Selected Poems* (1963).

l. 4. *Bow*: town in New Hampshire.

l. 92. *The Indians had a myth of Chicamoztoc*: according to the Aztec creation legend, the first of their race emerged from Chicamoztoc, the Cavern of the Seven Chambers.

l. 152. *Nausicaä*: Greek heroine mentioned in the Odyssey. She was the daughter of Alcinous, king of the Phaeacians, who befriended the shipwrecked Odysseus.

The Housekeeper

First published in *The Egoist*, January 15, 1914, this poem was written on the Derry farm and dated by Frost as 1905 [110:61], although it is possible the poem was written after December 1906 following the death of John Hall, the man about whom this poem was written. In a letter written to John Bartlett in 1913, "Slack Ties" was being considered as a possible title [66:89]. John Hall was a poultryman living in Atkinson, New Hampshire, whom Frost had met at a poultry show in Amesbury, Massachusetts. Frost arranged to call on Hall in 1902. According to Lawrance Thompson, Frost

> had expected to find an impressive outlay of equipment and was surprised to discover that Hall's farm was not as big as his own. The little house and barn were tucked in off a back road beyond a willow-shaded brook which was cluttered with ducks and geese. The barn yard sheltered a surprising congregation of plain and fancy birds [...]. Inside the farmhouse were more surprises: John Hall was not married, but he lived in relative peace and comfort with a common-law housekeeper-wife and her mother, plus a goodly number of Angora cats. Blue-ribbon prizes were tacked up all over the kitchen. It was clear that Hall got extraordinary pleasure out of life, and that prize-winning was his primary concern. He wasn't in the business to make money. Whenever anyone offered him a fancy price for one of his pets, he'd say that if she was worth that much to sell she was worth as much to keep, and that was the end of it. What he could earn from sales of ordinary hens, ducks, geese, and eggs he would spend with a flourish. He had even imported some of his birds from England and South America [142:283].

In a 1913 letter, Frost referred to Hall as the man "who lost his housekeeper and went down like a felled ox. [...] I never knew a man I liked better—damn the world anyway" [5:83]. Hall was also mentioned in "New Hampshire" [*l.* 259] as "Hall of Windham."

l. 146. *Langshang cock*: actually Langshan, a breed of domestic fowl introduced from China.

l. 151. *The Crystal Palace, London*: glass and iron exhibition hall in Hyde Park, London, which housed the great Exhibition of 1851.

The Fear

First published in *Poetry and Drama*, December 1913. According to Frost, this poem was "written at Bethlehem" [3:113], but he may have been referring only to the place where he first heard the story that inspired the poem. If he did actually write it in Bethlehem, New Hampshire, then it must have been written in the late summer of 1907, 1908 or 1910. The poem was probably begun during one of those visits, but was not finished until 1913. As Frost wrote to John Bartlett on August 7, 1913, "I have written one today that I may call 'The Lantern' [...]" [66:89].

"The Fear" had been inspired in 1907, 1908 or 1910 when Mary Lynch told Frost the story of a local girl who had gone to Boston to train as a nurse. There she married but later, falling in love with one of her patients, ran away with her lover to a small farm not far from the Lynches' farm in Bethlehem. Frost had encountered this woman one night when taking his son Carol, then five years old, for a walk along the South Road. On their return they saw the lamp of an approaching carriage and stepped off the road to let it pass. The carriage pulled in at the next house. Frost heard voices and was soon called to by a woman, who wanted to know what they were doing prowling about her property. He explained that they were only out for a walk. When he told Mary Lynch about her, he was told that the woman seemed to live in fear of being found and possibly murdered by her deserted husband [142:344].

ll. 19–21. *And the key ... another*: cf. "House Fear," *ll.* 5–7.

l. 34. *She pushed past ... herself*: in 1914 Frost referred to this line as "a particular line I like" [66:130].

The Self-Seeker

First published in *North of Boston*, this poem was written in England in 1913 [142:530]. In a letter to John Bartlett in 1913, Frost referred to it as "The Wrong" [66:89]. The poem was inspired by an incident which happened while the Frosts were on their honeymoon in Allenstown, New Hampshire, in 1896. They had rented a small cottage with the help of their friend from high school, Carl Burell, a farmer and amateur botanist who was working in a box factory in Pembroke, New Hampshire. In *The Early Years* Lawrance Thompson told the story of how one day when Carl Burell

> [...] was at work in the small factory where planks were sawed and planed and cut into shooks—the units of wood used in assembling a single box—

> the metal lacing on a leather pulley-belt caught the sleeve of his coat. Carl, pulled into the air, tried to hold fast to the belt, and succeeded until he was thrown over a pulley near the ceiling in such a way that his feet struck the roof girders. Falling to the floor heavily, and knocked unconscious, he seemed to be dead. When he recovered consciousness, he felt as though he had broken almost every bone in his body. The doctor's verdict was that his feet were so badly smashed that it might be necessary to amputate them both, but no decision could be made for some time. He was confined to his bed at his boarding house, where Rob visited him repeatedly. They both realized that all of Carl's devotion to the quest for his beloved flowers and plants would be curtailed pathetically if he were never able to walk again. As it happened, Rob himself became a witness to the scene in which Carl was paid a relatively small sum of money by an insurance representative, prior to the time when anyone could know for certain just how badly injured he might be. Amputation was not necessary [...] [142:220].

l. 85. *Burroughs*: John Burroughs (1837–1921), American naturalist, who lived in the Catskill mountain region of New York.

l. 86. *Cypripedium reginae*: queen's orchid.

l. 112. *Ram's Horn orchid*; *l.* 137 *Yellow Lady's Slipper*; *l.* 142 *Purple Lady's Slipper*: three lady's-slipper orchids, about which, according to Lawrance Thompson, Frost

> must have known he was taking poetic license in suggesting the possibility that these three lady's-slippers might be found blooming in the same days of spring [...] but it was befitting his tribute to Carl Burell that these three cherished members of the orchid family should be clustered in the same poetic bouquet [142:222].

l. 154. *Floating Heart*: small flower which grew in the water of local ponds.

The Wood-Pile

First published in *North of Boston*. According to Frost, this poem was written, or at least begun, in Derry [3:113; 133:119]. Frost's claim that he "played certain poems through without fumbling a sentence" included this poem [9:471].

ll. 10–17. *A small bird ... him*: this section about the bird may be a later addition inspired by Frost's reflection in a notebook which he kept in England, "As a bird that flies before you and thinks it is pursued" [156:221].

l. 30. *Clematis*: a vine or herb of the buttercup family.

l. 40. *slow smokeless burning*: the phrase was what Frost referred to as one of his "lucky snatches from an advertising page in the *Literary Digest* [...] one of those things a writer picks up by chance and steals them to new uses." The advertisement was for a firearms firm which described an "Infallible Smokeless" powder [13:164].

Good Hours

First published in *North of Boston*, the poem was written at Plymouth during the winter of 1911-1912 [142:433; 3:99, 104].

Mountain Interval

The first edition was published in New York by Henry Holt in 1916. The book was dedicated, "To you who least need reminding that before this interval of the South Branch under black mountains, there was another interval, the Upper at Plymouth, where we walked in spring beyond the covered bridge; but that the first interval of all was the old farm, our brook interval, so called by the man we had it from in sale." The "you who least need reminding" in the dedication is Frost's wife, Elinor. The "South Branch" interval refers to the Frosts' farm in Franconia, New Hampshire, purchased in 1915; the "Upper at Plymouth," their time in Plymouth, New Hampshire (September 1911 to September 1912); the "first interval [...] our brook interval," their period on the farm in Derry, New Hampshire (1900–1911), the brook being Hyla Brook [see the poem "Hyla Brook"]. It was not, however, acquired "in sale," but was bequeathed to Frost by his paternal grandfather.

In the original table of contents, six poems were emphasized by printing them in full capitals rather than small capitals as the other titles had appeared. These were "Christmas Trees," "In the Home Stretch," "Birches," "The Hill Wife," "The Bonfire" and "Snow." The opening poem, "The Road Not Taken," and the concluding poem, "The Sound of the Trees," were printed in italic.

In *Collected Poems* (1930 and all subsequent editions), "The Exposed Nest" was moved from its original placement between "A Girl's Garden" and "Out, Out—" to a position immediately following "An Old Man's Winter Night." Two poems which were not originally in *Mountain Interval*, "Locked Out" and "The Last Word of a Bluebird," were added.

Frost felt that this volume was rushed into print by Alfred Harcourt before he had sufficient time to impose on its design a thematic or structural unity equivalent to that of his first two volumes [110:272].

The Road Not Taken

First published in *The Atlantic Monthly*, August 1915.

Frost began writing the poem in England in 1914 and completed it in Franconia before his first public use of it on May 5, 1915 [143:546; 3:99, 117; 24:65].

"I'll bet not half a dozen people can tell who was hit and where he was hit by my 'Road Not Taken,'" Frost wrote to Louis Untermeyer [151:14]. The poem had, in fact, been inspired by Frost's amusement regarding a familiar habit of Edward Thomas, his closest friend while living in England. In 1914, Frost and Thomas often took long walks through the Gloucestershire countryside. Thomas would try to choose a way which might allow him to show his botanizing friend a rare plant or a special scene. Often, before the walk ended, Thomas would regret his choice, sighing over what they could have seen if they had chosen a better route [66:xiv]. After one particular walk, Frost said to Thomas, "No matter which road you take, you'll always sigh, and wish you'd taken another" [143:88]. Although it had been these walks with Thomas which inspired "The Road Not Taken," the image of the two roads occupied Frost's mind earlier when he wrote to Susan Hayes Ward on February 10, 1912:

> Two lonely cross-roads that themselves cross each other I have walked several times this winter without meeting or overtaking so much as a single person on foot or on runners. The practically unbroken condition of both for several days after a snow or a blow proves that neither is much travelled [133:87].

That the above image was a catalyst for this poem is partially confirmed by his once dating the poem "1912? 1914" [3:114].

The "two roads" theme has a long tradition in literature. Frost would have been aware of this archetypical pattern from a variety of sources. Following are a sampling of sources with which Frost would have been familiar.

In Virgil's *Aeneid* (book VI, *ll.* 540–543), the Sibyl tells Aeneas:

> Here is the place
> Where the road forks: on the right hand it goes
> Past mighty Dis's walls, Elysium way,
> Our way; but the leftward road will punish
> Malefactors, taking them to Tartarus [155:178].

In the section "Table-Talk" from *Drift-Wood,* Longfellow has this statement: "Round about what is, lies a whole mysterious world of might be [...] by turning down this street instead of the other, we may let slip some great occasion of good, or avoid some impending evil, by which the whole current of our lives would have been changed" [100:405–406].

Emily Dickinson wrote a poem beginning

> Our journey had advanced;
> Our feet were almost come
> To that odd fork in Being's road
> ... [1.2:276].

In his essay "Circles," Emerson wrote, "The difference between talents and character is adroitness to keep the old and trodden road, and power and courage to make a new road to new and better goals" [30:413].

Thoreau wrote in his journal on Sunday, August 31, 1851, that "our customs turn the hour of sunset to a trivial time as at the meeting of two roads—one coming from the noon and the other leading to the night [...]" [146.1:254].

William James, in the final paragraph to "The Will to Believe," wrote, "We stand on a mountain pass in the midst of whirling snow and blinding mist, through which we get glimpses now and then of paths which may be deceptive. [...] If we take the wrong road we shall be dashed to pieces" [91:479]. Even more to the point, James wrote in "The Dilemma of Determinism,"

> What is meant by saying that my choice of which way to walk home after the lecture is ambiguous and matter of chance as far as the present moment is concerned? It means that both Divinity Avenue and Oxford Street are called; but that only one, and that one *either* one, shall be chosen [91:573].

Frost was often dismayed at people reading more into his poems than he had intended. On interpreting the poem, Frost said during a reading at Wofford College in South Carolina:

> Should you take a hint when none is intended? Or should you, with more sensitive nature, only take hints when they *are* intended? And that's so in reading my poetry. That poem: there's a hint intended there. But you ought to know that yourself. One of the things I suffer from, you know, is being taken as intending a double meaning when I don't. Sometimes I do, and sometimes I don't. And I can't mark 'em [...] [143:547].

On the form of the poem, Frost said that when you read the poem you can just go past the rhymes as if they weren't noticed. Talking past the rhymes almost hides them. He said he was complimented whenever anyone said that when they read a poem of his they can hear him talking [25:123].

l. **16.** *I shall be telling this with a sigh*: speaking of the sigh, Frost warned a Bread Loaf audience that "the tone of that is absolutely saving" [25:112].

Christmas Trees
A Christmas circular letter

First published in *Mountain Interval.* According to Frost, this poem was written in Franconia on Christmas morning of 1915 [but it may have been the morning of the 24th—see below], on the spur of the moment. It was written for use on a handmade Christmas card, each card to be decorated with marginal illustrations which the Frost children were to make. The only known completed card in this form was the one sent to Louis Untermeyer, postmarked December 24, 1915 [143:540; 151:20–21]. The poem was read as "The Christmas Tree" on March 13, 1916, at Bates College [31:96]. See 151:20–21 for a variant version.

l. 12. *my Christmas trees*: Frost also referred to his trees in his 1917 poem, "For Allan, Who Wanted to See How I Wrote a Poem," *l.* 1–3.

l. 24. *The trial by ... to*: in a letter to Louis Untermeyer written on June 8, 1915, Frost wrote of poetry's trial by market:

> A thousand copies is a lot of any book of poetry to sell. Five hundred is more of an edition than many a good man sells in England. Big reputations are made on smaller sales. [...]
>
> Do you know, I think that a book ought to sell. Nothing is quite honest that is not commercial. Mind you I don't put it that everything commercial is honest [151:8–9].

An Old Man's Winter Night

First published in *Mountain Interval*, this poem was begun during the winter of 1906-1907, in Derry. Frost twice dated this poem as 1916 [3:100, 117] implying that the poem was completed shortly before its publication. This poem was chosen by Frost for an expanded edition of *North of Boston* that he was considering [144:178]. "An Old Man's Winter Night" may have been inspired by Charles Lambert, a local who lived for years as a hermit [143:540]. For an account of him see the *Derry Enterprise*, August 3, 1906, p. 3. More than once Frost said that this was the best poem in *Mountain Interval* [31:132; 133:179].

The Exposed Nest

First published in *Mountain Interval* following "A Girl's Garden." The poem recalls an event in the Derry period, but according to Frost it was written in 1915 in Franconia [143:541]. Frost also dated the poem as 1913 [3:100] and recalls having shown it to Edward Thomas, placing the poem before the Frosts' departure from England in February of 1915 [3:114].

A Patch of Old Snow

First published in *Mountain Interval.* The beginnings of the poem occurred in Frost's letter to John Bartlett, written from England on February 22, 1914. See 2:82–83.

In the Home Stretch

First published in *Century Magazine*, July 1916. According to Lawrance Thompson, this poem was probably written in Derry prior to 1909 [143:541]. Frost himself, however, referred to the poem as "very recent" in relation to its publication in *Mountain Interval* (1916) [3:117]. The poem, according to Newdick, "is a pretty close account of his [Frost's] and Elinor's first hours on their [Derry] farm, in their first home of their own [...]" [110:72]. Frost wrote into a copy of *Mountain Interval* that this poem was made of several places, but mostly the Derry farm [165:"RFA 16 1916 c.4" 30].

l. **118.** *the game "ten-step" the children play*: Frost's granddaughter, Lesley Lee Francis, describes the game as being "played with two lines of players: each line attempted to kick-catch the ball before it hit the ground, and thereby gained ten steps toward the opponent's goal" [36:206].

The Telephone

First published in *The Independent*, October 9, 1916. According to Lawrance Thompson, the poem was probably written between 1900 and 1910 on the Derry farm [143:541]. In 1930 Frost dated the poem as 1913 [3:100].

Meeting and Passing

First published in *Mountain Interval*, this poem was probably written, according to Lawrance Thompson, during Frost's sonnet writing period of 1906-1907 [143:541]. Frost dated the poem as 1912 [3:117].

The incident which inspired it took place in 1895 when Frost was renting space at the home of Henry Horne on Ossipee Mountain (now Mt. Shaw) in Moultonboro, New Hampshire. He had accompanied the White sisters, Elinor and Leona, who were staying in a rented cottage nearby. Leona White had been commissioned to paint the portraits of the grandchildren of the late Benjamin A. Shaw, owner of the Shaw Knit Stocking Company in Lowell, Massachusetts, who had built a summer home and small hotel in the White Mountains. Often the three would take walks together to explore the area. If Leona was busy with her art, it was better for Frost and Elinor. Frost felt, however, that there was something distant in Elinor's manner and he occasionally felt jealous at the way in which she easily responded to the needs of the Shaw family or their friends. Sometimes, as Elinor was heading down to Melvin Village on some errand, their paths might cross. Frost felt that there was a strange juxtaposition of intimacy and distance. Years later on the Derry farm the poet tried to capture the feeling of those brief meetings and passings [142:203-205].

Hyla Brook

First published in *Mountain Interval*, this poem was written on the Derry farm (1900–1910), according to Frost. Lawrance Thompson narrows that time frame down to probably 1906-1907 when Frost was writing sonnets and sonnet variants [143:541]. Frost dated the poem as 1904 [3:100] and also as 1912 [3:117].

Title *Hyla Brook*: brook on Frost's Derry, New Hampshire, farm. In a 1915 letter to John Haines, Frost wrote about "[...] the brook on my old farm. It always dried up in summer. The Hyla is a small frog that shouts like jingling bells in the marshes in the spring" [66:171].

l. 14. *brooks taken otherwhere in song*: see Tennyson's "The Brook," which has the refrain:

> For men may come and men may go,
> But I go on for ever [139:218, 220].

l. 15. *We love the things we love for what they are*: Frost said of this line at a Bread Loaf reading that it clinches the metaphor of the poem [25:55].

The Oven Bird

First published in *Mountain Interval.* According to Frost this poem was written on the Derry farm (1900–1910). Lawrance Thompson narrows that time-frame down to probably 1906-1907 when Frost was writing sonnets and sonnet variants [143:541]. Frost once dated the poem as 1902 [3:100] and once also as 1905 [3:117]. The autumnal images in this poem once prompted Frost to tell an audience that it might pair with "Nothing Gold Can Stay" [25:146].

l. 2. *a mid-summer and a mid-wood bird*: a possible echo of the opening of Dante's *The Inferno*:

> Midway in our life's journey, I went astray
> from the straight road and woke to find myself
> alone in a dark wood [29:3].

l. 5. *Mid-summer is to spring as one to ten*: Frost's poetic output slowed as he matured. He was very prolific as a youth and, as he told Daniel Smythe in 1940,

> I went to England with the material for several books. In every book I ever published, there is material from that early period. If I ever publish another book, there will be pieces in it from those first efforts [136:83].

True to his word, every book of poetry published in his lifetime, contained at least one of these "first efforts." Even in Frost's final volume, *In the Clearing*, the poem "[We Vainly Wrestle ...]" is really an excerpt from an unpublished 1911 poem entitled "New Grief." Of the more than a hundred poems left uncollected at the time of Frost's death, more than forty were written prior to his leaving the Derry farm in 1912.

l. 6. *the early petal-fall is past*: Frost's first outpouring as a youth. In his 1957 essay, "Maturity No Object," Frost wrote that "all poets I have ever heard of struck their note long before forty [...]" [109:11].

Regarding Wordsworth's power to summon up out of experience his creative imagination, which "after ten years Wordsworth had very nearly exhausted," Frost said, "The power, however, to do this does not last very long in the life of a poet" [143:36].

l. 12. *he knows ... sing*: as Frost wrote to John Bartlett in February 1914 in which he discussed his own poetic theories, "Get away from the singsong" [2:83].

Bond and Free

First published in *Mountain Interval.* This poem may have been written between 1896 and 1900 [143:541; 3:103], although Frost twice dated the poem as late as 1904-1905 [3:100, 117]. Frost once said that the poem was all about science [25:146]. See 31:26–27 for a variant version sent to Sidney Cox on July 10, 1913.

l. 12 *Sirius*: brightest star in the heavens. Frost used the same Sirius/serious pun in "One More Brevity," l. 58.

Birches

First published in *The Atlantic Monthly*, August 1915, this poem was written in England in 1913 [156:248]. At that time it was referred to as "Swinging Birches" [66:89]. Frost said he wrote the poem when he was a little homesick in England [142:433]. John Haines has said, "'Swinging Birches' he often read to us in 1914 and my wife and I have often thought that when published it was a great deal shortened" [103:133]. Despite Frost's claim that this poem was written "with one stroke of the pen" [132:300], Frost later said that "'Birches' is two fragments soldered together so long ago I have forgotten where the joint is" [9:471]. Frost once dated the poem as 1906 [3:100], which may refer to an early draft of one of the fragments.

Frost first learned to swing birches the summer of his twelfth year from his best friend, Charley Peabody, a boy whose fearless and extroverted traits contrasted with Frost's traits of shyness and cautious hesitancy [142:59–60]. Later, he taught this game to his daughter Lesley. Two passages from the journals Lesley kept when she was six deal with swinging birches:

> [...] on the way home i climbed up a hi birch and came down with it and i stopt in the air about three feet and pap cout me [40:II, 2].
>
> i like to climb trees very much but mama doesnt like me to becose i tare my stocings so i have to stop i do not like to but i have to at frst i was scared to swing with birchis but now i am not so much scared becose it wont hurt me. and i am not scared if it swings down with me if it goes klere down with me i dont like it if it dosunt i climb uther threes but they downt swing as the birchis do so i downt like them aswell i climb oak and mapel but with me they swing with me. i like that to but not as well but papa likes to swing beter [than I do] i climb apale trees but those dont swing a tall do they [40:II, 5–6].

l. 3. *some boy's been bending them*: see "Wild Grapes" for a girl's viewpoint of bending birches.

l. 43. *It's when I'm weary of considerations*: during a 1954 Bread Loaf reading, Frost said that over the years this line had come to mean the most to him [25:51].

ll. 48–49. *I'd like to ... over*: speaking to John Bartlett in 1934 about finding freedom by getting away from humankind and living an isolated life, Frost said: "It isn't in man's nature to live an isolated life. Freedom isn't to be had that way. Going away and looking at man in perspective, and then coming back ... an in and out existence ... that is what's sane and good" [2:175].

l. 55. *both going and coming back*: during a 1931 interview, Frost said, "I should expect life to be back and forward—now more individual on the farm, now more social in the city—striving to get the balance" [60:5]. As he phrased it in a June 7, 1937, letter,

> [...] there are no two things as important in life and art as being threatened and being saved. What are ideals of form for if we aren't going to be made to fear for them? All our ingenuity is lavished on getting into danger legitimately so that we may be genuinely rescued [98:101].

Pea Brush

First published in *Mountain Interval*, the poem was begun in Derry in 1905 [3:100] and appeared as the four stanza "Pea-sticks" in the typewritten magazine, *The Bouquet* (July 1914), compiled by the Frost children [143:541]. Lines 5–12 were later inscribed to Lawrance Thompson in a copy of *Mountain Interval* with the title, "A Spring Day in a New Clearing."

Title *Pea Brush*: stakes or sticks upon which a garden pea-plant is trained.

ll. 2–4. *John had been ... peas*: in a pocket notebook Frost carried while in England he wrote, "[John] Holis said I could have all the brushwood I wanted to brush my peas" [156:224].

Putting in the Seed

First published in *Poetry and Drama*, December 1914. Although Lawrance Thompson claims this poem for Frost's sonnet period on the Derry farm, 1906–1907 [143:541], in 1917 Frost recalled the poem being written in England in 1914 [66:220]. In 1930, however, Frost confirmed the Derry-years dating of the poem as 1905 [3:100].

A Time to Talk

First published in *The Prospect* (Plymouth Normal School, Plymouth, NH), June 1916. According to Lawrance Thompson, this poem was written in Franconia in 1915 or 1916 [143:541]. In 1930, Frost dated the poem as 1905 [3:100].

The Cow in Apple Time

First published in *Poetry and Drama*, December 1914, this poem was written in England in 1914 [143:541; 3:100]. At a 1935 reading Frost confessed that he used to tell his audiences that he got the idea from the Prince Albert Memorial in London, [see 25:113] although it was really written in England when he was homesick for Derry and a "heroic-sized" cow he once owned [26:356].

An Encounter

First published in *The Atlantic Monthly*, November 1916. According to Lawrance Thompson, this poem fits Frost's "bog-trotting days" during which he wrote "The Quest of the Purple-Fringed" in 1896 [143:541]. In 1930, Frost dated this poem as 1916 [3:100] but this may have been a confusion with its date of publication. Following this poem in a copy of *Mountain Interval*, Frost wrote that it was about the region in Vermont near Lake Willoughby [165:"RFA 16 1916 c.4" 47].

ll. **12–13.** *a resurrected tree ... again*: cf. "The Line-Gang," *ll.* 3–4.

l. **19.** *Where aren't you nowadays?*: telephone lines, something Frost had not seen as a boy, became ever-present as he grew older. As he explained to his grandson, William Prescott Frost, in a letter written on August 22, 1935:

> Electricity has come into use in my life time. When I came to New England in 1885, there wasn't a telephone in the city I lived in, Lawrence, Mass., and there wasn't an electric light. At least I didn't know of any. The telegraph had been going for quite a while. The wires were everywhere even in San Francisco. We used to loose [sic] our kites on them. But most electrical developments have taken place with me looking on [48:182].

l. 24. *the orchid Calypso*: *Calypsos Bulbosa*, a rare orchid, declining in New England and possibly extinct in New Hampshire.

Range-Finding

First published in *Mountain Interval*, this poem was written in Derry between 1900 and Christmas 1911, when it was sent to Susan Hayes Ward [143:541; 3:100, 118]. Frost wrote Amy Lowell that "Range-Finding" was one of several war poems written during peacetime, "circa 1902?" and that it was saved from being waste paper by Edward Thomas's having liked it [66:220]. This is confirmed by an unpublished annotation Frost made in a copy of *Mountain Interval* [165:"RFA 16 1916 c.4" 48].

The Hill Wife

Group of five poems first published in *The Yale Review*, April 1916 (except for poem III, "The Smile," which was previously published in *Poetry and Drama*, December 1914). "The Hill Wife" is the collective title for the following five poems:

I. Loneliness
Her Word

First published in *The Yale Review*, April 1916. Frost dated "Loneliness" as 1905 [143:541].

II. House Fear

First published in *The Yale Review*, April 1916. Frost dated "House Fear" as 1906 [143:541].

ll. 5–7. *They learned to ... flight*: this fear of unknown things which may be lying in wait is also expressed in "The Fear," *ll.* 19–21.

III. The Smile
Her Word

First published in *Poetry and Drama*, December 1914, it was later incorporated into "The Hill Wife" sequence and published in *The Yale Review*, April 1916. Frost dated "The Smile" as 1913 [143:541]. On Frost's fear of tramps, Lawrance Thompson wrote, "Any forlorn vagrant who knocked at the door to ask for a piece of bread or a cup of milk was—at least to Frost—a potential barn-burner, thief, murderer" [142:279]. Cf. "A Bed in the Barn," *ll.* 1–2.

IV. The Oft-Repeated Dream

First published in *The Yale Review*, April 1916. Frost dated this poem as 1916 [143:541].

V. The Impulse

First published in *The Yale Review*, April 1916. Frost dated this poem as 1913 [143:541].

The Bonfire

First published in *The Seven Arts*, November 1916. According to Lawrance Thompson, this poem was written in Franconia prior to June 1915, [143:541] although Frost was still revising it prior to his first public recitation of it before the Phi Beta Kappa Society at Harvard in June 1916 [143:79; 3:100]. Frost wrote to Amy Lowell in 1917 that "The Bonfire" was his only poem about World War I and that it was more about New England than what was happening in Europe [66:220].

Spring on the Derry farm was the time for raking up the dead leaves and branches for burning. Each year a great bonfire was built in the middle of the pasture across the road from the house. The April 1905 bonfire was one which got out of control. A breeze bent the tall flames down to the ground where it caught on the dead grass on the side near the road. Soon flames were rushing toward the stone wall and the road with the possibility of reaching the house. The dirt road prevented the fire from spreading any further to the east, but to the north and south, pasture was still burning. Frost extinguished the flames by beating on them with an old workcoat—or a board according to Frost's daughter Lesley (see 40:I.31). The last smoldering areas were doused with water from Hyla brook. They couldn't believe that so much had burned in so little time [142:301]. In her journal, six-year-old Lesley described this 1905 bonfire:

> we had a fire in the medow and we new it would not go across the brook and it set haf of the feld on fire and it went to the rod and it birnd are grap vine and rob thout it would get across in the other feld that a spark mite fly across but it did not and and when the brush had nely gone out we trid to put it out rob put it out with a bourd and i put it out with a pes of pine stik and i ran up and got a pail and rub the smoky places [40:I.31].

l. **58.** *Hyla brook*: brook on Frost's Derry farm. See "Hyla Brook."

ll. **104–108.** *About the ships ... towns*: references to the sinking of the *Lusitania* in 1915 and to the Zeppelin bombings of England during World War I.

A Girl's Garden

First published in *Mountain Interval*, this poem was written in Franconia in 1915-1916 [143:541; 3:100].

l. 1. *A neighbor*: in a copy of *Mountain Interval* Frost identified this neighbor as being a friend in Raymond, New Hampshire [165:"RFA 16 1916 c.4" 60].

Locked Out
As told to a child

First published in the typewritten magazine, *The Bouquet* (September 1914), compiled by the Frost children [36:120], it was later reprinted in *The Forge*, February 1917. This poem was not included in the first edition of *Mountain Interval*, but was added in 1930. Frost dated the poem between 1896 and 1900 [3:100, 104].

Subtitle *child*: if this refers to one of the Frost children and if Frost's dating of the poem is correct, the child would have to be Elliott.

The Last Word of a Bluebird
As told to a child

Not included in the first edition of *Mountain Interval,* this poem was added to *Mountain Interval* and first published in 1930. Composed in 1903 for his daughter Lesley as "The Message the Crow Gave Me for Lesley, One Morning Lately When I Went to the Well," the original version is similar to the twenty-two line version published in 1930. The following expanded version of forty-one lines was written in 1906 and sent to Susan Hayes Ward as "The Blue Bird to Lesley":

As I went out, a crow
In the dooryard said, "Oh,
I was looking for you!
How do you do?
Well, I just came to tell you
To tell Lesley—will you?—
That her little blue bird
Wanted me to bring word
That the north wind last night
That made the stars bright
And made ice on the trough
Almost made him cough
His little tail off.
He wanted to see her,
But winter's so near—
He just had to fly!
But he sent her, Good-bye,
And said to be good,
And bring in the wood,
And wear her red hood,
And look for fox tracks
In the snow with an ax
(But not catch a cold)
And get five years old,
And do everything,
And perhaps in the spring
He'll come back and sing.
He felt you don't know
How sorry to go
And leave the poor baby
(Her ribbon off, maybe)
And as wild as a bear,
And no one to care
And give her her supper
But mamma and papa.
But he told me to say
He would think every day—
Every time he began a
Coconut or banana—
And wonder about her
And cry some without her"
[40:II, 1,8-9 Notes].

Subtitle *child*: Lesley Frost.
l. 24. *And get five years old*: Lesley would have been five in 1904.

"Out, Out—"

First published in *McClure's*, July 1916. "Out, Out—" was inspired by talks with the Edward Connery Lathems about the tragedy which befell Raymond Tracy Fitzgerald, who lived on the South Road out of Bethlehem [142:567]. Although inspired by Fitzgerald's death, which took place in 1910, Frost did not write the poem until 1915-1916 [143:541]. The story about the Fitzgerald boy was reported in *The Littleton* [N.H.] *Courier* on March 31, 1910, as follows:

> Raymond Tracy Fitzgerald, one of the twin sons of Michael G. and Margaret Fitzgerald of Bethlehem, died at his home Thursday afternoon, March 24, as the result of an accident by which one of his hands was badly hurt in a sawing machine. The young man was assisting in sawing up some wood in his own dooryard with a sawing machine and accidentally hit the loose pulley, causing the saw to descend upon his hand, cutting and lacerating it badly. Raymond was taken into the house and a physician was immediately summoned, but he died very suddenly from the effects of the shock, which produced heart failure [...] [quoted in 142:567].

Title *"Out, Out—"*: from Shakespeare's *Macbeth* [V.v.23-28]:

> Out, out, brief candle!
> Life's but a walking shadow, a poor player,
> That struts and frets his hour upon the stage,
> And then is heard no more. It is a tale
> Told by an idiot, full of sound and fury,
> Signifying nothing [134:1337].

ll. 33–34. *No more to ... affairs*: on how far one is supposed to carry sympathy, Frost wrote to Louis Untermeyer on April 12, 1920: "And I suppose I am a brute in that my nature refuses to carry sympathy to the point of going crazy just because someone else goes crazy, or of dying just because someone else dies" [151:103]. On August 2, 1938, Frost wrote to J.J. Lankes: "God damn me when he gets around to it. I refused to be bowed down as much as she [Elinor] was by other deaths" [143:511]. Cf. "Home Burial," *ll.* 102–105, and "Departmental," *ll.* 40–41.

Brown's Descent

First published in *Mountain Interval*, this poem was written in Franconia in 1915 [143:542]. In *Mountain Interval* the poem was subtitled: "or, The Willy-Nilly Slide." Originally titled, "The Story of Brown and the Winter

Wind," the poem was based on a story told to Frost by George H. Browne. According to Browne, the descent was made by a man names Goss in Ashland, New Hampshire [143:537]. In a 1917 letter to Lewis N. Chase, Frost wrote that this poem "is not a good poem: I sort of did it on purpose to please a few people who gave me the subject" [5:75].

The Gum-Gatherer

First published in *The Independent*, October 9, 1916, this poem was written in Franconia in 1915-1916 [143:542; 3:100]. In a letter to Marguerite Wilkinson, Frost lightly remarked that this poem was a favorite of his if for no other reason than it "speak[s] poetically of chewing gum" [66:233].

The Line-Gang

First published in *Mountain Interval.* Lawrance Thompson places this poem in Frost's sonnet period of 1906–1907 [143:542].

ll. 3–4. *They plant dead ... thread*: cf. "An Encounter," *ll.* 12–13.

The Vanishing Red

First published in *The Craftsman*, July 1916, this poem was written in Franconia in 1915-1916 [143:542; 3.100]. According to an annotation made by Frost in a copy of *Mountain Interval*, the story was told to him by someone from Acton [165:"RFA 16 1916 c.4" 75]. Frost also referred to his father-in-law as his source for this story [3:114]. On the metrics of the poem, Frost wrote to Louis Mertins: "This was not intended for any kind of verse. It wanted to scan but I wouldn't let it" [103:151].

Title *The Vanishing Red*: used in this poem to refer to the disappearance of John, "the last Red Man in Acton," the phrase was commonly employed to refer to the diminution and disappearance of the entire race of native Americans.

l. 2. *Acton*: Frost said the place "was Acton, Mass., a hundred or more years ago" [103:151].

Snow

First published in *Poetry*, November 1916. "Snow" was written between 1912 and 1916 [3:100] but prior to March 8, 1916, on which date it was sent to *Poetry*. Lawrance Thompson dates it as 1915-1916 in Franconia [143:542]. The poem was chosen by Frost for an expanded edition of *North of Boston* that he was considering [144:178]. In an unpublished annotation Frost wrote that this was a combination of "Many people, places and winters [...]" [165:"RFA 16 1916 c.4" 98].

The Sound of Trees

First published in *Poetry and Drama*, December 1914, a second publication of the poem shortly followed in *The Atlantic*, August 1915. In *Mountain Interval* the poem was entitled "The Sound of the Trees." Although Lawrance Thompson claims that the poem was written at Lascelles Abercrombie's cottage in Ryton, England [143:37], and has an "implied reference to Abercrombie's elms called the Seven Sisters" [142:472], John W. Haines had this to say:

> A word about the trees. Written at Dymock for Lascelles Abercrombie, but *not* in connection with the *Ryton Firs* of L.A.'s poem. These were on a hill some way beyond the Gallows and cut down earlier. R.F. told me so, adding that at the back of his mind were a group of trees near his old home in America—I assumed New England [103:128].

Frost wrote to Amy Lowell in 1917 that if any poem was in danger of being influenced by Lascelles Abercrombie or Wilfrid Gibson it might be "The Sound of Trees" [66:220].

New Hampshire

The first trade edition was published in New York by Henry Holt in 1923. A limited edition of three hundred and fifty numbered and signed copies was also published. The book was dedicated, "To Vermont and Michigan." The title-page carried the subtitle, "A Poem with Notes and Grace Notes." The volume was originally divided into three parts: the title poem; a second section, "Notes" (from "A Star in a Stoneboat" through "I Will Sing You One-O"); and a third section, "Grace Notes" (from "Fragmentary Blue" through "The Need of Being Versed in Country Things"). Several lines in the title poem bore footnoted references to poems in the "Notes" section as did one line in "The Star Splitter."

New Hampshire

First published in *New Hampshire*, the poem was written in one night during the summer of 1922—in either June [133:249; 143:237, 594] or July [143:231]. An inscription in a copy of *Complete Poems* (1949) confirms that Frost had written "New Hampshire" all in one night [120:91]. As he told Louis Mertins:

> But the thing I worked on all night had no struggle in it at all. It's in print, called "New Hampshire." I sat in the same chair and wrote all night. Had a good time writing scatteringly about New Hampshire—how the state has nothing to sell in commercial quantities [103:82].

In 1938 Frost wrote to Louis Untermeyer, "I satisfied my conscience with hints at the truth, as in the last part of the poem 'New Hampshire' [...]" [151:305].

l. 1. *a lady from the South*: the manuscript has this woman coming from New York.

l. 7. *sell*: footnote in *New Hampshire*, "Cf. 'The Axe-Helve'."

l. 14. *Pullman*: a railroad passenger car furnished for day and night travel.

l. 19. *Vigilance Committees*: a volunteer committee of citizens organized to suppress and punish crime summarily when the law appears to be inadequate.

ll. 20–21. *Stefansson runs on ... Arctic*: Vilhjalmur Stefansson (1879–1962), Canadian Arctic explorer.

l. **30.** *Volstead Act*: National Prohibition Enforcement Act, named after U.S. Rep. Andrew J. Volstead of Minnesota, went into effect January 16, 1920, to enforce the 18th Amendment, which banned the manufacture and sale of liquor in the United States. In 1932 the 21st Amendment was passed, repealing the 18th Amendment.

l. **40.** *Constantinople*: Istanbul (Turkey).

l. **64.** *Purse*: Franklin Pierce (1804–1869), 14th President of the United States (1853–1857).

l. **67.** *Daniel Webster*: American statesman and orator (1782–1852).

l. **69.** *Dartmouth*: Dartmouth College, founded in 1769. Frost attended Dartmouth College for less than one semester in 1892.

l. **74.** *John Smith*: English colonist in America (1580–1631).

l. **76.** *Isles of Shoals*: group of nine rocky islands ten miles southeast of Portsmouth, New Hampshire.

l. **86.** *Nottingham*: county, and city within that county, in England.

l. **100.** *one I don't know what to call him*: Cornelius Weygandt (1871–1957). In a copy of *New Hampshire* Frost wrote that his difficulty in describing Weygandt is that he is "a cross between New Hampshire Yankee and Pennsylvania Dutch and between farmer and professor" [120:30].

l. **106.** *Dorkings because they're spoken of by Chaucer*: a Dorking is a five-toed, square-formed breed of poultry. Chaucer does not refer to Dorkings by name.

l. **107.** *Sussex because they're spoken of by Herrick*: a Sussex is a four-toed fowl from Sussex. Herrick does not refer to Sussex by name.

l. **108.** *She has a touch of gold. New Hampshire gold*: footnote in *New Hampshire*, "Cf. 'A Star in a Stone-boat' *l.* 5."

l. **117.** *Andover or Canaan*: Andover is a town in Massachusetts; Canaan is a town in Grafton County, New Hampshire.

l. **118** *beryl*: a mineral.

l. **125.** *style*: footnote in *New Hampshire*, "Cf. 'The Witch of Coös'."

l. **125.** *Colebrook*: town in Coös County, New Hampshire.

l. **135.** *The S'ciety for Psychical Research*: British society founded in 1882 to examine scientifically without prejudice or prepossession those faculties of man which appear to be inexplicable on any generally recognized hypothesis. A comparable American society was founded in 1884 by Sir William Barrett, a member of the British society. A prominent early member of the American society was William James.

l. **138.** *Salem*: town in New Hampshire.

l. **148.** *quality*: footnote in *New Hampshire*, "Cf. 'The Census Taker' *l.* 57, 'The Star-Splitter' *l.* 26, 'A Star in a Stone-boat' *l.* 21."

ll. **150–158.** *The farm I ... better*: after the Frosts returned to America in 1915, Frost searched for a small farm to settle down on, and found the farm he was looking for in Franconia, New Hampshire. As explained by Lawrance Thompson from information received from the widow of Willis Herbert:

> The serious hitch was that there seemed to be little chance of displacing the present owner, whom he found raking dead leaves away from the front of the house. Entering the dooryard and striking up a conversation, the intruder explained that he was just out tramping, but wasn't a tramp; he wanted to buy a farm, and this was the one he liked best. The owner, Willis E. Herbert, amused by the bluntness of the visitor's approach, said maybe they could help each other. Herbert, needing more pasturage than he had here for his livestock, had taken a fancy to a larger farm, half a mile farther up the road. The larger farm was being rented at present by Herbert's brother, who wanted to give it up and find work in the village. So if the blunt-spoken visitor wanted this little farm and was willing to pay a thousand dollars for it, Herbert would move in a hurry. [...] Apologetically, he said that he couldn't find a thousand dollars very fast, although he might be able to draw on the trust fund from which he received an annuity of $800, and he knew that John Lynch in Bethlehem would serve as reference for his credit. [...] [Herbert] closed the deal with a handshake, "nothing down" [143:27–28].

l. 161. *vitriol or arsenate of lead*: insecticides.

l. 164. *Far up the birches out of reach of man*: footnote in *New Hampshire,* "Cf. 'Wild Grapes'."

l. 171. *Poems produced than any other thing*: footnote in *New Hampshire,* "Cf. 'A Fountain, a Bottle, a Donkey's Ears and Some Books'."

l. 178. *Marches*: footnote in *New Hampshire,* "Cf. 'Maple'."

l. 195. *Election*: footnote in *New Hampshire,* "Cf. 'The Pauper Witch of Grafton'."

l. 209. *Whole townships ... population*: footnote in *New Hampshire,* "Cf. 'The Census-Taker'."

ll. 218–219. *Emerson said, "The ... men."*: Ralph Waldo Emerson (1803–1882), American essayist and poet. The quotation is from his "Ode Inscribed to W. H. Channing" (*ll.* 24–26).

ll. 220–227. *Another Massachusetts poet ... out."*: Amy Lowell (1874–1925), American poet and critic. In his essay "On Emerson," Frost commented parenthetically:

> "I have left New Hampshire," she told me. Why in the world? She couldn't stand the people. What's the matter with the people? "Read your own books and find out." They really differ from other New Englanders, or did in the days of Franklin Pierce [55:714].

l. 238. *From nearly everything that goes on round me*: footnote in *New Hampshire*, "Cf. 'The Grindstone'."

ll. 241–242. *Kit Marlowe ... it."*: Christopher Marlowe (1564– 1593), English dramatist. The quotation is from his *Doctor Faustus* (III.89).

ll. 246–247. *Because I wrote ... New Hampshire*: referring to his association with the New England states, Frost said that when he was first published in the United States his publisher emphasized "the New England of it" but when *Mountain Interval* was coming out, he requested that it be put on the jacket that he writes of "universals in terms of New England. I think they did—something like that. But I talk about the whole world in terms of New England" [25:174].

l. 259. *Hall of Windham*: John Hall (1845–1906), a poultryman of Atkinson, New Hampshire, not Windham, was the subject of "The Housekeeper."

l. 259. *Gay of Atkinson*: footnote in *New Hampshire*, "Cf. 'The Axe-Helve'." Napolean Guay (or Gay) lived to the south of Frost, on the Londonderry turnpike, in Derry, New Hampshire.

l. 260. *Bartlett of Raymond (now of Colorado)*: John T. Bartlett (1892–1947). Bartlett and his future wife, Margaret Abbott, met Frost when they were both his students at Pinkerton Academy in 1907. They moved to Colorado in 1917. They remained friends with the Frosts until their deaths; John in 1947 and Margaret in 1949.

l. 261. *Lynch of Bethlehem*: John Lynch. The Frosts had stayed with the Lynches, John and his wife, Mary, during the summers of 1906–1908 and 1911 and in February of 1915. Cf. "The Star-Splitter."

l. 266. *For art's sake ... worse*: footnote in *New Hampshire*, "Cf. 'The Star-Splitter'."

l. 275. *Dostoievskis*: reference to Fyodor Mikhailovich Dostoyevski (1821–1881), Russian novelist.

l. 282. *Pollyanna*: heroine of Eleanor Porter's novel *Pollyanna* (1913) who had an irrepressible optimism and a tendency to find good in everything.

l. 293. *"You hear those hound dogs sing on Moosilauke?*: footnote in *New Hampshire*, "Cf. 'The Pauper Witch of Grafton'."

l. 296. *Bryan*: William Jennings Bryan (1860–1925), American lawyer and politician.

l. 299. *John L. Darwin*: footnote in *New Hampshire*, "Cf. 'Wild Grapes' *l.* 53." John L. Darwin is a conflation of the names John L. Sullivan (1858–1918), the American pugilist, and Charles Darwin (1809–1882), the British evolutionist.

l. 303. *And spent the proceeds on a telescope*: footnote in *New Hampshire*, "Cf. 'The Star-Splitter'."

l. 305. *our place among the infinities*: this phrase (repeated in "The Star-

Splitter," *l.* 19) recalls one of Frost's favorite books as a child, of which he said, "When my father died and my mother and sister and I went east, I salvaged one book which I still have—one of my favorite books. It is [Richard Anthony Proctor's] *Our Place Among the Infinities*, a book of astronomical essays, written in the seventies. One of the first books I ever read" [103:360].

l. 345. *The way the … logjam*: footnote in *New Hampshire*, "Cf. 'Paul's Wife'."

l. 358. *a New York alec*: Frost was upset to discover that people at Amherst College believed that Alexander Meiklejohn, former president of Amherst College, later a resident of New York, was his "New York alec" and that the poem was a commentary on the controversy surrounding Meiklejohn's liberal and radical tenure and subsequent dismissal [66:295].

l. 363. *Mewling and puking*: echo of Jacques' "seven ages" speech in Shakespeare's *As You Like It* (II.vii.143-44) where he speaks of "the infant, / Mewling and puking in the nurse's arms" [134:381-382].

l. 364. *"Me for the hills … choose."*: footnote in *New Hampshire*, "Cf. 'An Empty Threat'."

l. 370. *Mathew Arnold*: English poet (1822–1888). Frost described Arnold as "confident and authoritative in his prose and a lost soul in his poetry" [51:125].

l. 371. *Nature is cruel, man is sick of blood*: from Mathew Arnold's "In Harmony with Nature" (*l.* 7).

l. 373. *Birnam Wood*: from Shakespeare's *Macbeth*.

l. 375. *dendrophobia*: fear of trees.

l. 379. *The line where man … starts*: footnote in *New Hampshire*, "Cf. 'A Fountain, a Bottle, a Donkey's Ears and Some Books'."

ll. 383–384. *"a foiled / Circuitous wanderer"*: from Mathew Arnold's "Sohrab and Rustum" (*l.* 887).

ll. 384–385. *"took dejectedly … throne"*: from Mathew Arnold's "The Scholar-Gypsy" (*l.* 183–184).

l. 388. *Ahaz*: 11th King of Judah who "did not do what was right in the eyes of the Lord his God like his forefather David […]. He sacrificed and burned offerings at the shrines and on the hilltops and under every spreading tree" [2 Kings 16.2–4]. Cf. "The Gold Hesperidee," *ll.* 51–54.

ll. 401–402. *words speak / Louder than actions*: inversion of the familiar proverb, "Actions speak louder than words."

l. 410. *a publisher in New York City*: Frost's New York publisher since 1915 was Henry Holt.

l. 413. *At present I am living in Vermont*: in 1922 when he wrote this poem, Frost was living in South Shaftsbury, Vermont. He wrote to Sidney Cox in 1937 that "New Hampshire improves on being looked at from Vermont" [31:226].

A Star in a Stoneboat
For Lincoln MacVeagh

First published, without the dedication, in *The Yale Review*, January 1921. The poem was written in 1920 [3:100].

Title *Stoneboat*: a sledge made of heavy planks used by upland Yankee farmers to clear their fields of rocks and boulders.

Dedication *Lincoln MacVeagh*: head of Holt's trade department from 1919 to 1923.

l. 16. *Bird of Paradise*: bird, native to New Guinea and adjacent areas, with brilliant plumage and long tail feathers in the male.

l. 29. *Pegasus*: winged horse of Greek mythology; also the constellation. Both are associated with poetic inspiration.

The Census-Taker

First published in *The New Republic*, April 6, 1921. According to Frost, the poem was written in 1920 [3:100]. An incomplete draft, possibly written between 1918 and 1921, was published in the April 1988 issue of the *Dartmouth College Library Bulletin* [28:78–80]. Frost wrote to Robert Hillyer, who had singled out "The Census-Taker" from the other poems in *New Hampshire*, that he had made no mistake in singling out this poem. Frost admitted having had "complacent moments" over it [120:233].

l. 53. *Where Asia wedges Africa from Europe*: Mesopotamia. The fertility and location of this region made this the seat of the early Babylonian and Assyrian civilizations.

The Star-Splitter

First published in *The Century Magazine*, September 1923. The poem was written in 1920 [3:100]. A draft variant was sent to Louis Untermeyer on February 12, 1923 [151:159–161].

Although it was not done to buy a telescope as in the poem, the incident which inspired "The Star-Splitter" was the burning down of Michael G. Fitzgerald's hotel for the insurance money. The story was told by Mary Lynch, a relative of Fitzgerald, as an example of her husband John's dry comments on life. The Frosts had stayed with the Lynches in the summers of 1906–1908 and 1911 and in February of 1915. John Lynch was in the process of putting new wallpaper up in the living room of his farmhouse when Fitzgerald, whose hotel was on fire, ran into the room, crying hysterically for help. Lynch was unperturbed. While fussing over the alignment of one sheet of wallpaper, and without looking over his shoulder at Fitzgerald, he said, "Let them as set the fire put it out" [142:343-344]. This incident, excluded from the published version, formed part of the original draft of this poem sent to Louis Untermeyer on February 12, 1923. See 151:160.

l. 1. *Orion*: constellation in the celestial equator, named for the great hunter of Greek mythology.

l. 19. *our place among the infinities*: during a 1960 interview Frost told Richard Poirier, "One of the earliest books I hovered over, hung around, was called *Our Place Among the Infinities*, by an astronomer in England named Proctor, noted astronomer. It's a noted old book. I mention that in one of the poems [Frost also used the phrase in "New Hampshire," *l.* 305]: I use that expression 'our place among the infinities' from that book that I must have read as soon as I read any book, thirteen or fourteen, right in there I began to read"[157:22–23].

l. 37. *Littleton*: town in New Hampshire. According to Frost, the actual hotel-burning incident occurred not far from the Lynch farm in Bethlehem [143:599].

l. 38–42. *After such loose ... tomorrow*: for a ten-line variant of these five lines, see 151:160.

l. 47. *For to be social is to be forgiving*: during a 1960 reading Frost said, "You've got to forgive the other side" [25: 143].

l. 65. *one at auction?*: original draft has extra line following this line. See 151:161.

l. 68. *Concord*: city in New Hampshire.

l. 86. *Said some of ... said*: footnote in *New Hampshire*, "Cf. 'A Star in a Stone-boat,' 'I Will Sing You One-O'."

l. 99. *ever stood?*: in the original draft this is the penultimate line, followed by one further question. See 151:161.

Maple

First published in *The Yale Review*, October 1921.

l. 46. *Lesley, Carol, Irma, Marjorie*: Frost's surviving children in 1921.

l. 106. *Wave offering*: in the Levitical law, an oblation or offering moved from side to side, possibly elevated. The term appears many times in the Bible, which fact prevents one from identifying the page in the Bible marked with the "bookmark maple leaf," if Frost had a particular passage in mind.

The Ax-Helve

First published in *The Atlantic*, September 1917 (the title was spelled as "The Ax-Helve" from 1949 on). Written on the Derry farm, according to Lawrance Thompson, "The Axe-Helve" may have been Frost's first dramatic narrative poem [142:553], although the poet was still revising it prior to his first public recitation of it before the Phi Beta Kappa Society at Harvard in June 1916 [143:79]. During an interview in April 1916, Frost said, perhaps with this poem in mind:

> Love, the moon, and murder have poetry in them by common consent. But it's in other places. It's in the axe-handle of a French Canadian woodchopper [...].
>
> You know the Canadian woodchoppers whittle their axe-handles, following the curve of the grain, and they're strong and beautiful. Art should follow lines in nature, like the grain of an axe-handle. False art puts curves on things that haven't any curves [79:48–49].

As Frost was later to admit, this was as close as he liked to come to writing "about art in a work of art (such as it is)" [3:109].

The French-Canadian woodchopper in "The Ax-Helve" was Napolean Guay (or Gay) who lived to the south of Frost, on the Londonderry turnpike, in Derry, New Hampshire. It was he who condemned machine-made axe-helves and showed Frost the lines of a good helve [142:284]. Guay is also referred to in "New Hampshire" (*l.* 259) as "Gay of Atkinson."

To John Bartlett, Frost wrote in 1919, "The first part of 'The Axe-helve' was a good poem, the last part not" [2:120].

l. 96. *The snake stood up for evil in the Garden*: evil was introduced to the world in Genesis 3:1–7 when the serpent, which "was more subtil than any beast of the field," tempted Eve to eat the forbidden "fruit of the tree which is in the midst of the garden" [131:8].

The Grindstone

First published in *Farm and Fireside*, June 1921. This poem, chosen by Frost for an expanded edition of *North of Boston* that he was considering [144:178], was inspired by Frost's experiences during the summer of 1889 when he worked on Loren Bailey's farm in Salem, New Hampshire. Bailey had an old grindstone which stood in the shade of a gnarled apple tree. Frost was taught how to turn the crank with one hand to give just the right speed to the stone, while the other hand, which held a tin can, poured a trickle of water to keep the stone moist under the pressure of the scythe-blade. As a boy Frost was impatient with Bailey's dissatisfaction with anything less than a razor-sharp blade [142:86].

Frost once wrote that there was a lot of himself in this poem, that it took "many years of living" to make it [3:109]. During a reading Frost referred to "The Grindstone" as a metaphor [25:55]. In a 1949 annotation Frost also referred to this poem as a "figure of [the] great round world. A metaphor [...]" [3:115].

l. 29. *Father-Time*: personification of time as an elderly man, bald but with a forelock, carrying a scythe and hourglass.

Paul's Wife

First published in *The Century Magazine*, November 1921. According to Frost, the poem was written between 1912 and 1920 [3:101]. This poem was chosen by Frost for an expanded edition of *North of Boston* that he was considering [144:178]. Frost referred to "Paul's Wife" as "one of the important ones" from *New Hampshire* [25:86]. The source for this poem was Ida Virginia Turney's *Paul Bunyan Comes West* (Boston: Houghton Mifflin, 1928). On page 8 of this chapbook appears the following unique tale: "A feller by the name o' Murphy tells 'bout how Paul found his wife in the heart o' a great white pine an' didn't never let no one see her, but 'taint so. Paul's wife wuz reg'lar folks, an' she never set in no moonlight spoonin' with Paul." Frost wrote that "This is merely about the kind of person who refuses to share socially his spiritual possessions" [3:109].

Title *Paul*: Paul Bunyan, legendary giant lumberjack of North America.

Wild Grapes

First published in *Harper's Magazine*, December 1920. Frost wrote that this poem was "as near being a thing written to order as I ever got. Susan Hayes Ward my first discoverer (1893) said I must write her for girls a companion piece to 'Birches' which she took to be for boys; and she would furnish me with the material. Some years afterward to my own great surprise I found myself doing as she commanded" [97:71].

ll. 1–2. *What tree may ... birch?*: echo of Matthew 7:16 which asks "Do men gather grapes of thorns, or figs of thistles?" [131:1004].

l. 27. *The way they ... German*: Leif Ericson (died circa 1020), Norse mariner who discovered land that he named Vinland for the vines growing there.

l. 99. *The mind—is not the heart*: for a contrast of the mind with the heart, see "Bond and Free."

Place for a Third

First published in *Harper's Magazine*, July 1920. The poem had at one time been titled "Eliza" [151:104]. Frost referred to it in a letter to G.R. Elliott as "one of my less amiable poems in character" [66:243].

Two Witches

Collective title for the following two poems:

I. The Witch of Coös

First published in *Poetry*, January 1922. Frost referred to "The Witch of Coös" as an important poem from *New Hampshire* [25:86]. It was chosen by Frost for an expanded edition of *North of Boston* that he was considering [144:178]. Note in first publication and in *New Hampshire*: "Circa 1922." Frost dated the poem once as 1920 [3:101]. Frost said that this witch is "a veritable witch in a county in upper New Hampshire. [...] Do not approach this witch with condescension" [26:358]. The source of the poem is a local history of Coös County, New Hampshire [66:473], which has not been identified.

Title *Coös*: county in New Hampshire.

l. **110.** *"The Wild Colonial Boy"*: ballad, Australian in origin, the refrain of which is:

Come, all my hearties, we'll roam the mountains high,
Together we will plunder, together we will die.
We'll wander over valleys, and gallop over plains,
And we'll scorn to live in slavery, bound down with iron chains [154:374].

II. The Pauper Witch of Grafton

First published in *The Nation*, April 13, 1921, the poem, dated as 1920 by Frost [3:101], was inspired by the following history found in William Little's *The History of Warren, a Mountain Hamlet located among the White Hills, New Hampshire* (Manchester, N.H.: 1870; pages 461–466), which had been lent to Frost by Raymond Holden in 1919 or 1920 [87:16]:

> But gossiping slanderers of that day said that the wife of Mr. Benjamin Weeks, Mrs. Sarah Weeks, had ten times the power that the above mentioned ladies possessed. Invisible on her good steed, a broom-stick, she rode the country round and was a sort of revenging angel for her husband.
>
> [...] Mrs. Sarah Weeks, of whom we have spoken before, and who had the very enviable reputation of being a witch, wife of Benjamin Weeks, Jr., had become chargeable to the town of Wentworth for support as a pauper. She had once lived in Warren on the Height-o'-land, and Wentworth thought our good town should support her. Wentworth requested Warren to do so. Warren refused. Wentworth was indignant—mad—and said she should. Warren was stubborn and a suit was brought.
>
> [...] The case was in the Eastern Judicial District of Grafton county, and was tried at Plymouth. It turned upon this point: Did Benjamin Weeks, Jr., have a residence in Warren? He had never paid taxes there seven years in succession; but on the books was this record: "1817, Benj. Weeks elected hogreeve." There was no record of his taking the oath of office, and unless he had done so, he would not have gained a residence.
>
> [...] And now the battle began. Wentworth's witnesses testified that Benjamin Weeks, Jr., was chosen hogreeve; but they could not swear that he was sworn in. Warren's witnesses testified that he was chosen, but that he was not sworn in.
>
> [...] The arguments were made, the Judge delivered his charge, the jury retired, and returning in a few minutes, gave a verdict for Wentworth. Warren's agent and his witnesses went home feeling cheap enough.
>
> [...] Wentworth's celebration had a wonderful effect. It waked up the musty recollection of every old man in Warren. They began to remember how the case was. [...] There were two men, father and son, by the name

of Benjamin Weeks, Benjamin, Sen., and Benjamin, Jr. The son was chosen hogreeve, but as he was not in the meeting at the tie, to take the oath, his father, Benjamin Weeks, stepped forward at once and said, "Choose me and I will serve." He was immediately chosen, took the oath, and the record on the town book, "1817, Benj. Weeks elected hogreeve," was correct; but it had no relation to Benjamin Weeks, Jr. [...]

The facts and the action of the town came to the ears of the agent of Wentworth. At first he was incredulous, then he made inquiries, then went to the old men of Warren and learned how they would testify, and finally after the winter and the spring had passed, he came to Warren, backed down, and paid up. Thus ended Warren's great lawsuit [...].

Title *Grafton*: county in New Hampshire.

ll. 7–8. *Double trouble's ... motto*: from Shakespeare's *Macbeth* (IV.i) in which the three witches chant, "Double, double, toil and trouble; / fire burn, and cauldron bubble" [134:1329].

An Empty Threat

First published in *New Hampshire*. In a letter to Louis Untermeyer, dated November 11, 1915, Frost makes an escapist statement with "Me for Hudson Bay!" and then goes on to describe an accompanying sketch [151:17–18]. This may have been the origin of his "An Empty Threat."

l. 3. *Hudson's Bay*: inland sea in Canada's Northwest Territories.

ll. 43–47. *the old captain's ... sailed*: Henry Hudson (died 1611), British navigator and explorer, who undertook four voyages to find a northwest passage from Europe to Asia. During his fourth voyage his crew mutinied, setting Hudson and eight others adrift in a small boat. Nothing is known of the fate of the nine men.

l. 52. *Great Auk*: diving seabird of the colder parts of the Northern Hemisphere, extinct since 1844.

A Fountain, a Bottle, a Donkey's Ears, and Some Books

First published in *The Bookman*, October 1923, the poem was written in the early 1920s [3:101].

ll. 8–10. *on Kinsman ... font*: Raymond Holden, in his "Reminiscences," offers the following background information on this section of the poem:

> I recall walking with Robert through the valleys of Grafton County [New Hampshire] and over its mountains, he stopping often to look at and identify for me some plant or tree or bush that would send him off reminiscing about what someone had told him about the plant in question, or enlarging upon what it reminded him of. He would often go from the vegetable world to the world of human history, fascinated by the half-known, half-forgotten relics of New Englanders of an earlier day. [...] Robert often told me of the legend he had heard when he lived in Derry to the effect that the Mormons had once built a stone temple in the forest somewhere in New Hampshire, the ruined altar or fount of which was sometimes stumbled upon by hunters. It could be said that Robert and I never took a walk without the sometimes spoken and sometimes tacit understanding that we were looking for that altar. We never found it. [...] The only reference to this romantically elusive spot in Robert's work is, so far as I know, in the poem, "A Fountain, a Bottle, a Donkey's Ears, and Some Books," which appeared in the volume, *New Hampshire*. Here, the Mormon temple is referred to as on Kinsman, Mount Kinsman, overlooking the eastern valley a little to the northeast of Moosilauke. I never heard Robert in conversation be as definite as he is in the poem. In any case, neither we nor anyone else have ever found it [87:42–43].

ll. 77–85. *Clara Robinson ... bed*: Clara Weaver Robinson (1854–1905) was indeed a poet who wrote about posies and birds, but that is about as far as she resembles the Clara Robinson of Frost's poem. She did not have a book of poems published in her lifetime. In 1959, a small edition of her translation of Sophocles' *Antigone* was privately published and in 1970 an edition of 300 copies was printed of her poems. She did not live in New Hampshire. Although separated by some years, twice Clara Robinson's life and Frost's crossed. It is possible that somewhere along the way he heard a story or some gossip about this woman. Her father was the pastor of the Universalist Church in Lawrence, Massachusetts, in the 1860s; in 1885 the young Frost with his mother and sister moved to Lawrence to live with his paternal grandparents. In the late 1870s through 1882, Clara Robinson was a tutor in Greek, Latin and botany and assistant professor of Latin at St. Lawrence University in Canton, New York; Elinor Frost attended St. Lawrence University from 1892 to 1895, prior to her marriage. Ethel Robinson Murphy, Clara's daughter, was also a poet and some of her poems were published in various books and journals between 1902 and 1958. It is possible that Frost had her poetry in mind when he wrote of the "poetess who wrote the book of verses" [Biographical information from 127].

I Will Sing You One-O

First published in *The Yale Review*, October 1923, the poem may, according to Frost, have been written in 1905 [3:101] or as early as 1896–1900 [3:104].

Fragmentary Blue

First published in *Harper's Magazine*, July 1920, this poem was written at least as early as 1919 [120:22]. Frost wrote to G.R. Elliott that "Fragmentary Blue" was designed to tease his friends who wanted him to stop writing lyrics [66:248].

Fire and Ice

First published in *Harper's Magazine*, December 1920, the poem was written in 1919 [3:101] at his Main Street house in Amherst [3:115].

l. 5. *But if it ... twice*: a more personal variant of this line—"I" replacing "it"—appeared in the version sent to Sidney Cox on July 17, 1920 [31:138].

In a Disused Graveyard

First published in *The Measure*, August 1923.

Dust of Snow

First published as "A Favour" in *The London Mercury*, December 1920, the poem was shortly thereafter published as "Snow Dust" in *The Yale Review*, January 1921. According to Frost, the poem may have been written in 1906 [3:101] or as early as 1896–1900 [3:104], although he referred to this poem in November 1920 as having been "done rather recently by me about as I am" [151:123]. In 1940 he told a group of friends, as recorded by Daniel Smythe:

> It is all one sentence, two little stanzas. I have called it "the favor." I often feel a special favor to find a flower I have not seen for a long while, or hear a strange bird I haven't heard in years [136:57].

Frost would refer to such a moment when he had been "spoken to—favored" as a "nature-favor" [26:357].

To E.T.

First published in *The Yale Review*, April 1920, the poem was reprinted later that year as "To Edward Thomas" in *American and British Verse from The Yale Review* (New Haven: Yale University Press, 1920). Frost dated the poem as 1917 [3:101] and said he wrote it as a tribute to his friend Edward Thomas, who was killed in France during World War I by the concussion from an exploding shell on April 9, 1917. Thomas was, Frost wrote, "the closest friend I ever had [...] and this was something I didn't wait to realize after he had died [...] [143:550]. Frost said of Thomas, "He did much for me, and I can never repay his memory" [103:135]. In his 1948 essay, "A Romantic Chasm," Frost wrote, "I wish Edward Thomas (that poet) were here to ponder gulfs in general with me as in the days when he and I tired the sun with talking on the footpaths and stiles of Leddington and Ryton" [54:5]. In defending the poem to Louis Untermeyer, who disliked it, Frost said that the poem "is complicated with the war in such a way that you are afraid it may be a tract in favor of heroism. (But it isn't.)" [151:104].

On the writing of this tribute, Frost has variously said:

> I have wanted to say a word to you [Wilbur Cross] to explain my failure to do anything about Edward Thomas. I find he was too near to me. Some time I shall write about him. Perhaps it will come to me to write in verse. As yet I feel too much the loss of the best friend I ever had. And by that I don't mean I am overwhelmed with grief. Something in me refuses to take the risk—angrily refuses to take the risk—of seeming to use grief for literary purposes. When I care less, I can do more [66:225].
>
> Some time I shall have something of my own to show you [Wilbur Cross] about Thomas (it will probably be in verse), but not right away. These are overwhelming times [143:549].

> I am going to send you [George Whicher] the E T poem to show you that it is something more than a mere project. The truth is it is probably as complete as it will ever be. I'm not keeping it back to go on with it. Perhaps I can tell you why I have hesitated over it. Edward Thomas was the closest friend I ever had [...] and this was something I didn't wait to realize after he had died [...] [143:550].

Title *E.T.*: Edward Thomas.

l. **14.** *Vimy Ridge*: ridge near Vimy commune, north of Arras, France.

l. **18.** *the Rhine*: river in Europe flowing from Switzerland to the North Sea in the Netherlands.

Nothing Gold Can Stay

First published in *The Yale Review*, October 1923. There are six extant variants of this poem. The earliest was sent to G.R. Elliott on March 20, 1920, as "Nothing Gold Can Stay." This version contains three octets. The third octet was adapted into "It Is Almost the Year Two Thousand." The first sixteen lines were compressed into the eight-line "Nothing Gold Can Stay" [143:565]. Frost himself confirmed, "The last three lines of 'Nothing Gold Can Stay' were ones entirely different" [9:471]. The first four lines were written in 1900 [3:101]. The autumnal images of this poem caused Frost to suggest that this poem "might go with" his "The Oven Bird" [25:146], with its images of fall and diminished things.

l. 1. *Nature's first green is gold*: cf. "The Gold Hesperidee," *l.* 71.

The Runaway

First published in *The Amherst Monthly* (Amherst, Mass., June 1918), the poem was written in 1916 [3:101]. A draft of "The Runaway," possibly a revision written between 1918 and 1921, was published in the *Dartmouth College Library Bulletin* [(April 1988):80–81]. Frost had repeatedly said that his little farm fable was inspired by students at Amherst—"I wrote it with college boys in mind" [118:16] and "The middle is about college boys" [43:8]—that it cast oblique light on one problem in education in that it expressed Frost's complaint about young men so immature that they refused to accept the guidance offered by teachers and parents [143:551]. As Frost wrote about the Amherst students under the presidency of Alexander Meiklejohn, "They had picked up the idea somewhere that the time was past for the teacher to teach the pupil" [151:170].

Frost referred to the poem's structure as having "such a complicated rhyme scheme that you would have to see it to get anything out of it" [43:8].

l. 3. *Morgan*: an American breed of light-statured horses which originated in Vermont.

ll. 19–21. *"Whoever it is ... in."*: Frost is reported to have said that he "added the moral at the end just for the pleasure of the aggrieved tone of voice" [10:5].

The Aim Was Song

First published in *The Measure*, March 1921, according to Frost, the poem was written in 1915 [3:101].

l. 4. *caught*: following this line, an early draft contains a deleted quatrain. See 121:201.

Stopping by Woods on a Snowy Evening

First published in *The New Republic*, March 7, 1923, the poem was written early one morning in the summer of 1922 after Frost had spent the entire night before working on the poem "New Hampshire" [143:237; see also notes to "New Hampshire"]. As Frost once explained to Louis Mertins about his writing of this lyric,

> There had been days of terrific strain on the farm. You see, I can manage a poem in the singular very well and not feel the strain, not too much. In the midst of my work at the farm I could handle such a task. Sometimes one would grow out of an idea, leaving me relaxed. At other times the idea would produce a second growth, forcing itself as a Siamese twin on its predecessor. That would bring trouble of spirit, and more than likely right in harvest time. I would be in a terrible stew, fever, likely. My legs would ache, my head would ache. Eating was out of the question. Sleep? There wasn't any. [...] As I remember it, "Stopping by Woods on a Snowy

> Evening" was written in just about that way, after I had been working all night long on "New Hampshire." But I must admit, it was written in a few minutes without any strain.
>
> Critics think I had that sort of all-night struggle before I could write the little poem I'm talking about. They must have heard me say, sometime or other, years back, that I wrote all night, in connection with "Stopping by Woods." But the thing I worked on all night had no struggle in it at all. It's in print, called "New Hampshire." [...] Then, having finished "New Hampshire," I went outdoors, got out sideways and didn't disturb anybody in the house, and about nine or ten o'clock went back in and wrote the piece about the snowy evening and the little horse as if I'd had an hallucination—little hallucination—the one critics write about occasionally. You can't trust these fellows who write what made a poet write what he wrote. We all of us read our pet theories into a poem [103:81–82].

A facsimile of the draft of *ll.* 5–16 was published in Charles W. Cooper's *Preface to Poetry* (New York: Harcourt, Brace, 1943; page 604). It was reprinted in *Reading Modern Poetry* by Paul Engle and Warren Carrier (Glenview, Ill.: Scott, Foresman, 1968; facing page 1).

On the structure of the poem, Frost wrote in his 1946 essay, "The Constant Symbol":

> There's an indulgent smile I get for the recklessness of the unnecessary commitment I made when I came to the first line in the second stanza of a poem [...] called "Stopping by Woods on a Snowy Evening." I was riding too high to care what trouble I incurred. And it was all right so long as I didn't suffer deflection [45:51].

Reacting to the interpretation of this as a "death poem," Frost said during a 1958 reading at Bread Loaf:

> Ciardi and others have said—some people have said—it's a suicide poem. That's going some. But he thinks it's a death poem. And you can see how you could say: "Life is lovely, dark and deep." See. "But I have promises to keep. I have heaven to go to, you know." Like that. You could do that. That analogy's in it. Many others. You say, just as I could right now: this is a lovely dark and deep situation, but I've got something [else], I ought to teach a class tomorrow, or something like that. Promises to keep. Company of an evening. One o'clock in the morning—two o'clock. An appropriate thing to say—that stanza is lovely, dark and deep, but I've got to be getting along. And it doesn't mean that you're going to do anything bad. Sounds rather good to me. I can see that someone might turn it the other way, like the old saying, "I used to be afraid to go home in the dark, but now I'm afraid to go home at all." They think it's like that. And all this metaphorical play and all! [25:123].

Frost wrote to Sidney Cox, "The more I think of it the surer I am of that there poem" [31:147]. He considered this poem his "best bid for remembrance" [151:163]. It contains "all I ever knew" [26:357].

l. 7. *frozen lake*: according to Frost's daughter, Lesley, there was a family legend to the effect that the lake was the pond regularly passed by Frost on his drive from his Derry farm to West Derry [142:548].

l. 13. *lovely, dark, and deep*: possible echo of line 13 of the early nineteenth-century poet, Thomas Lovell Beddoes' "The Phantom Wooer": "Our bed is lovely, dark, and sweet" [7:48].

ll. 15–16. *And miles to ... sleep*: on the ending of this poem, Frost confessed that he had written the third line of the last stanza in a way that called for another stanza. Frost didn't want another and then was struck with the idea to repeat the line to close the poem [9:471].

For Once, Then, Something

First published in *Harper's Magazine*, July 1920. Begun in Franconia around 1917 [3:101], this poem was first entitled "Well" and later "Wrong to the Light" before it received its present title [143:561]. One afternoon, having explained some metrical patterns of Latin poetry to his teenage daughter Lesley, Frost proposed a competition to her in which each would write a poem in lines of eleven syllables. Later that day Frost presented the beginnings of what would become "For Once, Then, Something" [13:131]. Frost was still experimenting with the form in May 1919 as he wrote to his daughter Lesley, "I've been trying Hen Dekker syllables [i.e. hendeca syllables] but without much luck lately." The poem was apparently finished shortly thereafter since he sent it to Louis Untermeyer as one of two "new ones" on June 30, 1919 [48:67]. Proud of the form, he wrote to G.R. Elliott in 1920 that it was "calculated to tease the metrists [...]" [66:248].

For another example of Frost's belief that glimpses of truth are given only to those not in a position to look too closely, see "A Passing Glimpse."

ll. 9–10. *something white ... depths*: possible echo of chapter 42, "The Whiteness of the Whale," from Melville's *Moby-Dick*.

l. 15. *Truth?*: refers to Democritus's phrase, "Of truth we know nothing, for truth lies at the bottom of a well."

During a 1940 conversation with Daniel Smythe, Frost said, "'What is truth?' Age-old. Most of us only get to near-truths—and luck at that—in poetry" [136:62].

Blue-Butterfly Day

First published in *The New Republic*, March 16, 1921, this poem was written between 1896 and 1900, probably on the Derry farm [3:104]. During an interview in 1921 Frost asked, in reference to this poem, "You have seen those thousands of little blue butterflies that come in the muddy season of the spring, haven't you?" [51:33].

The Onset

First published in *The Yale Review*, January 1921, the poem was written in 1917 [3:101].

l. **12.** *Yet all the ... side*: cf. "Our Hold on the Planet."

ll. **18–21.** *the snow all ... snake*: cf. "A Hillside Thaw," *ll.* 1–3.

To Earthward

First published in *The Yale Review*, October 1923, the poem was written in England [3:101, 104]. Frost once said specifically that it was written "under a plum tree" while he was staying at Little Iddens [133:125]. In a letter to Bernard DeVoto of October 1938, Frost wrote:

> One of the greatest changes my nature has undergone is of record in "To Earthward" and indeed elsewhere for the discerning. In my school days I simply could not go on and do the best I could with a copy book I had once blotted. I began life wanting perfection and determined to have it. I got so I ceased to expect it and could do without it. Now I find I actually crave the flaws of human handwork. I gloat over imperfection [66:482].

l. **10.** *honeysuckle*: shrub or vine with tubular, fragrant, yellow, white or pink flowers.

l. **24.** *clove*: East Indian evergreen, the aromatic unopened buds of which are used as a spice.

l. **31.** *rough*: in a 1928 letter to R.P.T. Coffin, Frost wrote of the relationship between roughness and the poet, "A real artist delights in roughness for what he can do to it" [66:465].

Good-By and Keep Cold

First published in *Harper's Magazine*, July 1920, the poem was written in the summer of 1919 as the following account by Raymond Holden explains:

> The happiest and most memorable days of my friendship with Robert were in spite of the difficulties which arose there for me and for him—those at Franconia between 1915 and 1920. I can point to many of his poems and say, "This was written after we did such-and-such." He had the habit, when he had finished a new poem, of writing out a copy of it in longhand, signing it, and giving it to me. [...]
>
> I remember also one morning when I appeared at his house to go for a walk with him before he returned to Amherst to take up his new teaching. This must have been in the late summer of 1919.
>
> While we were waiting for Elinor to make us the cucumber sandwiches which were standard rations for our walks, Robert handed me a poem which he said he had finished the night before. It was "Goodbye [sic] and Keep Cold," in his own hand-writing, with his signature at the bottom. I read it while he explained to me how he had learned that apple trees are better off if they do not thaw out during the winter. I have noticed that Elizabeth Sargeant [sic] in her book about Frost says that he told her that the poem was written in Amherst [see 133:231]. It wasn't. He must have forgotten. I haven't forgotten. It was probably the idea for the poem, that is, generated while he was in Derry, but he didn't complete it until that night in 1919 [87:11–15].

Frost once dated the poem as 1918 [3:101].

Two Look at Two

First published in *New Hampshire*, the poem was written in Amherst, possibly circa 1919 [3:101]. This poem was chosen by Frost for an expanded edition of *North of Boston* that he was considering [144:178]. Frost's claim that this poem was written "with one stroke of the pen" [110:397] is belied by the presence of an early draft sent to Sidney Cox in a letter dated July 17, 1920, containing fourteen more lines [160].

Not to Keep

First published in *The Yale Review*, January 1917. According to Lawrance Thompson, "Not to Keep" was partly inspired by Edward Thomas's letters to Frost written while on leave during Christmas, 1916, prior to his departure for France [143:90] although Frost also, perhaps because of the Thomas association, dated the poem as having been written in England [3:101].

A Brook in the City

First published in *The New Republic*, March 9, 1921. Frost once wrote that the brook is partially based on a brook in Greenwich Village [3:110].

ll. 1–3. *The farmhouse lingers ... in*: the image of the house which will not "square" with the street can also be found in Frost's 1903 story "The Question of a Feather," which he wrote during his days as a poultryman: "The city streets were there, too, though it was plain that the house he sought had been there before the streets, for it was set down without reference to their direction, like some mirage through which you might expect to see the more substantial objects behind it" [64:54].

The Kitchen Chimney

First published in *The Measure*, August 1923, according to Frost, the poem was written in 1918 [3:101].

Looking for a Sunset Bird in Winter

First published in *New Hampshire*, the poem was written in 1920 [3:101].

A Boundless Moment

First published in *The New Republic*, October 24, 1923, the poem was written in 1920 [3:101].

Evening in a Sugar Orchard

First published in *Whimsies* (University of Michigan) November 1921, this poem was written in 1920 [3:101]. It is based on an incident which took place in late March, 1920, when Frost spent the night with Raymond Holden stoking the fire in the sugar house on Frost's Franconia farm [143:142]. As Holden recalled:

> The happiest and most memorable days of my friendship with Robert were in spite of the difficulties which arose there for me and for him—those at Franconia between 1915 and 1920. I can point to many of his poems and say, "This was written after we did such-and-such." He had the habit, when he had finished a new poem, of writing out a copy of it in longhand, signing it, and giving it to me. I remember particularly the appearance of one called "Evening in a Sugar Orchard," and of another entitled "A Hillside Thaw," both of which were written in the early spring of 1919 [i.e., 1920], after he and I had sat up all one night tending the fire and keeping the sap flowing in the sugar orchard close to Robert's house [...] [87:11–12].

l. 15. *Leo, Orion, and the Pleiades*: constellations.

Gathering Leaves

First published in *The Measure*, August 1923.

The Valley's Singing Day

First published in *Harper's Magazine*, December 1920, according to Frost, this poem was written in 1913 [3:101].

ll. 19–20. *I should be ... day*: in a typescript (circa 1920) in the Jones Library, Amherst, Massachusetts, this couplet appeared as a quatrain, two lines being inserted between lines 19 and 20 [163].

Misgiving

First published in *The Yale Review*, January 1921, this poem had been sent in a letter to Sidney Cox from England on July 10, 1913 [31:25]. In a 1921 letter to Louis Untermeyer, Frost refers to the poem's having been written "fifteen years ago and now accepted by an editor for the first time" [151:125], which would place its date of composition during the Derry period (circa 1905). Frost himself dated the poem as between 1896 and 1901 [3:101, 103].

A Hillside Thaw

First published in *The New Republic*, April 6, 1921, the poem was written in 1920 [3:101]. In a letter to Sidney Cox written in July 1920, the poem was referred to as "Silver Lizards" [31:138]. It is based on an incident which took place in late March, 1920, when Frost spent the night with Raymond Holden stoking the fire in the sugar house on Frost's Franconia farm [143:142]. As Holden recalled:

> The happiest and most memorable days of my friendship with Robert were in spite of the difficulties which arose there for me and for him—those at Franconia between 1915 and 1920. I can point to many of his poems and say, "This was written after we did such-and-such." He had the habit, when he had finished a new poem, of writing out a copy of it in longhand, signing it, and giving it to me. I remember particularly the appearance of one called "Evening in a Sugar Orchard," and of another entitled "A Hillside Thaw," both of which were written in the early spring of 1919 [i.e., 1920], after he and I had sat up all one night tending the fire and keeping the sap flowing in the sugar orchard close to Robert's house [...].
>
> Several times, during the night, Robert and I went out to fetch more wood from the shed attached to the sugar house. We stood for a while in the moonlight, watching the glitter of the frozen rivulets which, in the warm sun of the afternoon before, had been runnels of thaw-water, running down the sloping floor of the sugar orchard [87:11–15].

l. 3. *Ten million silver ... snow*: cf. "The Onset," *l.* 18–21.

Plowmen

First published in *A Miscellany of American Poetry 1920* (New York: Harcourt, Brace, 1920), the poem was written in 1919 [3:101].

l. 1. *A plow, they ... snow*: the version of the poem sent to Louis Untermeyer on January 24, 1920, contains a minor variant. See 151:95.

On a Tree Fallen Across the Road
(To hear us talk)

First published, without subtitle, in *Farm and Fireside*, October 1921. The poem may have been written in 1920 [3:101]. Frost wrote to Louis Untermeyer, upon a 1949 printing of this poem, "Most accidents are just to ask us who we think we are. And after all who in Hell are we?" [151:351].

Our Singing Strength

First published in *The New Republic*, May 2, 1923, according to Frost, this poem was written in 1915 [3:101].

l. 22. *Hudson's Bay*: inland sea in Canada's Northwest Territories.

The Lockless Door

First published in *A Miscellany of American Poetry 1920* (New York: Harcourt, Brace, 1920). The incident which inspired this poem took place in 1895 when Frost was renting space at the home of Henry Horne on Ossipee Mountain (now Mt. Shaw) in Moultonboro, New Hampshire. He had accompanied the White sisters, Elinor and Leona, who were staying in a rented cottage nearby. One night Frost was severely frightened by the sudden appearance of an uninvited visitor. Awakened by what sounded like a knock on the lockless front door, Frost lay in bed, half-awake, trembling. He then heard three unmistakable knocks. He crawled to the open kitchen window, climbed out, and finally mustered enough courage to shout "Come in" through the window. He could hear the door creak open. Petrified, Frost fled. Barefooted, barechested, wearing only a pair of pants, he ran toward the hotel to get help. After a few moments, however, he decided to walk back to the Horne house. Finding the house still dark, he again aimed for the hotel. Back and forth he walked through the night. In the morning, he climbed back through the window to find a man, at first thought dead, but only asleep on the floor, snoring. A harmless neighbor, when Frost woke him, the man explained that he had only desired to spend the night in the Horne house so he could sober up before going home [142:206–207]. Frost's experiences in the Horne home inspired two of his prose plays, "A Way Out" and "The Guardeen."

l. **20.** *and alter with age*: the version of the poem sent to Louis Untermeyer on January 24, 1920, contains a minor variant. See 151:95.

The Need of Being Versed in Country Things

First published in *Harper's Magazine*, December 1920, the poem was written in 1900 [3:102]. Frost wrote to Louis Untermeyer on March 10, 1938, that he had "satisfied my conscience with hints at the truth" in this poem [151:305]. On the visual versus the vocal imagery in this poem, Frost wrote, "The concrete visual image is one chief thing and the concrete vocal image is another. Nothing special of the concrete vocal image here" [3:110].

West-Running Brook

First published in New York by Henry Holt in 1928. A limited, signed edition of one thousand copies was also published. The book was dedicated, "To E.M.F." The initials were for Frost's wife, Elinor Miriam Frost. The contents of *West-Running Brook* was divided into six sections:

I. Spring Pools ("Spring Pools" through "Acceptance")
II. Fiat Nox ("Once by the Pacific" through "Acquainted with the Night")
III. West-Running Brook ("West-Running Brook")
IV. Sand Dunes ("Sand Dunes" through "The Flower Boat")
V. Over Back ("The Times Table" through "The Birthplace")
VI. My Native Simile ("The Door in the Dark" through "The Egg and the Machine")

In *Collected Poems* (1930 and all subsequent editions) three poems which did not appear in the first edition of *West-Running Brook* were added: "The Lovely Shall Be Choosers," "What Fifty Said," and "The Egg and the Machine."

Spring Pools

First published in *The Dearborn Independent*, April 23, 1927, this poem was written in 1925 "sitting alone late at night in Ann Arbor, Michigan" [23:137] while reminiscing of spring in New England. During a 1925 interview in Michigan, Frost said:

> I never write about a place in New England, if I am there. I always write about it when I am away. In Michigan I shall be composing poetry about New Hampshire and Vermont with longing and homesickness better than I would if I were there, just as in England" [90:12].

The Freedom of the Moon

First published in *West-Running Brook*.

The Rose Family

First published simultaneously in *The Yale Review* and *The London Mercury*, July 1927.

l. 1. *The rose is a rose*: echo of Gertrude Stein's 1913 poem, "Sacred Emily": "Rose is a rose is a rose is a rose."

Fireflies in the Garden

First published in *West-Running Brook*. At an October 26, 1938, talk at Ohio Wesleyan University, Frost said that poems "are fireflies. They represent our lucid intervals and glow only for a moment" [110:209].

Atmosphere
Inscription for a garden wall

First published as "Inscription for a Garden Wall" in *Ladies' Home Journal*, October 1928.

Devotion

First published in *West-Running Brook*.

On Going Unnoticed

First published as "Unnoticed" in *The Saturday Review of Literature*, March 28, 1925. A note in *West-Running Brook* dates the poems as "1901," which is confirmed by Frost in a 1929 letter [66:355]. In 1930, however, Frost dated the poem as 1895 [3:102] and in 1931 as 1896–1900 [3:104]. The earlier date may refer to an earlier variant, entitled "Nature's Neglect"

[162:HM7646] and consisting of five quatrains. The first ten lines only survived as lines 1–8, 13–14 of "On Going Unnoticed"; the remaining ten lines are unpublished. A later manuscript was entitled "Unnoticed, Nature's Neglect" [120:167].

l. 5. *coralroot*: a nonphotosynthetic leafless orchid which lives on organic debris found in the woods during July and August.

l. 13. *You linger your ... gone*: possible echo of Shakespeare's *Macbeth* [V.v.24–26]: "Life's but a walking shadow, a poor player, / That struts and frets his hour upon the stage, / And then is heard no more" [134:1337].

The Cocoon

First published in *The New Republic*, February 8, 1927. In 1930, Frost dated the poem as "1913(?)" [3:102].

A Passing Glimpse
To Ridgely Torrence
on last looking into his "Hesperides"

First published as "The Passing Glimpse" in *The New Republic*, April 21, 1926, according to Frost, this poem was written in 1924 [3:102]. For another example of Frost's belief that truth is given in glimpses that are easily lost, see "For Once, Then, Something."

Dedication *Ridgley Torrence ... "Hesperides"*: the original dedication in *West-Running Brook* was simply "To Ridgley Torrence." Torrence (1875–1950) was a Midwestern poet whom Frost met in 1917. His "Hesperides" was not published until 1925 in *Hesperides* (New York: Macmillan). The phrase "on last looking into his 'Hesperides'" may be an echo of Keats' "On First Looking into Chapman's Homer."

ll. 1–2. *I often see ... are*: during a 1955 reading, Frost was asked what kind of flower it was which he hadn't seen from the train. He answered that it "was probably lupine. I never looked back. That's the point of that" [25:98].

ll. 11–12. *Heaven gives its ... close*: cf. "A Soldier," *l.* 5–6.

A Peck of Gold

First published as "The Common Fate" in *The Yale Review*, July 1927, according to Frost, this poem was written in 1924 [3:102]. A note in *West-Running Brook* dates the subject of the poem "As of about 1880." Frost said that it was about his childhood in San Francisco [66:500; 25:43–44].

l. 9. *Golden Gate*: strait in California connecting San Francisco Bay with the Pacific Ocean, separating San Francisco from Marin County.

Acceptance

First published in *West-Running Brook*.

Once by the Pacific

First published in *The New Republic*, December 29, 1926. Frost wrote that he began to write this poem at Dartmouth College in 1892 and completed it years later [3:115]. See note to *l.* 5–6 below. A note in *West-Running Brook* dates the subject of the poem "As of about 1880." Frost said that this was about his childhood in San Francisco, [66:500] particularly the Cliff House beach [25:133]. Reminiscing in California in 1932, Frost said, as recorded by Louis Mertins:

> It was a very long time ago that it happened. It was before Coney Island had come in to spoil the beach here at the Cliff House. I was very small and very impressionable—a child full of imagination and phobias. I watched the big waves coming in, blown by the wind. I recall that I was playing on the sand with a long black seaweed, using it for a whip. The sky must have clouded up, and night begun to come on. The sea seemed to rise up and threaten me. I got scared, imagining that my mother and father, who were somewhere about, had gone away and left me by myself in danger of my life. I was all alone with the ocean water rising higher and higher. I was fascinated and terrorized watching the sea; for it came to me that we were all doomed to be engulfed and swept away. Long years after I remembered the occasion vividly, the feeling which overwhelmed me, and wrote my poem "Once by the Pacific" [103:6].

Given the interpretation of "Once by the Pacific" as a war poem, Frost told a 1958 audience that it was written before either of the world wars [25:124]. However, Frost more than once considered this poem as a prophecy of the calamities associated with the two world wars [143:626].

ll. 5–6. *Like locks blown ... eyes*: Frost said that "Once by the Pacific" was originally a fragment written at Dartmouth, "an entirely different poem." Frost kept this couplet from the fragment and incorporated it into the new poem [133:31].

Lodged

First published in *The New Republic*, February 6, 1924. Frost's inscription to Louis Mertins, "Interesting to know I felt this way as early as thirty years ago when this was written" [103:140] places the date circa 1915, the time of the Frosts' return to America.

A Minor Bird

First published as "The Minor Bird" in *The Inlander* (University of Michigan), January 1926, the poem was written in 1924 [3:102].

A note in *West-Running Brook* dates the subject of the poem "As of about 1893." In 1893 Frost was teaching in Methuen, Massachusetts; in 1894 he was teaching in Salem, Massachusetts. The poem reflects Frost's annoyance as a teacher with having to read and correct the writings of his students. As he told Louis Mertins, "[...] you can't teach a child poetry-writing, or a bird to sing" [103:88]. For another example of Frost's annoyance with being a "charity clinic for incipient poesis" [66:312], see "Build Soil," *ll.* 270–275.

Bereft

First published in *The New Republic*, February 9, 1927. In 1930, Frost dated this poem as "189–" [3:102]. A note in *West-Running Brook* dates the subject of the poem "As of about 1893," the spring and summer of which

Frost spent at the Oliver Saunders place in Salem, New Hampshire, as the caretaker and protector of the White family women. Elinor's older sister, Ada, suffered from physical and psychological ailments which confined her to a shade-drawn bedroom in the Whites' Lawrence, Massachusetts, home. Recognizing a need for the quiet of the country, Mrs. White suggested the possibility of renting the Saunders place near Canobie Lake. Since Mr. White refused to go along, Frost volunteered to accompany them. Soon Ada and Mrs. White were joined by Elinor's other older sister, Leona, who, although married and pregnant, had run away from her husband, Nathaniel Harvey. Leona began to depend more and more on Frost's sympathies and friendship. Mrs. White, concerned about their closeness, summoned Elinor to join them from St. Lawrence University, saying that Ada was very ill. Elinor joined them, Ada's health improved, and Leona returned to her husband. When fall came, the Whites returned to Lawrence, and Frost remained behind alone, feeling that there was no reason to return home at that time if Elinor were returning to college. The pleasure Frost felt in feeling sorry for himself in his deserted state after the four women left became the inspiration for this poem [142:149–153].

Tree at My Window

First published in *The Yale Review*, July 1927. Just outside the poet's bedroom window on the Derry farm grew a white birch tree with long branches. These branches would scrape against the house and even against the window [142:309].

ll. **5–8.** *Vague dream-head ... profound*: in reference to the inclusion of this poem in an anthology Louis Untermeyer was preparing in 1931, Frost wrote about possibly deleting this stanza

> for the sake of perfection? Does that keep the 'head' in the last stanza from ringing as it should? I've always been a shade unsure about what the second stanza did to the poetic logic which is the thing I set above all things in poetry [151:208].

ll. **13–16.** *That day she ... weather*: on the form of this stanza, Frost said in 1958 that "No matter what I think it means, I'm infatuated with the way the rhymes come off there" [25:124].

The Peaceful Shepherd

First published in *The New York Herald Tribune* Books Section, March 22, 1925, "The Peaceful Shepherd" was grouped with "On a Star-Bright Night" under the general title "A Sky Pair." Referring to the "Rule/renewal" and "warred/Sword" rhymes, the poet wrote that he "Would hate to make a system of off-rhyme. But one now and then for the roughness of handcraft—" [120:92]. Frost wrote that this was about World War I [3:115].

ll. 3–4. *line the figures ... stars*: to outline the constellations.

The Thatch

First published in *West-Running Brook*, according to Lawrance Thompson, this poem was written shortly before its publication in *West-Running Brook* [143:631]. In 1930, however, Frost dated the poem as 1921 [3:102]. A note in *West-Running Brook* dates the subject of the poem "As of 1914."

Title *The Thatch*: in 1914 the Frosts were living at The Gallows, home of Lascelles Abercrombie. As Frost wrote to Sidney Cox, "We are in another old house, this time under a very ancient thatch: the bottom layer of straw is rye—perhaps put on two or three hundred years ago" [31:51].

l. 1. *Out alone*: apparently this reflects an often repeated marital routine of the Frosts. Whenever Frost felt overcome by his desire to steal away because too much tension had built up between the couple, he would leave the house, walking until nearly exhausted, finally returning, repentant [142:310].

ll. 6–7. *I would not ... in*: a similar stalemate is described in "A Dream Pang," *ll.* 7–8.

ll. 17–27. *And as I ... flyer*: about the incident which inspired this part of the poem, Frost said:

> One of the amusing things was I used to walk in the night along a thatched roof—a very old thatched roof that came clear down from way up; came down to my shoulders—and I used to scare the birds out of that in the night if they lived in the thatch.... It bothered me a lot because I didn't know where they went when they roosted on the ground the rest of the night, and I was in distress my self, but I was sorrier to distress the birds. And that's always been with me—the notion of what becomes of a bird that is scared off its perch. Just that line, that little thing I don't get credit for [25:233].

A Winter Eden

First published in *The New Republic*, January 12, 1927, according to Frost, this poem was written in 1925 [3:102].

l. 2. *conies*: rabbits.

The Flood

First published as "Blood" in *The Nation*, February 8, 1928, the poem was written in 1926 [3:102].

l. 6. *power of blood itself releases blood*: possible echo of *Macbeth* (III.iv.121): "It will have blood, they say; blood will have blood" [134:1327].

l. 14. *blood will out*: echo of Chaucer's "The Prioress's Tale" (*l.* 576): "Mordre wol out, certeyn, it wol nat faille" [17:244].

Acquainted with the Night

First published in *The Virginia Quarterly Review*, October 1928, according to Frost, this poem was written in 1925 [3:102]. Frost claimed in 1959 that "Acquainted With the Night" was written for the tune [25:135].

Title *Acquainted with the Night*: the title, according to Lawrance Thompson, "may be considered as echoing Isaiah 53:3: ... a man of sorrows, and acquainted with grief..." [143:627].

l. 13. *the time was ... right*: Frost explained during readings in the 1950s that this phrase was made for A.E. (George Russell) who often said, from reading Henry Adams, that the times are not right [25:52, 87]. Frost's reaction is expressed in this line. Cf. "The Lesson for Today," "Build Soil," *l.* 53, and "Letter to *The Amherst Student*."

The Lovely Shall Be Choosers

First published in booklet form (New York : Random House, 1929) in "The Poetry Quarto" series. This poem was not originally published in *West-*

Running Brook, but was added in 1930. Frost said that "the poem was written—not all of it at the same time—in Franconia, on a high chair perched on a platform I built to keep the winter draughts from my feet" [13:171]. This statement places the date of the poem circa 1915–1920 and contradicts Frost's claim, which he made about many of his poems, that it was played "through without fumbling a sentence" [9:471]. In the 1930s, Frost dated this poem as between 1915 and 1917 [3:102, 104]. The first draft contains two trial-titles: "Retribution" and "Defeat in [Life]" [142:555; bracketed word inserted by author or editor of 142].

Title *The Lovely*: Frost's mother, Isabelle Moodie (Mrs. William Prescott) Frost.

l. 22. *her wedding*: Isabelle Moodie and William Prescott Frost were married on March 18, 1873, in Lewistown, Pennsylvania.

l. 26. *her grief is secret*: Frost mistakenly thought that his parents had married hastily after his conception. It was his belief that the marriage and birth records were destroyed during the San Francisco earthquake and fire of 1906. Frost learned late in life that his parents had been married over a year before his birth.

l. 29. *too far off*: Frost's parents had settled in San Francisco in November 1873.

l. 31. *a child at either knee*: Robert Lee Frost was born on March 26, 1874; his sister, Jeanie Florence Frost, was born June 25, 1876.

l. 33. *once she walked in brightness*: Frost's mother had inherited a belief in the power of second sight. Her grandfather, on the night he died, told her of his first glimpse of bright angels encircling the gates of heaven. Her intense interest in matters of the spirit would cause her face to appear to brighten or glow [142:4]. A more mundane explication of this line would be in reference to Isabelle Moodie Frost's having come "from too high too late" [*l.* 45].

l. 46. *some one with eyes to see*: Frost himself.

West-Running Brook

First published in *West-Running Brook*, this poem was chosen by Frost for a possible expanded edition of *North of Boston* [144:178]. "West-Running Brook" was begun in the spring of 1920 and had been in part inspired by Edward Ames Richards, an Amherst student, who had published in the *Amherst Monthly* (March 1920) a poem entitled "'Joe Wright's Brook'" about two lovers who talk briefly about the name of the brook. Frost said in a discussion with Richards in 1920 that if he were to build a poem around the name of a brook he would make something quite different out of it. The discussion brought back to Frost's mind a stream which flowed westward in Derry, New Hampshire, and which he had admired for its apparently ignoring its destination in the east, the Atlantic Ocean. The poem remained unfinished until 1926 when Frost was in Franconia, New Hampshire, after his return from the University of Michigan, where he had argued with a group of scientists about the Darwinian theory of evolution [143:299–300].

In a 1937 letter, Frost linked "West-Running Brook" with "Reluctance," "The Tuft of Flowers," and the passage about home in "The Death of the Hired Man," as having the "same subject [...] my position [...] between socialism and individualism" [118:5].

Title *West-Running Brook*: a small west-running brook ran to the south of the Frost farm in Derry, New Hampshire, and was fed by a pasture spring (see "The Pasture").

l. 59. *Not just a swerving*: the reference is to Lucretius's *De rerum natura* (book II, *ll.* 216–293), which begins with a discussion of the fact that

> Though atoms fall straight downward through the void
> by their own weight, yet at uncertain times
> and at uncertain points, they swerve a bit—
> enough that one may say they changed direction [101:34].

Sand Dunes

First published in *The New Republic*, December 15, 1926. In 1931, Frost dated this poem as having been written between 1896 and 1900 [3:104] and in 1949 as having been written prior to going to England [3:115]. The poem is a possible echo of Oliver Wendell Holmes's poem, "The Chambered Nautilus," which ends [*ll.* 29–35]:

> Build thee more stately mansions, o my soul,
> As the swift seasons roll!
> Leave thy low-vaulted past!
> Let each new temple, nobler then the last,
> Shut thee from heaven with a dome more vast,
> Till thou at length art free,
> Leaving thine outgrown shell by life's unresting sea [1.1:558].

Canis Major

First published as "On a Star-Bright Night" in *The New York Herald Tribune* Books Section, March 22, 1925, "Canis Major" was grouped with "The Peaceful Shepherd" under the general title "A Sky Pair."

Title *Canis Major*: constellation, Frost's "great Overdog" (*l.* 1) which contained the Dog Star, Sirius.

l. 9. *underdog*: reference to the constellation, Canis Minor, the lesser dog, which contains the star Procyon, meaning "fore-dog," because it rises before the Dog Star.

A Soldier

First published as "The Soldier" in *McCall's Magazine*, May 1927. Frost referred to this poem in 1961 as "one kind of way of taking life about war or peace" [25:181].

l. 6. *like men we look too near*: cf. "A Passing Glimpse," *ll.* 11–12.

Immigrants

First published in George P. Baker's *The Pilgrim Spirit* (Boston: Marshall Jones Co., 1921), as *ll.* 21–24 of Frost's "The Return of the Pilgrims." This quatrain was written between 1896 and 1900 [3:104]. Cf. "The Return of the Pilgrims," pages 239–240.

l. 3. *the Mayflower*: the ship on which the Pilgrims sailed to America in 1620.

Hannibal

First published in *West-Running Brook*, this poem was written before 1895 [3:103]. In 1949 Frost commented, "I loved Hannibal and Scipio" [3:116].

Title *Hannibal*: Carthaginian general (247–183 B.C.) who, in the

Second Punic War, left New Carthage, defeated the Gauls and crossed the Alps in fifteen days.

The Flower Boat

First published in *The Youth's Companion*, May 20, 1909, this poem was subsequently printed later that year in *The Pinkerton Critic*, December 1909. A note in *West-Running Brook* dates this poem as "Very early." Frost wrote to R.B. Haselden that the poem was written around 1894–1895 [66:355]. In 1930 Frost dated this as part of a group of poems written in or before 1895 [3:103].

l. 8. *Georges Bank*: submerged sandbank east of Massachusetts, well-known Atlantic fishing area.

l. 9. *Elysian*: of or relating to Elysium, the abode of the blessed after death in classical Greek mythology.

The Times Table

First published in *The New Republic*, February 9, 1927, the poem is an expansion of an idea originally expressed in five lines on a sheet containing various, probably unrelated, fragments on the verso of a manuscript of "A Minor Bird," written 1924–1926 [164]. Cf. *ll.* 9–13 of "The Mountain Road" [125].

l. 1. *a spring with ... glass*: a similar image appears in "Directive," *ll.* 55–57.

The Investment

First published in *West-Running Brook.*

The Last Mowing

First published in *West-Running Brook.*

The Birthplace

First published in *The Dartmouth Bema* (Dartmouth College) June 1923, according to Elinor Frost in 1931, this poem was written in Franconia, N.H., between 1915 and 1917 [3:104].

The Door in the Dark

First published in *West-Running Brook*, this poem was written in June 1928 and sent to Louis Untermeyer on June 21, 1928, as "Speaking of Metaphor." In an accompanying letter, Frost wrote, "The only thing that can disappoint me in the head is my own failure to learn to make metaphor. My ambition has been to have it said of me: He made a few connections" [151:189].

ll. 8–9. *So people ... before*: the version sent to Louis Untermeyer had for the closing couplet a more personal tercet referring to Untermeyer's recent divorce from his second wife, Virginia, and remarriage to his first wife, Jean [151:190].

Dust in the Eyes

First issued in broadside form as an advertisement for *West-Running Brook.*

Sitting by a Bush in Broad Sunlight

First published in *West-Running Brook.* In 1930 Frost dated this poem as 1928 [3:102]. The poem apparently was begun from notes made in a 1925 notebook. The notes were worked into a first-draft quatrain [see 143:627–628] before being reworked into the poem as published. An undated manuscript [163] consisting of three stanzas—variants of the first, fourth and fifth stanzas of the final version—entitled "There Were Miracles in Those

Days" apparently falls between the first-draft and the final form published in *West-Running Brook*. According to Wilbert Snow, Frost told him that "he considered the account of man's creation as recorded in the first chapter of Genesis as no more miraculous than the combined factors of air, heat, light, moisture, climate, and other conditions brought into exact harmony to make life upon this planet possible [...]" [137:22–23].

ll. 13–16. *God once declared ... bush*: God's revelation to Moses from the burning bush in Exodus 3:1–4:17 in which "the angel of the Lord appeared unto him in a flame of fire out of the midst of a bush: and he looked, and, behold, the bush burned with fire, and the bush was not consumed" [131:73].

The Armful

First published in *The Nation*, February 8, 1928. Frost was easily upset by distractions which took him away from his writing, but the demands of family life often interrupted his work. One such demand, such as running to the nearest grocery store for whatever may have been needed, provided Frost with the basis for this poem [143:307].

What Fifty Said

This poem was not originally published in *West-Running Brook*, but was added in 1930. It was probably written sometime in 1925, when Frost believed he had turned 50 (he was actually 51; see note to *l.* 26 of "The Lovely Shall Be Choosers"), but no later than February 1927 when it was sent to Sidney Cox [31:177].

Riders

First published in *West-Running Brook*.

On Looking Up by Chance at the Constellations

First published in *West-Running Brook*, according to Frost in 1930, this poem was written in 1927 [3:103].

l. 3. *the Northern Lights*: the aurora borealis, luminous atmospheric phenomenon consisting usually of streamers radiating from above the northern magnetic pole.

The Bear

First published in *The Nation*, April 18, 1928. In 1930, Frost dated this poem as 1927 [3:103]. This poem was inspired by a "descent of bears" in the Franconia region of New Hampshire during the summer of 1925 [151:176].

The Egg and the Machine

First published as "The Walker" in *The Second American Caravan* (New York: 1928), edited by Alfred Kreymborg, Lewis Mumford and Paul Rosenfeld. This poem was not originally published in *West-Running Brook*, but was added in 1930.

A Further Range

First published in New York by Henry Holt in 1936. A limited, signed edition of eight hundred and three copies was also published. The book was dedicated, "To E.F. for what it may mean to her that beyond the White Mountains were the Green; beyond both were the Rockies, the Sierras, and, in thought, the Andes and Himalayas—range beyond range even into the realm of government and religion."

The contents of *A Further Range* was arranged into six sections:

Taken Doubly ("A Lone Striker" through "A Record Stride"; each poem in this section has a subtitle [see below]
Taken Singly ("Lost in Heaven" through "Provide, Provide")
Ten Mills ("Precaution" through "In Dives' Dive")
The Outlands ("The Vindictives" through "Iris by Night")
Build Soil ("Build Soil" and "To a Thinker")
Afterthought ("A Missive Missile")

At a 1937 talk at Haverford College, Frost referred to this book as having "got a good deal more of the times in it than anything I ever wrote before" [74:14].

A Lone Striker

First published as "The Lone Striker" in booklet form (New York: Knopf, 1933) as number 8 of the Borzoi Chap Books. The poem was subtitled in *A Further Range*: "Without Prejudice to Industry."

Referring to the poem's first publication, Frost wrote to John Bartlett, "I shall soon be out with a ponderous book of one poem on how I detached myself from the mills of Man in Lawrence Mass but without prejudice to machinery, industry or an industrial age so that there will be no mistake in the record" [2:170–171]. The incident which inspired "The Lone Striker" occurred in a late winter 1894 morning. Approaching the Arlington Mill where he was employed, Frost heard the mill bell change from a vigorous clang to a more somber tone indicating that the gate would soon be shut. Those who were not inside before the gate shut were destined to remain outside for half an hour and find a corresponding reduction in pay in their next pay envelope. Frost had often found himself on the wrong side of the gate. This particular morning, hearing the gate clang shut, he summoned what Lawrance Thompson referred to as a "Shelleyan gesture of scornfully rebellious defiance." He turned away as a lone striker, putting an end to his days as a millhand [142:160–161]. At a talk given at Haverford College on October 24, 1937, Frost said, "It is all right to be a striker, but not a lone striker. [...] the trouble with me is that I was a lone striker; if I called it a 'collectivist striker,' that would be another matter" [74:12].

l. 29. *harplike spread of strings*: according to Newdick, "RF was shocked when he found he had repeated himself, e.g., the harp-like figure in 'A Lone Striker' and in 'The Death of the Hired Man' [*l.* 107]. He tries always for different tones, and of course to avoid any repetition" [110:334].

Two Tramps in Mud Time

First published in *The Saturday Review of Literature*, October 6, 1934. The poem was subtitled in *A Further Range*: "A Full-time Interest." The poem was inspired by Frost's memory of an incident which had occurred on his Franconia, New Hampshire, farm [143:425]. In a 1938 letter Frost wrote, "I am philosophically opposed to having one Iseult for my vocation and another for my avocation, as you may have inferred from a poem called 'Two Tramps in Mud Time'" [66:462]. In a 1935 lecture in Colorado, Frost remarked, "A poet may be concerned with the jails, the poor-houses, the slums, the insane asylums, and wars; or, because he sees no possibility of change, he may try to find what happiness he can for himself and be cruelly happy" [143:425].

A few days after Elinor underwent surgery for cancer in 1937, Frost wrote to Louis Untermeyer, that she had been "the unspoken half of everything I ever wrote, and both halves of many a thing from 'My November Guest' down to the last stanzas of 'Two Tramps in Mud Time' [...]" [66:450].

Title *Mud Time*: at a 1937 talk, Frost said in a reminiscent mood,

> Few back roads are left now; mud time is going by. We used to be shut in by mud longer than by snow. All the old pleasures of mud time are nearly gone. When we first went to another farm, we helped get somebody out of the mud. But this is in memory of those good days [74:15].

ll. 49–64. *Out of the ... agreed*: this stanza is not present in the manuscript. Above the final stanza is a quatrain. See 121:169.

l. 69. *Only where love ... one*: possible echo of Henry David Thoreau's "Life Without Principle" in which Thoreau wrote, "Do not hire a man who does your work for money, but him who does it for love of it. [...] You must get your living by loving" [147:159–160]. During a 1937 talk at Haverford

College, Frost commented, "It is a very general thing: getting your need and your love together in everything. I don't say we do it. [...] We almost do it. That's the object of everything. To get your love and need together" [74:15].

The White-Tailed Hornet

First published with subtitle "or Doubts About an Instinct" in *The Yale Review*, spring 1936. The poem was subtitled in *A Further Range*: "The Revision of Theories." One of the theories to which both the earlier and later subtitles refer is that expounded by J. Henri Fabre in his *Souvenirs entomologiques*, one part of which was published in America as *The Hunting Wasps*. Discussing instinct as represented in the Sphex, Fabre states, "The Sphex has shown us how infallibly and with what transcendental art she acts when guided by the unconscious inspiration of her instinct [...]. To instinct nothing is impossible [...]" [32:188]. At a reading at Bread Loaf, Frost introduced this poem by saying that the anecdotal or parabolic surface meaning has got to be good and sufficient in itself, above or beyond anything further the poem may represent [25:43]. Frost wrote to L.W. Payne, Jr., in 1936 that this was one of the best poems from *A Further Range* [66:426].

l. 47. *very like a fly*: echo of Shakespeare's *Hamlet* (III.ii.382), "Very like a whale" [134:1166].

ll. 61–62. *We were men ... angels*: echo of Psalms 8:5, "For thou hast made him a little lower than the angels [...]" [131:602].

A Blue Ribbon at Amesbury

First published in *The Atlantic Monthly*, April 1936. The poem was subtitled in *A Further Range*: "Small Plans Gratefully Heard Of."

Title *Amesbury*: town in Massachusetts where many poultry shows were held.

l. 12. *Sewell*: Franklane L. Sewell (1867–1948), prominent illustrator of fowl and game birds.

A Drumlin Woodchuck

First published in *The Atlantic Monthly*, June 1936. The poem was subtitled in *A Further Range*: "Be Sure to Locate." Frost claimed that his poem "Triple Bronze" was written as a "pendant" to "A Drumlin Woodchuck," which he separated and published at different times [3:116]. Trial lines for "A Drumlin Woodchuck" appear on the first draft of "Departmental" [35:11].

Title *Drumlin*: an elongated or oval hill formed by a glacial drift.

The Gold Hesperidee

First published in *Farm and Fireside*, September 1921. The poem was subtitled in *A Further Range*: "How to Take a Loss." Frost got the story for this poem from an unidentified town history [3:116].

Title *Gold Hesperidee*: in Greek mythology, golden apples from the garden of the Hesperides, the daughters of Evening.

l. 17. *what was green would by and by be gold*: cf. "Nothing Gold Can Stay," *l.* 1.

l. 51. *Ahaz*: 11th King of Judah who, in 2 Kings 16.2–4, "did not that which was right in the sight of the Lord his God, like David his father. [...] And he sacrificed and burnt incense in the high places, and on the hills, and under every green tree" [131:441]. Cf. "New Hampshire," *ll.* 388–389, 393–394.

l. 57. *Gath*: one of five royal cities of the Philistines. Biblically this city is associated with the story of David, in that Goliath came from Gath.

In Time of Cloudburst

First published in *The Virginia Quarterly*, April 1936. The poem was subtitled in *A Further Range*: "The Long View."

A Roadside Stand

First published in *The Atlantic Monthly*, June 1936. The poem was subtitled in *A Further Range*: "On Being Put Out of Our Misery." Frost had considered entitling the poem, "Euthanasia" [143:439].

l. 19. *the life of ... promise*: during a 1931 interview, Frost said, "Many of our country people don't value anything unless they buy it in the town—where townspeople buy it. Country people go to the movies instead of looking around them" [60:5].

ll. 23–31. *It is in ... way*: refers to the New Deal, a domestic program of the Franklin D. Roosevelt administration (1933–1945) designed to bring about economic relief and reform.

l. 44. *the country scale of gain*: Frost said in 1931, "The country's advantage is that it gives many pleasures and supplies many needs for nothing. The tendency of our day is to throw away all of these things and count them worthless" [60:5].

Departmental

First published in *The Yale Review*, winter 1936. The poem was subtitled in *A Further Range*: "The End of My Ant Jerry." The poem was written in early January 1935, as the following statement from a letter to George Whicher, posted January 14, 1935, states: "The enclosed went across my mind the other night like a cloud across the moon." The poem, which was excluded from the January 14 letter, was included with Frost's next letter to Whicher, dated January 23, 1935, in which he wrote, "Take my word for it and internal evidence my Ant is not a Stinging Ant. He is merely an amusing little piece of nature faking so bare faced that I found I was ashamed of [it]—was and still am" [124]. The first draft of "Departmental" contains trial lines for "A Drumlin Woodchuck" [35:11].

Frost once referred to this poem as "my iridium poem; it's hard and useful" and claimed that "This one has all my erudition in it." He also cautioned an audience, "Don't be too interested in it, except for the rime pairs" [26:355, 358].

l. 23. *McCormic*: in the first draft, following this line was a couplet which was eventually eliminated [124]. See 35:11.

ll. 40–41. No one stands ... affair: Frost wrote to Louis Untermeyer in 1920 in reference to Jeanie Frost, "And I suppose I am a brute in that my nature refuses to carry sympathy to the point of going crazy just because someone else goes crazy, or of dying just because someone else dies" [151:103]. For similar notions of taking sympathy to a certain point but no farther, see "Home Burial," *ll.* 102–105, and "Out, Out—," *ll.* 33–34.

l. 43. *thoroughly*: the first draft had the word "frightfully." When Louis Untermeyer found fault with the word, Frost defended his original choice in a letter to Untermeyer written in January 1936, in which he wrote: "To tell you the truth I thought that word was part of the joke—just like 'mortician' and 'out of there' [...]" [151:268]. Ultimately, however, Frost changed the word.

The Old Barn at the Bottom of the Fogs

First published in *A Further Range*. The poem was subtitled in *A Further Range*: "Class Prejudice Afoot."

ll. 38–39. *In chestnut now ... trees*: in the 1930s a destructive fungal disease, referred to as "chestnut blight," was introduced from Europe, and it quickly killed all of the larger chestnut trees. Young trees still grow, but these too will eventually be killed by the blight.

On the Heart's Beginning to Cloud the Mind

First published in *Scribner's Magazine*, April 1934. The poem was subtitled in *A Further Range*: "From Sight to Insight." The poem was created out of something Frost saw from his Pullman window in the darkness of the desert while he was traveling by train from Denver to Salt Lake City in August of 1931 [143:414]. As Frost said during a reading, "I was looking out of a train window away out in Utah and way in the night, and I saw one lonely light way off, you know, far from any other all around. I made a whole poem out of that" [25:110]. Frost said he wrote the poem "in a hotel bedroom in Wilkes Barre Pennsylvania one midnight about five years ago [circa 1931–1932]" [123:36]. Cf. "The Figure in the Doorway."

l. 1. *Something I saw or thought I saw*: Reuben Brower suggests a possible allusion to Virgil's *Aut videt aut videsse putat* [10:16].

The Figure in the Doorway

First published in *The Virginia Quarterly*, April 1936. The poem was subtitled in *A Further Range*: "On Being Looked At in a Train." Frost introduced the poem at a reading by saying that it was "Out of the Ozarks. I don't know how I happened to write this poem, but it is (I guess it was) at somebody I saw looking out of the train window" [25:110]. Cf. "On the Heart's Beginning to Cloud the Mind."

At Woodward's Gardens

First published in *Poetry*, April 1936. The poem was subtitled in *A Further Range*: "Resourcefulness Is More than Understanding." Frost wrote to Whit Burnett that this poem was reminiscent of his childhood in San Francisco [66:500].

Title *Woodward's Gardens*: botanical gardens, zoo and amusement park in San Francisco.

A Record Stride

First published in *The Atlantic Monthly*, May 1936. The poem was subtitled in *A Further Range*: "The United States Stated." This poem was "written in California at the time of the Olympic games [1932]" [66:500], although, according to Lawrance Thompson, it was written in South Shaftsbury in late 1931 a few months after Frost's 1931 visit to California [143:396]. In December 1932, Frost said that he wrote "A Record Stride" for his family when he was torn between Montauk, Long Island, and Long Beach, California, the previous summer. He also joked about his claim to have written the poem on the spur of the moment at a party as a challenge to T.S. Eliot [151:231].

l. 1. *a Vermont closet*: South Shaftsbury [103:194].

l. 13. *Montauk*: point on the eastern extremity of Long Island, New York.

l. 15. *Cliff House*: according to John Bartlett, claiming the poet as a source, Frost "really wet the second shoe at Long Beach, California, but that he wasn't going to give Long Beach a place in any poem because he didn't like it well enough; that, on the other hand, he did like the beach at the Cliff House" [143:655]. This is confirmed by an annotation made to Louis Mertins [103:194].

l. 16. *extra-vagant*: this word may be hyphenated simply to control the rhythm of the line (ex'-tra-va'-gant vs. ex-tra'-va-gant), but it may also be an allusion to Thoreau, who wrote in *Walden*:

> I fear chiefly lest my expression may not be *extra-vagant* enough, may not wander far enough beyond the narrow limits of my daily experience, so as to be adequate to the truth of which I have been convinced. *Extra vagance!* it depends on how you are yarded [148:580].

l. 17. *Two entirely different grandchildren*: the "Atlantic" grandchild was Lesley's daughter, Elinor; the "Pacific" grandchild was Carol's son, Prescott.

Lost in Heaven

First published in *The Saturday Review of Literature*, November 30, 1935, although it had been accepted, but not published, by *The American Mercury* in December 1933.

Desert Places

First published in *The American Mercury*, April 1934. Frost's claim to have "played certain poems through without fumbling a sentence" included this poem [9:471].

Leaves Compared with Flowers

First published in *The Saturday Review of Literature*, February 2, 1935.

A Leaf-Treader

First published in *The American Mercury*, October 1935, it was written at least as early as November 1934 when it was sent in a letter to Louis Untermeyer [151:246]. Recalling how a friend misinterpreted the poem by what he often referred to as "pressing too hard for meaning," Frost said that this poem was about a year he kept getting sick. "That's all that means" [26:356].

On Taking from the Top to Broaden the Base

First published in *A Further Range*.

They Were Welcome to Their Belief

First published in *Scribner's Magazine*, August 1934. The manuscript was entitled "The Truth of It" [120:168].

l. 12. *of snow*: between this stanza and the next, the manuscript contains a rejected quatrain. See 121:169.

The Strong Are Saying Nothing

First published in *The American Mercury*, May 1936.

*l*6. *Men work alone*: this recalls "The Tuft of Flowers" [*ll.* 8–10] where the narrator of the poem says:

> And I must be, as he had been—alone,
>
> "As all must be," I said within my heart,
> "Whether they work together or apart."

l. 16. *the strong are ... see*: in his 1931 essay "Education by Poetry," Frost wrote, "There are four beliefs that I know more about from having lived with poetry. One is the personal belief, which is a knowledge that you don't want to tell other people about because you cannot prove that you know. You are saying nothing about it till you see" [67:46].

The Master Speed

First published as "Master Speed" in *The Yale Review*, winter 1936, this sonnet was written as a wedding present for Irma Frost and John Cone on their marriage in Franconia in the summer of 1926 [143:304].

ll. 1–9. *No speed of ... say*: Frost said that his "favorite theory is that we are given this speed swifter than any stream of light time or water for the sole purpose of standing still like a water beetle in any stream of light time or water off any shore we please" [133:xxi].

l. 11. *Cannot be parted*: unintentionally ironic in that the Cones were divorced in 1947.

l. 14. *wing to wing*: echo of the final line of Yeats' "The Countess Cathleen in Paradise" which ends: "All the heavens bow down to Heaven, / Flame to flame and wing to wing" [158:43].

Moon Compasses

First published in *The Yale Review*, autumn 1934.

l. 6. *measured*: in a letter replying to Leonida Payne's suggestions of corrections, Frost wrote:

> I have to be a pretty exact person when it comes to such a delicate poem as "Moon Compasses." Your suggestion there would spoil my meaning. *Was measured* doesn't mean the same thing as *measured*. My passive is perfectly idiomatic. You must remember I am not writing school-girl English [66:370].

Neither Out Far nor In Deep

First published in *The Yale Review*, spring 1934. This poem was "written in California at the time of the Olympic games [1932]" [66:500]. Although it is one of his "Californian poems," Frost claimed it "is made up of mixed memories" [103:194].

l. 1. *the sand*: Laguna Beach, California.

ll. 13–14. *They cannot look ... deep*: about these lines Frost said that "Sometimes in the by-product of science we lose the spirit entirely; but not in the act of scientific penetration—deeper, deeper, deeper, further, further, further [...]. But—as far as we can and as deep as we can, as far out as we can—still we penetrate into matter, further into matter [25:131].

Voice Ways

First published in *The Yale Review*, winter 1936, this poem was originally to be placed as the introductory poem in a book of 26 poems by Frost's daughter Marjorie, privately printed in 1936 as a memorial volume. Marjorie had died on May 2, 1934, from puerperal fever. The book, *Franconia*, was published without Frost's introductory poem. The poem was written prior to October 8, 1935, when it was sent in a letter to Frost's daughter Lesley.

l. 6. *Your*: Marjorie's.

Design

First published in *American Poetry 1922: A Miscellany* (New York: Harcourt, Brace, 1922). At a reading Frost commented that this was a poem which he had forgotten about but that someone found and so he put it in *A Further Range* [25:126]. An early draft, entitled "In White," was sent to Susan Hayes Ward on January 15, 1912. See 142:582.

l. 2. *heal-all*: any of several plants reputed to have healing powers, especially *Prunella vulgaris*, a low-growing plant with violet-blue flowers.

On a Bird Singing in Its Sleep

First published in *Scribner's Magazine*, December 1934.

Afterflakes

First published in *The Yale Review*, autumn 1934. Frost told Louis Mertins, "I believe I wrote ["Afterflakes"] [...] in California when we were round together [1932]" [103:195].

Clear and Colder

First published in *Direction*, autumn 1934.

l. 18. *Cotton Mather*: American clergyman and author (1663–1728).

Unharvested

This sonnet was first published as the eleven-line "Ungathered Apples" in *The Saturday Review of Literature*, November 10, 1934.

There Are Roughly Zones

First published in *A Further Range*. Frost said that although one likes "to say to young people that there's no sharp line between good and evil" [25:126], "there are bounds set in all company" [31:156].

A Trial Run

First published in *The Atlantic Monthly*, June 1936.

l. 8. *stand your ground*: at the beginning of the Revolutionary War, Captain John Parker, addressing his men at Lexington Green, April 19, 1775, said, "Stand your ground. Don't fire unless fired upon, but if they mean to have a war let it begin here."

l. 10. *cotter-pinned*: in which a cotter pin, a half-round metal strip bent into a pin, is inserted through a slot or hole and its ends flared to prevent its slipping out.

Not Quite Social

First published in *The Saturday Review of Literature*, March 30, 1935.

During a reading Frost made the claim that this poem "goes with" his "The Lost Follower" [25:43].

l. 8. *when its walls ... roof*: during medieval times when, for protection, the castle walls rose higher than roofs within.

l. 9. *You may taunt ... earth*: Frost expressed this desire to flee in many poems, as in "Birches" (*l.* 48.) in which he wrote: "I'd like to get away from earth awhile."

l. 10. *loosely, as I would be held*: cf. "The Silken Tent," *ll.* 9–10.

l. 11. *The way of understanding is partly mirth*: cf. "[It Takes All Sorts...]."

Provide, Provide

First published in *The New Frontier*, September 1934. The poem was inspired by a strike of charwomen in 1935 at Harvard organized by some Harvard reformers. The ensuing controversy seemed typical of some of the wrongs emanating from the New Deal, namely, as Lawrance Thompson phrased it, "sentimental humanitarianism" [143:437]. Proud of the poem's form, he once remarked that there was "plenty of tune" to it [25:135].

l. 3. *Abishag*: a beautiful Shunamite maiden, in 1 Kings 1:3, 15, brought to minister to the dying King David [131:385].

l. 21. *Provide, provide!*: in a political aside referring to the New Deal, Frost added once during a reading, "Or somebody else'll provide for ya" [114:258].

Ten Mills

Collective title for group of ten poems first published in *Poetry*, April 1936. "Ten Mills" as published in 1936 consisted of:

I. Precaution
II. The Span of Life
III. Pertinax
IV. Assertive
V. Tendencies Cancel
VI. Untried
VII. Money
VIII. Ring Around
IX. Not All There
X. In Dives' Dive

In *A Further Range* (1936), "Ring Around" was dropped (but later retitled "The Secret Sits" and published in *A Witness Tree*) while "The Wrights' Biplane" and "One Guess" were added, making a total of eleven, not ten, poems. In *A Further Range*, as collected in the 1949 and later editions of Frost's poems, "Assertive" was dropped. It had already been published in *A Further Range* as *ll.* 260–261 of "Build Soil."

Title *Ten Mills*: Frost was using the word "mill," which has a monetary value of 1/10 cent, to mean something small. Ten mills would have the value of one penny.

I. Precaution

First published in *Poetry*, April 1936, following an incidental appearance in the Baltimore *Sun*, February 26, 1936. The couplet was apparently first said in 1932 as the following statement by Frost explains:

> There has been too much talk about—too much emphasis on—my chance remark away back in 1932, out in Pasadena with atom-splitter Millikan—the one I made in answering a woman who wanted to know if I were a conservative or a radical—whether I was about to embrace the era of F.D.R. (He hadn't yet been elected.) I didn't take much time to think about a reply. I just snapped right back with [the couplet] [103:338].

Frost introduced the couplet at a 1937 interview by saying, "In my boyhood I read the radical works of Edward Bellamy and Henry George but I have never been a radical. I wrote a two line poem once. It was [recites couplet]" [20: 8]. Frost's saying in 1936 that "Two lines from one of my earlier verses really sum up my whole viewpoint" [51:85] implies that this couplet may have been part of a longer poem. On the form of this poem, Frost referred to it as "a couplet that isn't a couplet. It's a free verse couplet" [25:145].

II. The Span of Life

First published as "The Old Dog" in *Rainbow in the Sky*, edited by Louis Untermeyer (New York: Harcourt, Brace, 1935), prior to its publication as part of "Ten Mills" in *Poetry*, April 1936.

III. The Wrights' Biplane

First published in *A Further Range*, the poem was written at least as early as August 1932, when it was sent in a letter to Louis Untermeyer [151:229].

Louis Mertins recalls

> how greatly exercised Frost was over the fact that the encyclopedias were trying to take the honor of the first heavier-than-air flight away from the Wright brothers.
>
> "Why," he sputtered, "when all this thing is written, that about Lindbergh and all, there will still remain only the Wright boys, the Columbuses of the air. Orville is eating his heart out over in Dayton because of what's being done and what is not being done. Shabby treatment."
>
> Asked if he thought Orville would be willing to bring his plane back from Europe to the Smithsonian Institution if Congress would give him the credit for making the first flight, he continued:
>
> "Of course he would. Why, they have a little insignificant contraption in the institute marked as the one which made the first flight, when all it was able to do was nose up and take a dive into the bay, and that without a pilot. I wanted to do all I could to help establish them in their rights. So I wrote a poem about our having wheelwrights, wainwrights, and now we've got wingwrights. I want to print it and do what I can to help" [103:195–196].

Cf. "Kitty Hawk" and "Let Congress See To It."

Title *The Wrights*: Orville (1871–1948) and Wilbur (1867–1912) Wright, pioneers in aviation.

IV. Evil Tendencies Cancel

First published as "Tendencies Cancel" in *Poetry*, April 1936.

l. 1. *the blight*: in the 1930's a destructive fungal disease, referred to as "chestnut blight," was introduced from Europe, and it quickly killed all of the larger chestnut trees. Young trees still grow, but these too will eventually be killed by the blight.

V. Pertinax

First published in *Poetry*, April 1936. The poem refers to Frost's adherence to his belief in poetic form, as opposed to the "chaos" of free verse, but takes on larger dimensions when read against his March 1935 "Letter to The Amherst Student," in which he wrote,

> There is at least so much good in the world that it admits of form and the making of form. And not only admits of it, but calls for it. [...] When in doubt there is always form for us to go on with. [...] Fortunately, too, no forms are more engrossing, gratifying, comforting, staying than those lesser ones we throw off, like a poem [...] [67:106–107].

Twenty years later, on *Meet the Press*, Frost reiterated this idea in very similar terms:

> This matter of confusion. I think the thing that confuses the mind is loss of a sense of form, and if you lose the sense of form, the doctor can restore it by teaching you how to make a horseshoe or a basket or something like that, or to blow smoke rings or anything to restore your sense of form. And as long as so many of us, nearly all of us, have a chance to make a little rounding out of something—of family life or a magazine or an article or a poem [...] that is what keeps the sanity and that is what keeps and saves us from the sense of confusion [79:121].

Title *Pertinax*: thoroughly tenacious (Latin).

VI. Waspish

First published as "Untried" in *Poetry*, April 1936. The poem was sent to Louis Mertins as "Name Untried" on September 10, 1935 [103:212].

l. **6.** *But*: in a letter replying to Leonidas Payne's suggestions of corrections, Frost wrote, "Substituting *but that* for *but* in 'Waspish' would show school girl timidity and spoil my metrics. *But* alone will be found all the way down in our literature" [66:370].

VII. One Guess

First published in *A Further Range*, the poem was written circa 1911 with the title "A Riddle.—Who Is Intended" [162].

VIII. The Hardship of Accounting

First published as "Money" in Poetry, April 1936. Frost, apropos his grandfather, William Prescott Frost, Sr., paying him five dollars a week every week he stayed in Dartmouth University, said:

> Since he paid me five dollars a week for my keep, it was only natural, from his viewpoint, that he should desire a return on his investment, usury. He had the New England shrewdness which demanded a dollar back with interest. Now, inasmuch as I got my room for $30.00 a year, meals

> proportionately reasonable, the five dollars was plenty for ordinary needs. What made it bad was the fact that he insisted on an itemized account for every penny spent, where it went, and what it was for. I rebelled and wanted to tell him to go to hell. But I didn't, I held. It wasn't that I objected to being dependent on him. That sort of thing has never bothered me [...]. It was just that I hated to keep an account of every little dab I spent [103:47].

IX. Not All There

First published in *Poetry*, April 1936. An early manuscript draft was titled "Don't Anybody Laugh" [143:689].

X. In Dives' Dive

First published in *Poetry*, April 1936.

Title *Dives*: name traditionally given to the rich man in Jesus's parable of Lazarus and the rich man (Luke 16:19–31) from a mistranslation of the phrase "*homo quidam erat dives*" ("there was a certain rich man") [131:1098].

ll. 3–4. *the Declaration ... equal*: refers to the Declaration of Independence and its statement that "all men are created equal."

The Vindictives

First published in *A Further Range*. A note in *A Further Range* associates the poem with "The Andes."

The Bearer of Evil Tidings

First published in *The Yale Review*, winter 1936. A note in *A Further Range* associates the poem with "The Himalayas."

Frost told Louis Mertins in 1932, the possible inspiration for this poem:

> The old kings used to have a fine way of treating such [bearers of evil tidings] [...]. The general would send a runner on ahead with the bad news of retreat or defeat; and when the message was delivered the messenger would be taken out and killed. I like that, original [103:195].

Iris by Night

First published in *The Virginia Quarterly*, April 1936.

The poem describes an event which occurred in August of 1914 [142:455]. A note in *A Further Range* associates the poem with "The Malverns (but these are only hills)."

Title *Iris*: a double rainbow.

l. 2. *We two*: Frost and Edward Thomas. Thomas commemorated the many walks the two poets took in his "The Sun Used to Shine," which begins:

> The sun used to shine while we two walked
> Slowly together, paused and started
> Again, and sometimes mused, sometimes talked
> As either pleased, and cheerfully parted
>
> Each night. We never disagreed
> Which gate to rest on. The to be
> And the late past we gave small heed.
> We turned from men or poetry
>
> To rumours of the war [...] [141:106].

In his 1948 essay, "A Romantic Chasm," Frost wrote, "I wish Edward Thomas (that poet) were here to ponder gulfs in general with me as in the days when he and I tired the sun with talking on the footpaths and stiles of Leddington and Ryton" [54:5].

l. 2. *a Malvern side*: the Malverns are hills in England between Worcestershire and Herefordshire.

l. 5. *according to belief in Rome*: reference to Lucretius's *De rerum natura* (book V, *ll.* 666–679), which begins with a discussion of the fact that

> men see wide-scattered fires
> that flow then into a sort of ball or sphere.
> Yet, in all this, it should not seem surprising
> that at such definite times these seeds of fire
> should gather and build the sun's bright gleam anew [101:128].

l. 6. *Memphis*: city in, and once capital of, ancient Egypt.

l. 22. *And I alone of us have lived to tell*: echo of the formula used by the four messengers in Job 1:15–19, "and I only am escaped alone to tell thee" [131:570].

Build Soil
A political pastoral

First published in *A Further Range*. According to a note in *A Further Range*, the poem was "delivered at Columbia University, May 31, 1932, before the National party conventions of that year." A letter to Louis Untermeyer written May 13, 1932, headed by the motto, "Courage he said and pointed toward the land" from Tennyson's "The Lotus Eaters" [*l.* 1], is a prose working-out of ideas expressed in "Build Soil" [See 151:222–223]. As Frost told Louis Mertins, "You can never accuse me of being pro-red. There are my books, my poems. [...] Just read 'Build Soil' and you'll see" [103:190].

ll. 1–2. *Tityrus ... Meliboeus*: from Virgil's "First Eclogue." Meliboeus was a farmer; Tityrus, his friend, was a farmer-poet.

l. 6. *interval*: variant of intervale, chiefly a New England term meaning bottom or valley, as in Frost's title, *Mountain Interval.*

l. 44. *Whittier's luck with Skipper Ireson*: John Greenleaf Whittier (1807–1892), American poet, who wrote "Skipper Ireson's Ride." Cf. "New Hampshire," *l.* 143.

l. 46. *Stuart's portrait*: Gilbert Charles Stuart (1755–1828) painted three portraits of George Washington—one in 1795 and two in 1796 (one of them unfinished).

l. 53. *I doubt if ... bad*: see "The Lesson for Today" for a discussion of whether the present times are bad as compared with any other age.

l. 129. *I'd let things take their course*: simplified statement of the doctrine of laissez-faire which opposes governmental interference, particularly in economic affairs, and promotes individual freedom of choice and action.

l. 134. *I'm not afraid to prophesy the future*: although he might offhandedly refer to his "prophetic soul" [133:143], Frost had a real belief in the concept of poet as prophet. He inherited his faith in second sight from his mother (cf. "The Trial by Existance"). His readings in Shelley, Wordsworth, Carlyle, Emerson, Tennyson and Browning furthered this belief [143:626]. Cf. "The Wind and the Rain" [*ll.* 12–14] and "The Prophets Really Prophesy as Mystics, The Commentators Merely by Statistics" [*ll.* 6, 22].

l. 153. *pinxit*: he painted it (Latin).

l. 172. *To market 'tis our destiny to go*: cf. "Christmas Trees" (*l.* 24).

l. 175. *More that should be kept back*: a similar idea is expressed in Frost's poem "Unharvested."

l. 202. *all reasoning is in a circle*: cf. "[No matter how straight forward...]."

l. 220. *five-year plans*: beginning with the First Five-Year Plan of 1928–

1932, the Soviet economy was linked to five-year plans which are adjusted annually and sometimes quarterly to correct imbalances.

ll. 255–256. *I unostentatiously move ... resume*: Frost wrote to Sidney Cox that this is "what to do when anyone comes on you too overwhelming" [31:206].

ll. 260–261. *Let me be ... done*: this couplet was also published separately as "By Myself" in Louis Untermeyer's *Rainbow in the Sky* (New York: Harcourt, Brace, 1935) and as "Assertive" in the group "Ten Mills" in *Poetry*, April 1936.

ll. 270–275. *A youngster comes ... parents*: for another example of Frost's annoyance with his being a "charity clinic for incipient poesis" [66:312] and performing "perfunctory routine criticism of ordinary college writing" [143:358], see "A Minor Bird."

ll. 278–279. *Steal away, / The song says*: from the Black American spiritual, which has the chorus: "Steal away, steal away, steal away to Jesus! / Steal away, steal away home, / I hain't got long to stay here" [1.2:816].

To a Thinker

First published as "To a Thinker in Office" in *The Saturday Review of Literature*, January 11, 1936. The trial proofs of *A Further Range* list the title in the contents as "Our Darkest Concern" [120:58]. During a reading at the University of Colorado Writers Conference in Boulder on August 1, 1935, Frost described "To a Thinker" as a "suppressed poem" in that it had been written during the early years of the New Deal, and that, many things said in it having coming to pass, he felt it necessary to suppress its publication. After its eventual publication in January 1936, an article in the *Baltimore Sun* (February 26, 1936) connected the poem with President Roosevelt. Other articles followed. As a result of the controversy surrounding the poem, Henry Goddard Leach, editor of *The Forum*, wrote to Frost requesting permission to publish the poem. Frost replied on March 15, 1936

> that it was only by restriction of meaning that it was narrowed down to fit the President. [...] As a matter of fact it was written three years ago and was aimed at the heads of our easy despairers of the republic and of parliamentary forms of government. [...] I doubt if my native delicacy would have permitted me to use the figure of walking and rocking in connection with a person of the President's personal infirmities [66:427–428].

A Missive Missile

First published in *The Yale Review*, autumn 1934. The manuscript was titled "A Stone Missive" [120:168].

l. 1. *Mas d'Azil*: commune in Southern France. In 1887, in a nearby cave, prehistoric human remains were discovered belonging to a period immediately preceding the Neolithic.

A Witness Tree

First published in New York by Henry Holt in 1942. A limited, signed edition of seven hundred and thirty-five copies was also published.

Following a page containing two introductory poems, "Beech" and "Sycamore," the contents of *A Witness Tree* were arranged in five titled sections:

One or Two ("The Silken Tent" through "The Discovery of the Madeiras")
Two or More ("The Gift Outright" through "The Lesson for Today")
Time Out ("Time Out" through "It Is Almost the Year Two Thousand")
Quantula ("In a Poem" through "An Answer")
Over Back ("Trespass" through "The Literate Farmer and the Planet Venus")

This is Frost's first book not dedicated to his wife. It was dedicated, "TO K.M. FOR HER PART IN IT." K.M. was Kathleen (Kay) Morrison, Frost's secretary following Elinor's death in 1938. Frost had first met Kay at Bryn Mawr in 1920 when she, then Kathleen Johnston, had organized the other students to invite Frost to their campus for a reading. After his wife's death, it was Kay who helped put Frost back on his feet. As he told Louis Mertins:

> I owe everything in the world to her. She found me in the gutter, hopeless, sick, run down. She bundled me up and carted me to her home and cared for me like a child, sick child. Without her I would today be in my grave. If I have done anything since I came out of the hospital, it is all due to her [103:233].

Beech

First published in *A Witness Tree.*

Attribution *The Moodie Forester*: Moodie is Frost's mother's maiden name.

l. 9. *not unbounded*: for the way in which one is "not unbounded," see "The Silken Tent," *ll.* 9–10.

Sycamore

First published in *A Witness Tree*. "Sycamore" is not a Frost poem, but simply a direct quotation from the rhymed alphabet pages of the *New England Primer*.

Attribution *The New England Primer*: textbook, first published circa 1690, used in New England and other English settlements in North America. It contained alphabet rhymes, the catechism, and Calvinistic religious injunctions.

The Silken Tent

First published in *The Virginia Quarterly Review*, winter 1939. This poem was originally titled "In Praise of Your Poise" and presented to Kay Morrison in 1938 [144:23]. During a 1953 interview, Frost said, "What is man but all his connections? He's just a tiny invisible knot so that he can't discern it himself: the knot where all his connections meet" [51:119]. Cf. "On the Question of an Old Man's Feelings."

l. **1.** *She*: a controversy exists whether the "she" of this poem refers to Frost's wife, Elinor, or his secretary, Kay Morrison. We have Lesley Frost's word that "The Silken Tent" was written to Elinor, Lesley having typed out the poem while her mother was still living. Lesley quotes Frost as saying to her, "Every love poem I ever wrote was to one person—your mother" [39:314]. Lawrance Thompson, however, fueled the Kay Morrison theory when he wrote of "The Silken Tent" as a new poem written after Elinor's death, presented to Kay as a way of informing her how he felt toward her [144:23].

Although Kay Morrison was indeed presented with the poem, there is no reason to believe that she was ultimately its original inspiration. In all likelihood, the poem was written to Elinor, but after Elinor's death, the increased respect and love he felt for Kay prompted Frost to present this sonnet to her.

ll. **9–10.** *loosely bound ... thought*: this is an example of Frost's "proof of not being unbounded" ["Beech," *l.* 9]. Cf. "Not Quite Social," *l.* 10.

All Revelation

First published as "Geode" in *The Yale Review*, spring 1938. The idea for this poem began possibly in 1935 when Frost wrote in his introduction to Edwin Arlington Robinson's *King Jasper*:

> We began in infancy by establishing correspondence of eyes with eyes. We recognized that they were the same feature and we could do the same things with them. We went on to the visible motion of the lips—smile answered smile; then cautiously, by trial and error, to compare the invisible muscles of the mouth and throat. They were the same and could make the same sounds. We were still together. So far, so good. From here on the wonder grows. It has been said that recognition in art is all. Better say correspondence is all. Mind must convince mind that it can uncurl and wave the same filaments of subtlety, soul convince soul that it can give off the same shimmers of eternity. At no point would anyone but a brute fool want to break off this correspondence. It is all there is to satisfaction; and it is salutary to live in the fear of its being broken off [129:vi–vii].

l. 4. *Cyb'laean*: relating to Cybele, the Phrygian mother-goddess.

Happiness Makes Up in Height for What It Lacks in Length

First published in *The Atlantic Monthly*, September 1938. Although Frost wrote the poem "in those stormy March days at Harvard" [66:453] in 1936, the idea is "as old as Derry days" [142:563]. The idea springs from some notes on an undated piece of foolscap from his years on the Derry farm in which Frost recognizes the terms of the challenge of flight: "a little more pleasure than pain. Pain greater in length and breadth but exceeded by pleasure in height; one more pleasure than pain by actual count—the pleasure of being alive" [142:332]. Richard Poirier suggests that the title may have been derived from George Santayana's *Soliloquies in England* which states in its final paragraph, "The length of things is vanity, only their height is joy" [114:92].

Come In

First published in *The Atlantic Monthly*, February 1941.

ll. 5–7. *Too dark in ... night*: on these lines Frost once said at a Bread Loaf reading:

> I've been told by a birdman, somebody who knows a lot about birds, that birds never shift their perch at night, and I've felt corrected somewhat. I made a generalization out of having made birds shift ["The Thatch," *ll.* 17–27] and I've distressed myself about them [25:44].

I Could Give All to Time

First published in *The Yale Review*, autumn 1941. Frost had first intended to title the poem "I Could Give All to Change" [103:248; 35:11].

Carpe Diem

First published in *The Atlantic Monthly*, September 1938. Written shortly after his wife's death on March 20, 1938, this poem was sent to Louis Untermeyer with minor variants on April 17, 1938 [151:307]. About Elinor's death, Frost wrote to Untermeyer on May 16, 1938, from Amherst:

> I don't know myself yet and won't for a long time, if I ever do. I am so quickened by what has happened that I can't touch my mind with a memory of any kind. I can't touch my skin any where with my finger but it hurts like a sad inspiration [151:308].

In August 1938, he wrote to J.J. Lankes:

> I'm afraid I dragged her through pretty much of a life for one as frail as she was. Too many children, too many habitations, too many vicissitudes. And a faith required that would have exhausted most women. God damn me when he gets around to it. I refused to be bowed down as much as she was by other deaths. But she has given me a death now that I can't refuse to be bowed down by [143:511].

Title *Carpe Diem*: from Horace's Odes, Book I, Ode XI: *Carpe diem, quam minimum credula postero.* Popularly translated as "seize the day," it might better be translated as "Reap the harvest of to-day, putting as little trust as may be in the morrow!" [89:32–33].

l. **2.** *twilight*: possible reference to Frost's first book of poetry, *Twilight*. It had been privately printed by Frost for Elinor when he was courting her.

l. **10.** *seize the day*: English for *Carpe Diem*.

l. **13.** *gather-roses burden*: this is a reference to Robert Herrick's "Counsel to Girls," which begins:

> Gather ye rose-buds while ye may,
> Old Time is still a-flying:
> And this same flower that smiles today,
> Tomorrow will by dying [81:71].

A similar reference is made in a poem originally published in *A Boy's Will*, but left out of the collected editions of Frost's poetry, "Asking for Roses," *ll.* 17–20:

> A word with you, that of the singer recalling—
> Old Herrick: a saying that every maid knows is
> A flower unplucked is but left to the falling,
> And nothing is gained by not gathering roses.

ll. **23–24.** *The present is too much*: for a similar stance of not being able to deal with the present, see "Directive," *l.* 1.

The Wind and the Rain

First published in *A Witness Tree*, the poem was probably written in 1938 following Elinor's death.

Title *The Wind and the Rain*: from Shakespeare, in both the Clown's song at the end of *Twelfth Night* (V.i.389–408) and the Fool's song in *King Lear* (III.ii.74–77).

l. **9.** *I sang of death*: it is unknown whether Frost had any particular poem in mind here, but certainly he had sung of death many times by 1938. A list of titles would include "Despair," "Spoils of the Dead," "Ghost House," "My Butterfly," "Home Burial," and "Place for a Third."

l. **10.** *the many deaths*: by 1938, Frost had already faced the deaths of both his parents (his father in 1885, his mother in 1900); his only sister, Jeanie

(1929); three of his six children (Elliott in 1900, Elinor Bettina in 1907, and Marjorie in 1934); his close friend, Edward Thomas (1917); and his wife, Elinor (1938).

ll. 12–14. *Oh, should a ... prophesied?*: echo of Emerson's "Fate" from *The Conduct of Life*: "They who talk much of destiny [...] invite the evils they fear" [30:954]. Although he might offhandedly refer to his "prophetic soul" [133:143] Frost had a real belief in the concept of poet as prophet. He inherited his faith in second sight from his mother [see "The Trial by Existance"]. His readings in Shelley, Wordsworth, Carlyle, Emerson, Tennyson and Browning furthered his beliefs [143:626]. Cf. "Build Soil" [*l.* 134] and "The Prophets Really Prophesy as Mystics, The Commentators Merely by Statistics" [*ll.* 6, 22].

l. 40. *And there is ... said*: one possible exchange Frost may have had in mind as something "more than should be said" was the one with his daughter Lesley, shortly after Elinor's death. In this exchange Lesley refused her father's request that he be allowed to live with her, stating that he had caused so much injury to the lives of his children that she would not permit him to live in her home where he may cause injury to her family. She also blamed him for her mother's death, citing his selfishness in putting himself above the needs dictated by his wife's health. She concluded by saying that he was the kind of artist who should never have married, or at least should not have had a family [143:495–496]. He may also have had in mind his own statement to Louis Untermeyer, "I have had almost too much of her [Elinor's] suffering in this world" [151:296]. The horror of saying more than one should is captured in Frost's poem "Ends."

ll. 46–47. *To see to ... eyes*: a similar image is expressed in "The Offer," which Frost referred to as the "tears poem" about "proposing to supply the sorrow felt if the storm will supply the tears" [151:265]. Cf. "The Offer."

The Most of It

First published in *A Witness Tree*. Wade Van Dore, in such poems as "The Echo" and "Man Alone," displayed a certain sentimentalism regarding nature that annoyed Frost. As Lawrance Thompson explained, "Frost grew impatient with Van Dore's wistful attitude of asking nature for something nature could not give. One sought the solitude of wilderness, Frost believed, to make the most of it in terms of natural wonders, whatever they might be, without cultivating a 'troubled heart' over such companionship as it would obviously fail to provide" [143:361]. Frost wrote "The Most of It," originally entitled "Making the Most of It," in response to Van Dore. In his autobiography, Van Dore wrote:

> [...] taking one of my own not-quite-successful poems, "The Echo," as a starting point for his "The Most of It," he plainly used me as copy. I had spent months as a semi-hermit in Canada; and in response to my poem, he had me as one crying out "on life" across a lake for "counter-love, original response." I had often confided in him my strange adventures in silence and loneliness in the lake country northwest of Lake Superior; but, aside from a great answer I might have desired from nature, was I crying out for his and not someone else's sympathy after failing to find complete fulfillment in a great wilderness? The dark and primitive feeling of his poem suggested that he took my seeking as something that touched him personally [152:3–4].

Never Again Would Birds' Song Be the Same

First published in *A Witness Tree*, this poem was written for Kay Morrison [144:304].

l. 1. *He would declare ... believe*: possible echo of *Hamlet* (I.i.165), "So I have heard and do in part believe it" [134:1143]. In 1925 Frost wrote, "For sheer usefulness in every modern encounter, I consider 'So I have heard and do in part believe' the most beautiful single line of English verse" [120:250].

The Subverted Flower

First published in *A Witness Tree*. The first draft of this poem had been written early enough to have been published in *A Boy's Will*, but Frost had hesitated to publish it because of elements in the poem which might appear too daring and autobiographical [142:512]. It was originally entitled "The Inverted Flower" [120:179].

During a 1960 interview Frost told Richard Poirier:

> I wouldn't read "The Subverted Flower" to anybody outside. It isn't that I'm afraid of them [certain poems], but I don't want them out. I'm shy about certain things in my books, they're more—I'd rather they'd be read.

A woman asked me, "What do you mean by that 'subverted flower'?" I said, "Frigidity in women." She left [157:26].

Willful Homing

First published in *The Saturday Review of Literature*, February 26, 1938, as part of Louis Untermeyer's "Play in Poetry."

A Cloud Shadow

First published in *A Witness Tree*, this poem was sent to Louis Untermeyer on December 8, 1916 [151:46].

The manuscript was titled "A Poem on Spring (A Cloud Shadow)" [120:176].

The Quest of the Purple-Fringed

First published as "The Quest of the Orchis" in *The Independent*, June 27, 1901. Frost said this poem was "Probably written in 1895 or 6. Place in mind was near East Pembroke N.H. where we spent a summer." Lawrance Thompson places the East Pembroke summer in 1896 [142:530]. The poem may have been written in Allenstown, New Hampshire, in the summer of 1896 [142:223].

Title *Purple-Fringed*: in 1935 Frost wrote, "Only three or four times have I come on such a dazzling stand of the Purple Fringed [...]" [120:50]. The term "purple-fringed" could refer to either the orchis or the gentian. Frost changed the title of his poem when he collected it in *A Witness Tree* because of his realization that he had confused the orchis, which is an early-bloomer, with the gentian, which is a late-bloomer ["for summer was done," *l.* 28].

The Discovery of the Madeiras
A rhyme of Hakluyt

First published in *A Witness Tree*. An alternate title had been "The Discovery of the Madeira Islands" [120:70]. The source of this poem is Richard Hakluyt's *The Principal Navigations, Voyages, Traffiques and Discoveries of the English Nation*, originally published in 1589. As told by Hakluyt from the original Portuguese history of Anthonio Galvano:

> In the yeere 1344. King Peter the fourth of that name, raigning in Arragon, the Chronicles of his age, write, that about this time the Iland of Madera, standing in 32. degrees, was discovered by an Englishman, which was named Macham, who sayling out of England into Spaine, with a woman that he had stolne, arived by tempest in that Iland, and did cast anker in that haven or baye, which now is called Machico, after the name of Macham. And because his lover was sea sicke, he went on land with some of his companie, and the shippe with a good winde made saile away, and the woman died for thought. Macham, which loved her deerely, built a chappell, or heremitage, to bury her in, calling it by the name of Jesus, and caused his name and hers to be written or graven upon the stone of her tombe, and the occasion of their arrivall there: And afterward he ordained a boate made of one tree, (for there be trees of a great compasse about) and went to sea in it, with those men that he had, and were left behinde with him, and came upon the coast of Affricke, without saile or oare. And the Moores which saw it, tooke it to be a marveilous thing, and presented him unto the King of that Countrey for a wonder, and that king also sent him and his companions for a miracle unto the King of Castille [84.2:455].

Title *Madeiras*: group of Portuguese islands in the North Atlantic.

Subtitle *Hakluyt*: Richard Hakluyt (1552–1616), English geographer and historian.

l. **16.** *Paphian bourn*: literally, a destination in Paphos, Cyprus, but suggesting, because of the identification of the ancient city of Paphos as the center of worship for Aphrodite, a place of love and beauty.

l. **39.** *drink each other's eyes*: possible echo of Ben Jonson's "To Celia" which begins, "Drink to me only with thine eyes" [81:77].

ll. **48–105.** *Sometimes, with her ... pay*: the story of the murder of the slave lovers and its effect on the lady is apparently an interpolation by Frost. It does not appear in Hakluyt.

The Gift Outright

First published in *The Virginia Quarterly Review*, spring 1942, the poem was written at least as early as the summer of 1936 when it was inscribed, untitled, in Lawrance Thompson's copy of *West-Running Brook* [97:31]. A later manuscript contained the title "We Gave Ourselves Outright" [120:180]. This poem was later appended to "For John F. Kennedy His Inauguration" in *In the Clearing*. This note appears in *A Witness Tree*: "Read before the Phi Beta Kappa Society at William and Mary College, December 5, 1941."

Frost's claim that he "played certain poems through without fumbling a sentence" included this poem [9:471]. Frost said that "The Gift Outright" was "as poetic as I ever get" [44:54]. At various times, the poet commented on this poem:

> Yes, I have one on this subject of freedom. (What gives us our freedom is having a territorial basis belonging to the land.) That's one of my favorite poems. Because other people seem to like it [...]. It all lies in that first line [79:113].
>
> The little nation that was, and was to be, gave itself, as Virginia gave herself, westward, into the great nation that she saw coming, and so gave help to America [143:483].
>
> And that, I take it, is the whole thing. Lately I've been thinking more and more about it. All there is is belonging and belongings; belonging and having belongings. You belong and I belong. The sincerity of their belongings is all I have to measure those people by [144:171].
>
> [...] this is what I was talking about—our Revolutionary War, you know. Was it an escape or a pursuit? Pursuit of nationality—as simple as could be. Not an escape at all [25:80].
>
> My history of the Revolutionary War which was the beginning of the end of Colonialism [120:180].

l. 1. *The land was ... land's*: as early as 1919 Frost was writing that "America isn't American enough for her authors to be very American yet" [151:88]. Later, Frost summed it up by saying, "I tried to say in fourteen lines the whole history of the Revolutionary War. Maybe I should have left it in one line—one line there tells it all [...]" [103:399]. "It all lies in that first line," Frost said on *Meet the Press*, December 23, 1956 [79:119]. At a reading in 1962 he commented simply, "See, we didn't belong enough to where we lived" [25:194].

ll. 6–7. *Possessing what we ... possessed*: Frost said that "That's a whole story of just that—the realization that we've got to belong to what belonged to us" [25:80].

l. **13.** *many deeds of war*: regarding these deeds of war Frost said:

> Many deeds of war, little deeds of war—Bennington, one more, Kings Mountain. Named after a king. Down in North Carolina. Went by that within a year in a fast train. [...] Went by a little empty station. There wasn't a truck there. There was nobody there. There wasn't anything. I just happened to look up from a book or magazine or something and it said on the station "Kings Mountain." One of those great little battles [...] [25:112].

Triple Bronze

First published in booklet form as "Triple Plate," being Frost's 1939 Christmas poem. The poem was written at least as early as November 2, 1934, when it was sent to Louis Untermeyer as "Defense" [151:249]. The beginning of the idea for the poem appeared in a May 1932 letter to Untermeyer in which Frost wrote, "I'm in favor of a skin and fences and tariff walls" [151:223]. A 1949 annotation by Frost calls this poem, "Anti–New Deal," and claims it was written as a "pendant" to "A Drumlin Woodchuck," although he did not publish them at the same time [3:116].

Title *Triple Bronze*: from Horace's *Odes* Book I, Ode III, *ll.* 9–11, in which it says that "Oak and triple bronze must have girt the breast of him who first committed his frail bark to the angry sea [...]" [89:13].

Our Hold on the Planet

First published in booklet form, being Frost's 1940 Christmas poem. The poem's first periodical publication was in *The Virginia Quarterly Review*, spring 1942. The manuscript was titled "A Fraction of One Percent" [120:179]. The poem was apparently written sometime between 1938 and 1940, as the following account by John Holmes of a 1938 visit to Frost in South Shaftsbury indicates:

> [Frost] said he thought the balance of life and death—the forces of positive and negative, good and evil, success and failure, whatever one calls them—are roughly fifty-five for life and forty-five for death. He said he thought God or something else, call it what you would, had given man a slight advantage, maybe only two points over fifty.

> [...] and in that narrow margin, he said, we can find almost all of what it's about. We have to remember always, he said, what a small hold we have, and how hard we have to work even to keep it. I asked him, somewhere toward 2:30 or 3 [a.m.], if he had ever said this in a poem. He said he thought not, not that he could remember [...] [88:12].

The idea for this poem may have come as an answer to a prevalent pessimistic outlook which Frost expressed two years earlier in 1936: "They that are against us should be more than they that are for us by all present-day accounts" [19:ix]. Frost iterated a more positive belief in a 1937 letter, using terms similar to the wording found in "Our Hold on the Planet": "Nature in which is included our own human nature must be a little more for us that it is against us [...]" [118:4]. On being a "survivalist," Frost said:

> I believe in survival. That is my fundamental doctrine. I argued in a monologue lately that the fact of our race's having survived should be enough for others as it is for me. It proves those for us must be more than those against us—in nature and human nature [...] [143:459].
>
> And we'll never lack resources to stay here, to hang onto this globe. We'll never be shaken off [143:672].

For another "survivalist" statement, see "The Onset," *ll.* 12–14.

ll. 1–6. *We asked for ... drown*: the opening recalls Frost's concerns as a farmer, as expressed in 1915 to John Bartlett when there was a shower after a lack of rain for a short period, "A little rain today—not enough to pay for prayers at the regular pulpit price." A month later found Frost complaining about too much rain, "I'll bet there is nearly as much water here today as there is where you are. And we care personally. We have to care. We have a garden we don't want drowned" [143:49].

ll. 13–15. *Take nature ... man*: echo of John Burroughs, who in his essay "The Gospel of Nature" wrote, "More has been for us than against us" [15:40] and in *Accepting the Universe* wrote, "Some power other than ourselves [...] is more positive than negative, more for us than against us, else we should not be here" [14:45].

l. 14. *human nature, in peace and war*: in 1940, the Nazi's were advancing across Europe.

To a Young Wretch
(Boethian)

First published, without a subtitle, in booklet form, being Frost's 1937

Christmas poem, this poem was also published in *The Saturday Review of Literature*, December 25, 1937.

Subtitle *Boethian*: reference to Boethius (480–524 A.D.), who wrote *De Consolatione Philosophiae* while in prison.

l. 15. *opposing goods*: on this idea of opposing goods, Frost said, "I often say that most tragedy is like that great tragedy [the Revolutionary War]—a conflict of good and good" [25: 193].

The Lesson for Today

First published in *A Witness Tree*, the poem was begun in 1935 [144:79]. This note appears in *A Witness Tree*: "Read before the Phi Beta Kappa Society at Harvard University, June 20, 1941." During a 1955 interview, Frost said:

> People ask, "Is this the worst time for poetry?" Is it worse than the Middle Ages? I wrote a poem about that, "The Lesson for Today." I don't know how to measure. In our time, anyway, you are a rank insider. You can't tell [51:153].

As Frost told Selden Rodman:

> Life always ends badly. The idealists can't accept it that all ages since time began have ended badly. They resent my not thinking that *our* time is worse than any other [130:41].

l. 15. *ver aspergit terram floribus*: adapted from the second stanza of a medieval Latin song:

> *Ver purpuratum exiit,*
> *ornatus suos induit;*
> *aspergit terram floribus,*
> *ligna silvarum frondibus.*

Translation: The spring with purple dignified / Comes forth, wearing his robes of pride, / To scatter flowers about the land / And bid the leaves in woods expand [82:26].

l. 20. *Charles*: Charlemagne (742–814), Frankish king (768–814), and emperor of the West (800–814).

l. 27. *Virgil*: Publius Virgilius Maro (70–19 B.C.), Roman poet.

l. 87. *paladins*: champions of a prince or a cause.

l. 89. *Roland, Olivier*: heroes of the song of Roland and paladins of Charlemagne.

l. 93. *Horace*: Quintus Horatius Flaccus (65–8 B.C.), Roman poet and satirist.

ll. 94–95. *like a Christian ... end*: the Shorter Catechism in the *New England Primer* states that the chief end of man is to "glorify God and enjoy him forever."

l. 96. *Memento mori*: remember you must die (Latin). In a December 1931 letter to Louis Untermeyer referring to the death of Vachel Lindsay, Frost wrote, "*Memento mori,* the church says. I do. I will now more and more anyway" [151:219].

ll. 98–102. *Earth's a hard ... kingdom-come*: in his 1935 "Letter to The Amherst Student," Frost wrote what became the basis for this part of the poem:

> All ages of the world are bad—a great deal worse anyway than Heaven. [...] One can safely say after from six to thirty thousand years of experience that the evident design is a situation here in which it will always be about equally hard to save your soul. Whatever progress may be taken to mean, it can't mean making the world any easier a place in which to save your soul [...] [67:105–106].

Frost expressed the same idea in *A Masque of Reason, ll.* 316–322.

l. 103. *millennium*: according to Revelation 20, the thousand year period during which holiness is to prevail and Christ is to reign on earth.

ll. 126–155. *It sent me ... rest*: these lines were apparently inspired by a visit to a Key West cemetery on March 2, 1935. As he wrote to Louis Mertins the next day:

> Nothing is important at our age, you know. Why try to get the fussy details right when everything is coming right in a lump so soon. Let me not scare you. I am not fey. I merely mean that in fifty years from now we'll be about at the end of our old age pensions. The oldest person I could find in the Key West graveyard yesterday (Sunday) was a veteran of the War of 1812 who died in Key West at 108 years. But many have lived to be older than that. His inscription wound up "A good citizen for 65 years." He must have been a bad citizen for 43 years then. That's what undermined him and shortened his life [103:212].

l. 161. *I had a lover's quarrel with the world*: the earliest known instance of this phrase occurs in a letter written to Kay Morrison, circa September 1938, in which Frost wrote:

> I am like an ocean that in its restlessness may have brought up every imaginable shape to the surface, but won't be satisfied till it brings up the sea serpent. You two [Kay and Ted Morrison] rescued me from a very dangerous self when you had the idea of keeping me for the whole season at Bread Loaf. I am still infinitely restless, but I came away from you as good as saved. I had had a long lover's quarrel with the world. I loved the world, but you might never have guessed it from the things I thought and said. Now the quarrel is made up [144:13].

In 1958 Frost reiterated, "I've waged a lover's quarrel with the world ever since I felt old enough to woo it with dash" [142:594].

Time Out

First published in *The Virginia Quarterly Review*, spring 1942, this poem was inscribed in Lawrance Thompson's copy of *Collected Poems* with the title "On the Ascent" and dated 1939 [144:390]. The manuscript was entitled "It Took That Pause" [120:176]. This note appears in *A Witness Tree*: "Read before the Phi Beta Kappa Society at William and Mary College, December 5, 1941."

To a Moth Seen in Winter

First published in *The Virginia Quarterly Review*, spring 1942, this poem was written sometime between 1900 and 1911. The 1900 date was established from two sources. A note in *A Witness Tree* dates the poem as "Circa 1900." Underneath this poem in a 1941 manuscript of sixteen of the *A Witness Tree* poems, Frost wrote, "This is a very early treatment of a theme now uppermost in the general mind. Date about 1900" [120:174]. The 1911 date came from a statement Frost made to Robert Newdick who had unearthed this forgotten poem in 1937: "I made it walking down a foggy icy mountain one thaw in March the year we were at Plymouth. Not everything is as easy to date as that" [110:163]. These notes appear in *A Witness Tree*: "Read before the Phi Bet a Kappa Society at William and Mary College, December 5, 1941" and "Circa 1900."

A Considerable Speck (Microscopic)

First published, without subtitle, in *The Atlantic Monthly*, July 1939. In a 1941 manuscript of sixteen of the *A Witness Tree* poems, Frost dated the poem as 1938 and tied it thematically to "To a Moth Seen in Winter" [120:174].

The Lost Follower

First published in *The Boston Herald*, September 13, 1936. Frost said that "The Lost Follower" is about Jean Flexner and Carter Goodrich, [66:591] both of whom "forsook poetry to do something for the next election. They thought one good election and the world would be saved. They tried three or four" [25:43]. "And the time was about 1917 [...] I ought to say this of them: that they were two whom I had set my heart on for the poetry they were going to write, and both of them left the poetry to do social work. Both of them" [25:110–111].

Title *The Lost Follower*: the title is an echo of Robert Browning's "The Lost Leader." Browning's poem discusses his dismay with William Wordsworth's growing political and social conservatism.

ll. 2–3. *golden line / Of lyric*: possible reference to Francis Turner Palgrave's *The Golden Treasury*, which Frost discovered in 1892 and which remained a favorite of his for the rest of his life.

l. 11. *Shelleyan dejection*: the kind of despair expressed by Percy Bysshe Shelley (1792–1822), English poet, in such poems as "Alastor" or "Stanzas Written in Dejection Near Naples."

l. 19. *the Muse*: one of the nine sister goddesses in Greek mythology presiding over the arts and sciences; as used in this poem, the sister who presided over poetry.

l. 30. *Ghibelline or Guelph*: in medieval Italy, a Ghibelline was a member of an aristocratic political party supporting the authority of the German emperors, while a Guelph (or Guelf) was a member of a papal and popular political party opposing that authority.

November

First published as "October" in *The Old Farmer's Almanac 1939* (Boston, 1938). The title was changed when it was discovered that it had already been used for an earlier poem published in *A Boy's Will.* The manuscript title was "In Praise of Waste" [120:174]. An alternate title, "For the Fall of Nineteen Thirty Eight" [120:70], confirms the dating of the poem in a note in *A Witness Tree* as 1938, although a letter of John Holmes dated September 11, 1938, states, "In the limited edition of *West Running Brook*, which I owned, he wrote out a new poem, which he titled 'Lines Written last Autumn,' with a footnote to say he meant 1937. It begins 'We saw leaves go to glory—' [...]" [110:346]. Frost's claim that he "played certain poems through without fumbling a sentence" included this poem [9:471].

The Rabbit-Hunter

First published in *A Witness Tree.* This poem was written while Frost was living in Derry, N.H. (1900–1911) [40:Notes IV.21 1–11]. A manuscript in the Dartmouth College Library has the title "Death" [162:HM 7237]. Apropos rabbit hunters, cf. "Mending Wall," *ll.* 7–9.: "[...] they have left not one stone on a stone, / But they would have the rabbit out of hiding, / To please the yelping dogs."

A Loose Mountain (Telescopic)

First published in *A Witness Tree.* The manuscript title was "Telescopic—A Loose Mountain" [120:177].

l. 1. *the Magi*: the three wise men who came from the East to pay homage to the infant Jesus.

l. 2. *Leonid*: one of the shooting stars which constitutes the meteoric shower that occurs near November 14.

l. 18. *the Zodiac*: band of the celestial sphere representing the path of the principle planets, the moon and the sun.

l. 21. *absorb it*: a working manuscript presented to Robert Newdick contained the following closing couplet after this line: "The way we did the Great War and the curse / That followed after of defeatist verse" [110:214].

It Is Almost the Year Two Thousand

First published in *A Witness Tree*, this poem was begun in March 1920. It was adapted from the third and final stanza of the draft for a poem entitled "Nothing Gold Stays," the first two stanzas of which became "Nothing Gold Can Stay" [143:565]. An alternate title was "It Is Nearly the Year Two Thousand" [120:70].

l. 6. *The true Millennium*: according to Revelation 20, the thousand year period during which holiness is to prevail and Christ is to reign on earth.

In a Poem

First published in *A Witness Tree.*

On Our Sympathy with the Under Dog

First published in *A Witness Tree.* The manuscript title was "On the Difficulty of Keeping Up in Sympathy" [120:177].

A Question

First published in *A Witness Tree.* Asked about this poem during a 1956 interview, Frost commented, "That is a mood, when you sometimes wonder if it is worth it, all the pain" [79:123].

Boeotian

First published in *A Witness Tree.*

Title *Boeotian*: of Boeotia, an ancient Greek district proverbially known for its dull inhabitants.

The Secret Sits

First published as "Ring Around" in *Poetry*, April 1936, as part of the group "Ten Mills." It was inscribed to Roy Virgil Thornton in 1953 as "Ring around a Rosy" [120:69]. The original title refers to the nursery rhyme "Ring around the roses, a pocket full of poesies [...]."

An Equalizer

First published in *A Witness Tree*.

A Semi-Revolution

First published in *A Witness Tree*.

Assurance

First published in *A Witness Tree*, this poem may have been written on or been a memory of any one of Frost's sea voyages. A letter by Frost describes one such voyage, from Cherbourg to New York, in November 1928: "We ran right out of Cherbourgh [sic] into a hundred-and-fifty mile gale that knocked her nose in and brought us to a standstill for three hours a thousand miles from anywhere among some of the biggest waves they say you ever see" [36:192].

An Answer

First published in *A Witness Tree*.

Trespass

First published in *American Prefaces* (University of Iowa), April 1939.

A Nature Note

First published as "A Nature Note on Whippoorwills" in *The Coolidge Hill Gazette* (Cambridge, Mass.), December 1938.

Of the Stones of the Place

First published as "Rich in Stones" in *The Old Farmer's Almanac 1942* (Dublin, N.H., 1941).

Not of School Age

First published in *A Witness Tree* with the note "1932," the poem was written in California [151:227] during the summer of 1932 when the Frosts were in Monrovia visiting the Carol Frosts. The manuscript was titled "An Admirer of the Flag" [120:177].

A Serious Step Lightly Taken

First published in *A Witness Tree*. An early draft of this poem was sent to George Whicher from Key West, Florida, with a letter postmarked

January 14, 1935. Written in pamphlet form, the draft, which varies considerably from the printed text, contains "marginalia" by Frost [165:MS Frost 120].

The Literate Farmer and the Planet Venus

A dated popular-science medley on a mysterious light recently observed in the western sky at evening

First published in *The Atlantic Monthly*, March 1941, this poem was written at least as early as 1932 when it was first read to Louis Mertins [103:193]. According to line 140, it may have been begun as early as 1926. The manuscript was subtitled "A Dated Popular Science Medley on the Bane of War" [120:177]. For variants, see 121:178.

l. **90.** *manumitter*: one who releases a slave.

Steeple Bush

First published in New York by Henry Holt in 1947. A limited, signed edition of seven hundred and fifty-one copies was also published. The book was dedicated to Frost's grandchildren: "For Prescott, John, Elinor, Lesley Lee, Robin and Harold." The contents of *Steeple Bush* were originally arranged in five sections:

[untitled] ("A Young Birch" through "To an Ancient")
Five Nocturnes ("The Night Light" through "In the Long Night")
A Spire and Belfry ("A Mood Apart" through "Iota Subscript")
Out and Away ("The Middleness of the Road" through "Lucretius Versus the Lake Poets")
Editorials ("Haec Fabula Docet" through "To the Right Person")

The title refers to the plant hardhack, an American shrub of the rose family, which grew in abundance near Frost's cabin in Ripton, Vermont.

A Young Birch

First published in booklet form, being Frost's 1946 Christmas poem. This poem was written prior to 1944 [120:183].

l. 5. *To double day*: the image of birches doubling daylight first occurred in a letter written January 6, 1929. Writing to Louis Untermeyer, Frost described his new farm in South Shaftsbury, Vermont, on which "There is a small grove of white paper birches doubling daylight" [151:194].

l. 21. *a thing of beauty*: recalls the opening of Keats' "Endymion," which begins:

> A thing of beauty is a joy for ever:
> Its loveliness increases; it will never
> Pass into nothingness; but still will keep
> A bower quiet for us [...] [95:49].

Something for Hope

First published in *The Atlantic Monthly*, December 1946, this poem was written prior to 1944 [120:183]. The manuscript was titled "A Living on Hope" [120:184].

ll. 2–3. *meadowsweet / And steeple bush*: shrubs of the rose family.

l. 11. *their wooden rings*: note in *Steeple Bush*: "'their wooden rings.' Ripton rings."

l. 18. *laissez-faire*: French for let it be, or let it happen—a doctrine which opposes governmental interference, particularly in economic affairs, and promotes individual freedom of choice and action, or, as Frost states it simply in *l.* 21: "leaving some things to take their course."

l. 24. *spes alit agricolum*: from Tibullus II.vi.20, *spes alit agricolas,* which means "Hope sustains the farmer" [16:280–281].

One Step Backward Taken

First published in *The Book Collector's Packet,* January 1946, as part of Ray Nash's "Robert Frost and His Printers." Frost said that in this poem he "remembers the time of the big flood [1927] when I set out to see Mr [Arthur Stanley] Pease inaugurated here [Amherst College] and didn't get here" [103:174]. He was travelling by train from Arizona and saw from the window a small washed-out bridge and an auto nearby which moved back a little each time a small cake of earth washed away [24:66].

Directive

First published in *The Virginia Quarterly Review,* winter 1946.

l. 1. *all this now ... us*: World War II. For another example of this sentiment of being overwhelmed by the present, see "Carpe Diem" (*ll.* 23–24).

l. 9. *getting lost*: this is an echo of one of Frost's favorite books, Thoreau's *Walden,* which, in the chapter "The Village," has the line, "Not till we are lost, in other words, not till we have lost the world, do we begin to find ourselves, and realize where we are and the infinite extent of our relations" [148:459]. As Frost himself wrote, "Most lives are meant to be lost. At least any that are found have to be lost first" [57:321].

l. 19. *Panther Mountain*: peak in the Adirondack Mountains in central New York.

l. 44. *little things*: Lesley Lee Francis describes some of the "little things" the Frost children did, how "resourceful the Frost children were on meager resources [...] convey[s] a sense of making do with whatever they could find lying around: boards from the path to make a store in the summerhouse; barrel staves to make a tree house; crushed berries to make colors for paints; a make-shift windmill" [36:59].

l. 57. *A broken drinking goblet*: this image also appears in "The Times Table," *l.* 2.

l. 57. *Grail*: dish (in later legend, a cup) used by Christ at the Last Supper. According to legend, Joseph of Arimathea brought it to Glastonbury. At Pentecost, an image of it appeared at King Arthur's table and His knights set out on a quest to find it.

l. 59. *Saint Mark*: in Mark 4:11–12, Jesus says, "Unto you it is given to know the mystery of the kingdom of God: but unto them that are without, all these things are done in parables. That seeing they may see, and not perceive; and hearing they may hear, and not understand: lest at any time they should be converted, and their sins should be forgiven them" [131:1049].

Frost said at a reading that "it's always coming into my head: that these things are said in parable so the wrong people can't understand them and so get saved. It says that twice in the New Testament. It seems very harsh and undemocratic, doesn't it?" [25:76–77].

l. 62. *confusion*: during a 1956 interview on NBC's "Meet the Press," Frost said:

> This matter of confusion. I think the thing that confuses the mind is loss of a sense of form, and if you lose the sense of form, the doctor can restore it by teaching you how to make a horseshoe or a basket or something like that, or to blow smoke rings or anything to restore your sense of form. And as long as so many of us, nearly all of us, have a chance to make a little rounding out of something, of family life or a magazine or an article or a poem or a basket or a horseshoe or a tumbler—that is what keeps the sanity and that is what keeps and saves us from the sense of confusion [79:121].

Cf. "Pertinax."

Too Anxious for Rivers

First published in *Steeple Bush*.

ll. 23–26. *Lucretius the ... love*: Titus Lucretius Carus (96?–55 B.C.), Roman poet and philosopher. He is the author of the six-volume poem *De Rerum Natura*. Of his life little is known, but Jerome says he was driven insane by a love potion, writing his poem during intervals of lucidity, and eventually committing suicide. His "master" was the Greek philosopher Epicurus (342?–270 B.C.).

An Unstamped Letter in Our Rural Letter Box

First published in booklet form, being Frost's 1944 Christmas poem.

l. 51. *in forma pauperis*: literally, Latin for "in the form of a pauper," but also having the meaning of one who acts in a humble or abject manner.

To an Ancient

First published in *The Atlantic Monthly*, December 1946, this poem was written prior to 1944 [120:183].

Five Nocturnes

Collective title for the following five poems, the first three of which were first published together under the title "Nocturnes" in *The Yale Review*, autumn 1946:

I. The Night Light

First published in *The Yale Review*, autumn 1946, this poem was written in September 1928. A letter from John W. Haines to Louis Mertins written in 1949 explains:

> It may interest you that I have just found a letter from Robert received September 23, 1928 from the Imperial Hotel, Russell square, where I stayed with him, concerning "The Night Light," put into his head by a talk we had. I do not know anything about the origin of the poem. It bore the postmark London, Sep. 21, 1928, and was sent off no doubt a day or two after my stay with him, except that we must have been talking about night lights, as there was precious little we didn't talk about. The letter ran: "Dear Jack: This is a small one put into my head by our talk about

> the night light." Then follows the manuscript of the poem he had written with his initials [103:178].

The origin of the poem, according to Edward Hyde Cox, as described by Lawrance Thompson below could not possibly be correct given the dating of the poem above:

> [Hyde] Cox rented the Euber house from RF several summers during the mid-forties, and while living there he was taken care of by his (and formerly his grandmother's) black cook, Mary Douglas. [...] Frightened by the foxes and raccoons which often approached the Euber farmhouse at night, she comforted herself during her stays there by leaving a small lamp burning all night beside her bed. RF was a frequent visitor to Hyde's and had many meals with him, often returning on foot to the Homer Noble farmhouse hours past midnight. When he did, he always noticed the light in Mary's window as he started back [144:411].

l. 4. *her soul to keep*: echo of the prayer which first appeared in the 1781 edition of the *New England Primer* printed in London:

> Now I lay me down to sleep
> I pray the Lord my soul to keep
> If I should die before I wake
> I pray the Lord my soul to take [108:46].

II. Were I in Trouble

First published as "Were I in Trouble with Night Tonight" in *The Yale Review*, autumn 1946, this poem was written prior to 1944 [120:184].

III. Bravado

First published as "Bravery" in *The Yale Review*, autumn 1946, this poem was written prior to 1944 [120:185].

IV. On Making Certain Anything Has Happened

First published in booklet form, being Frost's 1945 Christmas poem, this poem was written prior to 1944 [120:185].

ll. 12–16. *To make sure ... night*: Frost once remarked, "I always advise my friends to be sure they have something to get hysterical about before they do it" [144:405].

V. In the Long Night

First published in *Dartmouth in Portrait 1944* (Hanover, N.H.: Dartmouth College, 1943) as "Till the Day Breaks."

l 5. *ingle*: fire.

l 9. *Etookashoo and Couldlooktoo*: note in *Steeple Bush*: "Etookashoo and Couldlooktoo who accompanied Dr. Cook to the North Pole."

A Mood Apart

First published, untitled (following an incidental, unauthorized appearance in an auction catalog), in *Fifty Years of Robert Frost*, edited by Ray Nash (Dartmouth College exhibition catalogue: Hanover, 1944). The manuscript was dated June 14, 1943. As early as circa 1918 in Amherst Frost was thinking about being intruded on during "a mood apart" when he wrote in some class notes, "Is it permissible to erect barriers against the intrusion of other peoples' thought[s] on our own thinking? [...] On what ground do we ask to be let alone when we are engaged with a piece of work?" [120:256].

The Fear of God

First published in *Steeple Bush*, this poem was written prior to 1944 [120:184]. This note appears in *Steeple Bush*: "The Fear of God—Acknowledgment to the Papyrus Prisse." After reading "The Fear of God" during a 1961 interview published in *Life*, Frost said, "That's all I'm answerable to" [51:269].

l 6. *examination*: in the manuscript this line has the following notation: "And so disarming such malignancy as may be smiling darkly on the side in the wings" [120:184].

l 10. *subordinating look or tone*: first of the seven deadly sins, pride.

The Fear of Man

First published in *Steeple Bush*, this poem was written prior to 1944 [120:185]. The manuscript titles were "The Common Danger The Fear of Man" [120:185] and "Her Fear" [120:188].

l 10. *Mammon*: material wealth and possessions, from the Sermon on the Mount (Matthew 6:24, Luke 16:13), which states "Ye cannot serve God and mammon" [131:1002].

ll. 15–16. *May I in ... mean*: in a 1935 introduction to E.A. Robinson's *King Jasper,* Frost wrote about "the fear of Man—the fear that men won't understand us and we shall be cut off from them" [129:vi].

A Steeple on the House

First published in *Steeple Bush,* this poem was written prior to 1944 [120:184]. The manuscript was titled "The Spire" [120:188].

l. 6. *to live*: for a manuscript variant, see 120:184.

Innate Helium

First published in *Steeple Bush,* this poem was written prior to 1944 [120:184].

The Courage to Be New

First published in *Steeple Bush,* although the first two stanzas were previously published separately with the title "1946" as a broadside for the dedication services of Orris C. Manning Memorial Park, Ripton, Vermont, July 28, 1946. The poem was written prior to 1944 [120:184]. In *Steeple Bush* this poem has an additional quatrain in the form of a footnote. See 59:570.

l. 8. *Federation of Mankind*: during an August 1915 visit with Frost, Sidney Cox wrote that Frost "sees a possibility of a world federation and police which may limit war, and would be glad to see it" [31:83].

Iota Subscript

First published in *Steeple Bush,* this poem was written prior to 1944 [120:185]. The manuscript title was "Upsilon Iota Subscript" [120:185].

Title *Iota Subscript*: the Greek *iota* can subscripted to the vowels *alpha, eta* or *omega* (*l.* 6). By punning on the Greek letters—*iota* for I, *upsilon* for you—Frost is placing himself in a subservient position to the "you" of the poem.

The Middleness of the Road

First published in *The Virginia Quarterly Review*, winter 1946, this poem was written prior to 1944 [120:183]. The manuscript title was "The Middleness of the Road/Blue and Green" [120:183].

Astrometaphysical

First published in *The Virginia Quarterly Review*, winter 1946, this poem was written prior to 1944 [120:184].

l. 11. *One to Seven*: in Muslim and cabalist doctrines, there exist seven heavens, of which the seventh is the highest.

Skeptic

First published in *Steeple Bush*, this poem was written prior to 1944 [120:183].

Two Leading Lights

First published in the 1944 Christmas booklet of the California collector Earle J. Bernheimer.

l. 21. *Sheba came to Solomon*: in 1 Kings 10:1–13, "And when the queen of Sheba heard of the fame of Solomon concerning the name of the Lord, she came to prove him with hard questions. [...] And she said to the king, It was a true report that I heard in mine own land of thy acts and thy wisdom. Howbeit I believed not the words, until I came, and mine eyes had seen it [...]" [131:401].

l. 23. *not her quest*: following this line, the first printing has an additional couplet. See 59:571.

A Rogers Group

First published in *The Atlantic Monthly*, December 1946, this poem was written on the Derry farm, between 1900 and 1912 [3:117].

Title *A Rogers Group*: John Rogers (1829–1904), American sculptor, whose plaster groupings were popular in the nineteenth century.

On Being Idolized

First published in *Steeple Bush*, this poem was written prior to 1944 [120:183].

A Wish to Comply

First published in *Steeple Bush*, this poem was written prior to 1944 [120:185]. The manuscript title was "On Being Shown a Cosmic Ray" [120:186].

l. 2. *Millikan*: Robert A. Millikan (1868–1953), who did research on the electron ("Millikan mote") and cosmic rays in the 1920s and 1930s.

l. 11. *eye*: the manuscript ends with this line, lacking the final couplet [120:185].

A Cliff Dwelling

First published in *Steeple Bush*, this poem was written prior to 1944 [120:184]. The manuscript title was "The Cliff Dwelling" [120:184].

It Bids Pretty Fair

First published in *Steeple Bush*, this poem was written prior to 1944 [120:185]. The manuscript titles were "It Bids Fair" [120:185] and "The Play" [120:188].

Beyond Words

First published in *Steeple Bush*, this poem was written prior to 1944 [120:185].

A Case for Jefferson

First published in *Steeple Bush*, this poem was written prior to 1944 [120:185]. At a reading at Bread Loaf, Frost referred to "A Case for Jefferson" as a dated period poem, which was written "out of the irritation of a certain time when people were talking [...]" [25:125]. Another time he said, "My, that's bad. I don't ever want to write like *that* again!" [130:44].

l. 5. *It isn't*: "It is" in a 1944 draft of *Steeple Bush* [120:185], although this may have been a copying error in the draft rather than a conscious variant.

Lucretius Versus the Lake Poets

"Nature I loved; and next to Nature, Art."

First published in *Steeple Bush*, this poem was written prior to 1944 [120:185]. The manuscript title was "Nature I Loved and Next to Nature Art or Lucretius Versus the Lake Poets" [120:185].

Title *Lucretius Versus the Lake Poets*: Titus Lucretius Carus (96?–55 B.C.), Roman poet and philosopher. He is the author of the six-volume poem *De Rerum Natura*. Of his life little is known, but Jerome says he was driven insane by a love potion, writing his poem during intervals of lucidity, and eventually committing suicide.

The Lake Poets were a group of early nineteenth century poets living in the English Lake District. The most famous of the group were William Wordsworth and Samuel Taylor Coleridge.

Legend *"Nature I loved; and next to Nature, Art."*: *l.* 2 of Walter Savage Landor's poem "Dying Speech of an Old Philosopher." According to Lawrance Thompson, in the spring of 1944 Frost quarreled with Howard Mumford Jones over the meaning which Landor implicitly assigned to "Nature" in this quatrain. Their quarrel was continued by Frost in his "Lucretius Versus the Lake Poets" [143:581]. The quatrain referred to was:

> I strove with none, for none was worth my strife:
> Nature I loved, and, next to Nature, Art:
> I warm'd both hands before the fire of Life;
> It sinks; and I am ready to depart [81:318].

l. 5. *Epicurus*: Greek philosopher (342?–270 B.C.).

l. 7. *college*: rather than the general word "college," the manuscript had the specific name of "Harvard" [120:185].

Haec Fabula Docet

First published in *The Atlantic Monthly*, December 1946, this poem was written prior to 1944 [120:183]. The manuscript had the title "Blind Individualist" [120:183].

Title *Haec Fabula Docet*: this story teaches (Latin). This formula is often found in Pheadrus's Latin translations of Aesop's fables.

l. 1. *La Fontaine*: Jean de La Fontaine (1621–1695), French fabulist.

l. 20. *grief*: a note in *Steeple Bush* with an additional quatrain follows this line in the first printing. See 59:571.

Etherealizing

First published in *The Atlantic Monthly*, April 1947, this poem was written prior to 1944 [120:184].

Why Wait for Science

First published as "Our Getaway" in *The New Hampshire Troubadour*, November 1946. This poem was written prior 1944 [120:184]. Frost told Louis Mertins:

> I'll just make a little fun of it [science] though, right here. It's all in one of my late evil poems, entitled "Why Wait for Science?" It's a sonnet of a sort. You see a sonnet is composed of 14 lines, no more, no less. It goes along for eight lines, and after the eighth line it takes a turn for the better—or the worse [103:268].

Any Size We Please

First published in *Steeple Bush*, this poem was written prior to 1944 [120:184]. The manuscript titles were "On Our Deciding to Have Our Universe Smaller," "They Decided on a Smaller Universe" [120:184] and "We Can Have It Any Size We Please" [120:187].

An Importer

First published as "The Importer" in *The Atlantic Monthly*, April 1947, this poem was written prior to 1944 [120:184]. The manuscript title was "The Importer" [120:184].

The Planners

First published in *The Atlantic Monthly*, December 1946, this poem was written prior to 1944 [120:184].

l. 1. *This*: the world.

No Holy Wars for Them

First published in *The Atlantic Monthly*, April 1947, this poem was written prior to 1944 [120:184]. The manuscript title was "No Holy Wars" [120:184].

l. 2. *three*: the three states Frost probably had in mind were the United States, England and Russia.

Bursting Rapture

First published in *Steeple Bush*.

l. 14. *certain bomb*: hydrogen bomb.

U.S. 1946 King's X

First published in *The Atlantic Monthly*, December 1946, this quatrain was originally the opening four lines of an unpublished, untitled sonnet. Two drafts of the sonnet, with minor variants, are extant: in the Clifton Waller Barret Collection, University of Virginia [see 121:187], and in the McCain Library, Agnes Scott College [see 122:62]. This note appears in *Steeple Bush*: "U S 1946 King's X—Recent Riptonian."

l. 1. *a new Holocaust*: the atomic bomb.

The Ingenuities of Debt

First published in *The Atlantic Monthly*, December 1946. A note in *Steeple Bush* dates the poem as "PreFranconian," placing it prior to 1915. It was begun on the Derry farm between 1900 and 1912 [143:598]. The poem was not completed until 1946 when Frost thought of a satisfactory final line [151:349]. Frost said of the poem in 1950 that he had left it lying around for forty years because he had trouble finding a good fourth line. A friend, possibly Ezra Pound, in 1913, was less bothered by the fourth line than by Frost's using the word "tessellation" in the fourteenth line [9:471].

l. 6. *Ctesiphon*: an ancient city in Iraq, now ruins.

The Broken Drought

First published as "But He Meant It" in *The Atlantic Monthly*, April 1947, this poem was written prior to 1944 [120:185]. The manuscript title was "The Broken Drought But He Meant It" [120:185]. An early, variant draft, entitled "A Convention," was first printed in 123:8–9.

ll. 7–8. *as Shakespeare says ... out*: in *As You Like It* (IV.i.75–76), Rosalind says, "Very good orators when they are out, they will spit [...]" [134:391].

To the Right Person

First published at the end of Frost's essay "The Constant Symbol" with the subtitle "Fourteen Lines" in *The Atlantic Monthly*, October 1946, this poem also appeared in *The Poems of Robert Frost* (Modern Library, 1946). This poem was written prior to 1944 [120:183].

l. 1. *one state of ours that is a shire*: New Hampshire.

"An Afterword" from Complete Poems (1949)

In *Complete Poems* (1949), following the text of *Steeple Bush* and before the two masques, was a section entitled "An Afterword." It contained three poems, "Choose Something Like a Star" (subsequently changed to "Take Something Like a Star"), "Closed for Good," and "From Plane to Plane." "Closed for Good" was later incorporated into *In the Clearing*, where it remains in *The Poetry of Robert Frost.*

Take Something Like a Star

First published as "Choose Something Like a Star" in Frost's *Come In and Other Poems*, compiled by Louis Untermeyer (New York, 1943). During a reading at Bread Loaf, Frost remarked that "Take Something Like a Star" was written as much to himself as to anyone else, for fluctuating through fifty years of politics. He said that you need to focus on something far enough away, like a star or an ancient poet [25:183].

l. 1. *O Star*: on his use of the word "star," Frost commented, "And by star—I've just used that as though it might be some poet of a thousand years ago—two thousand years—something way out of all of this" [25:136].

l. 6. *Some mystery becomes the proud*: referring to this line at Bread Load readings, Frost remarked about the mystery of modern poetry, with an implied reference to T.S. Eliot [25:136, 191].

l. 11. *Say something! And ... burn."*: during a 1960 interview Frost replied to a question about the younger poets who made San Francisco their headquarters, "I'm waiting for them to say something that I can get hold of. The worse the better. [...] Like you say to somebody, 'Say something. Say something.' And he says, 'I burn'" [157:32].

l. 18. *Keats' Eremite*: refers to Keats' sonnet which begins:

Bright star, would I were steadfast as thou art!
   Not in lone splendour hung aloft the night,
And watching, with eternal lids apart,
   Like Nature's patient sleepless Eremite [...] [95:232].

ll. 20–25. *It asks a ... staid*: Frost said, "We may take something like a star, somewhere, or a poem, or God or something, to stay our minds on, and be staid" [63:118]. To stay his mind, Frost would "read Catullus, and astronomy is like that to me and so is hoeing and so on" [25:191].

From Plane to Plane

First published in *What's New* (Abbott Laboratories, North Chicago), December 1948. Sidney Cox, in January of 1949, refers to various points from this poem as being discussed over the last eighteen months [31:263]. "From Plane to Plane" was originally conceived as a novel, and later converted to a play, before being adapted as a poem. When Lawrance Thompson asked Frost in 1959 about the novel he had tried to write in England, Frost

> said he had intended to build the story around the differences of opinion between two farm workers: a young man fresh out of college and an old rich man with first-hand experiences on the farm. RF said that he transferred the subject matter to the start of a play, but that he had only the idea of the tension between two opposite points of view and that he could never find adequate situations to represent, dramatize, and develop this tension [142:583–584].

ll. 21–22. *Bradford Interval / By the Connecticut*: low-lying grassland area in Bradford, New Hampshire, along the Connecticut River.

l. 70. *Tecumsah*: William Tecumseh Sherman (1820–1891), American general.

l. 90. *The sun then had his longest day*: the summer solstice.

l. 109. *Cygnus*: a northern constellation.

l. 136. *innocent of Milton*: reference to *ll.* 124–133.

l. 143. *Mount Hecla, Iceland*: a volcano in Iceland.

l. 146. *"So I have ... it"*: *Hamlet* (I.i.165). In 1925 Frost wrote to a Mr. Tewson, "For sheer usefulness in every modern encounter, I consider 'So I have heard and do in part believe' the most beautiful single line of English verse" [120:250].

In the Clearing

First published in New York by Holt, Rinehart and Winston in 1962. A limited, signed edition of fifteen hundred copies was also published. The volume was dedicated: "Letters in prose to Louis Untermeyer, Sidney Cox, and John Bartlett for them to dispose of as they please; these to you in verse for keeps." The three named dedicatees were close, longtime friends of Frost. Frost met Untermeyer in 1915, Cox in 1911 and Bartlett in 1907. The unnamed "you" was Kay Morrison [144:304].

The table of contents of *In the Clearing* was preceded by an excerpt from the poem, "Kitty Hawk" (*ll.* 219–224, 246–257 with no break between segments. Line 254 had one textual variant: Is for Was) which was called "But God's Own Descent" in the contents. The volume had two titled sections:

Cluster of Faith ("Accidentally on Purpose" through "[Forgive, O Lord ...]")

Quandary ("Quandary" through "[In Winter in the Woods ...]")

The second half-title has *l.* 3 of "The Pasture" printed in italics: *And wait to watch the water clear, I may.*

Frost's intention was to call what he knew would be his final volume of poetry *The Great Misgiving*, from line 229 of "Kitty Hawk" [13:159]. It was finally determined, upon the urging of friends, to name the volume for one of its poems. The title of the volume was taken from the title of the poem "A Cabin in the Clearing."

Pod of the Milkweed

First published as "From a Milkweed Pod" in booklet form, being Frost's 1954 Christmas poem.

ll. 15–16. *flows / With milk and honey*: the phrase was used to describe the Promised Land in the Old Testament, as in Exodus 3:8 when God said to Moses, "And I am come down to deliver them out of the hand of the Egyptians, and to bring them up out of that land unto a good land and a large, unto a land flowing with milk and honey [...]" [131:73].

l. 54. *must be fairly faced*: first publication through 1963 is followed by the note: "And shall be in due course."

Away!

First published in booklet form, being Frost's 1958 Christmas poem.

ll. 11–12. *Like Adam and ... Park*: in Genesis 3:23–24, "the Lord God sent him forth from the garden of Eden, to till the ground from whence he was taken. So he drove out the man [...]" [131:10].

l. 20. *"I'm—bound—away!"*: from one of Frost's favorite folksongs, "Shenandoah," which has the chorus: "Ah ha I'm bound away, 'cross the wide Missouri" [11.2:807]. Cf. *A Masque of Mercy*, *l.* 172.

A Cabin in the Clearing
For Alfred Edwards

First published, without dedication, in booklet form, being Frost's 1951 Christmas poem. The poem was written circa August 1950, when Frost referred to the "recent" poem in a letter to Louis Untermeyer as "Come, Come Ye Disconsolate, or Mist Smoke and Haze" [151:363]. For the variant 1950 version, see 151:364–366. Frost once introduced this poem as being "about knowing ourselves" [25:190].

Dedication *Alfred Edwards*: friend and publisher of Frost. Edwards joined Henry Holt and Company in 1945 as treasurer, later becoming executive vice president and then president. He was chosen by Frost to serve as his literary executor.

ll. 13–14. *No one—not ... are*: for the idea of being "lost enough to find yourself," see "Directive."

Closed for Good

First published in booklet form, being Frost's 1948 Christmas poem. This poem was chosen by Frost as the final poem for an expanded edition of *North of Boston* that he was considering [144:179]. Frost said this poem is "It's just about a road that's been abandoned [...]" [25:125].

ll. 1–6. *Much as I ... away*: when the poem was published in *In the Clearing*, Frost deleted this stanza, but, as he said at a 1962 reading, "Here's one I'm going to put a stanza back into [...]. See that stanza I threw out and it ought to be back in" [25:191–192].

l. 9. *My slowness with their speed*: Frost wrote in a 1925 letter to Leonidas W. Payne, "All I ask in this age of speed is to be allowed to go slow" [66:305].

l. 30. *as my proxy*: prior to inclusion in *In the Clearing*, this poem as published in 1948 had an additional sextet following this line. See 59:574.

America Is Hard to See

First published as "And All We Call American" in *The Atlantic Monthly*, June 1951. This poem was entitled "For Columbus Day" when it was first read at Amherst College in December 1950 [144:204]. Frost claims to have written "the whole eighty-four lines of it without consulting a single book in one night" but it was also "true in a sense that I had been all my life writing it" [48:263].

l. 1. *Columbus*: Christopher Columbus (1451–1506), Italian navigator who is given credit for discovering America. Of Columbus, Frost wrote in a note dating from his Derry days, that it was not for crossing the Atlantic and suffering hardships and privation that "is he Columbus. Why is he immortal, then? [...]. Well, because he had the faith that so few people are capable of; the faith of an idea" [142:332].

l. 2. *Ind*: India.

l. 3. *proved the world a ball*: it was Columbus's intention to prove during his expedition that the world was round.

l. 6. *the Queen*: Isabella I (1451–1504), Queen of Castille (1474–1504) and wife of Ferdinand II of Aragon.

l. 10. *Ormuz*: Hormuz, an island in the Strait of Hormuz. The Strait of Hormuz connects the Persian Gulf and the Gulf of Oman.

l. 20. *da Gama*: Vasco da Gama (1469?–1524), Portuguese navigator.

l. 24. *Ophir*: ancient city of unknown location mentioned in 1 Kings 9:28.

l. 31. *Valladolid*: town where Columbus died in 1506.

l. 36. *Moses' exodus*: see Exodus.

l. 57. *Culebra Cut*: Gaillard Cut, southeastern section of the Panama Canal, approximately eight miles through Culebra Mountain.

l. 78. *Cathay*: name used during the Middle Ages for China.

ll. 83–84. *easy raid ... made*: Hernando Cortes (1485–1547), Spanish conqueror of Mexico. Cf. Frost's high-school poem, "La Noche Triste."

One More Brevity

First published in booklet form, being Frost's 1953 Christmas poem. The manuscript had the title "Down to Earth" [120:193]. Lawrance Thompson points out that this poem concerns a dog similar to Gillie, Frost's companion from 1940 to 1949 [144:204].

l. 4. *Sirius*: part of the constellation Canis Major, also known as the Dog Star, brightest star in the heavens.

l. 61. *avatar*: an incarnation, usually in human form, of a deity. The manuscript has an additional couplet between this line and *l.* 62. See 120:194.

l. 65. *in song*: first publication through *In the Clearing* is followed by this note: "But see 'The Great Overdog' and 'Choose Something Like a Star,' in which latter the star could hardly have been a planet since fixity is of the essence of the piece."

Escapist—Never

First published in *The Massachusetts Review*, winter 1962. On escapism, Frost said at various times:

> I have been asked if I consider myself an escapist, and I have been called a pursuitist. Well, a man may climb a tree and still not be an escapist. He may go up there to pick something [143:425].
>
> What one person calls an escapist might really be a pursuitist, like the man who climbed the apple tree not to get away from the ground and the world but to reach the apples [2:192].
>
> [...] everybody is escaping from something or somebody. So you're an escape from an escape from an escape from an escape until you get to hell [...] [25:80].
>
> Cut and run away from every care: that is the rule. Nothing else will do. No faltering [2:111–112].
>
> I'm a very artful dodger of unnecessary pains [143:451].
>
> No escape theory will explain me [143:323].

Elizabeth Shepley Sergeant recalled

> a conversation with him in the twenties about the word "escapist." He objected to the negative meaning. The point he said was: what are you escaping from? Possibly something that is strangling you. What are you escaping to? Possibly something you need and must have [133:57].

l. 5. *A crooked straightness*: as early as March, 1925, Frost wrote, "A straight crookedness is most to be desired in a stick or line. Or a crooked straightness. That's why a free-hand-drawn line is pleasant" [3:111].

For John F. Kennedy His Inauguration
Gift outright of "The Gift Outright"
(With some preliminary history in rhyme)

First published (variously titled) in newspapers immediately following Kennedy's inauguration on January 20, 1961. Asked to read "The Gift Outright" at the inauguration ceremonies, Frost wrote a prefatory dedication. The first version of the dedication was a prose essay entitled "A New England Tribute." It was published in early January, prior to the inauguration, in *Official Program. Inaugural Ceremonies of John F. Kennedy [...] and Lyndon B. Johnson [...]* (Washington, D.C.: Kennedy-Johnson Inaugural Committee, January 20, 1961), 43. The dedicatory poem, 42 lines, was published in *The New York Times* (city edition) on January 21, 1961 (page 9), as "Dedication Poem," and in other newspapers, variously titled. The poem was published as "Dedicatory Poem," 42 lines, in *A Pictorial Review 1961 Inauguration [...]* (Washington, D.C.: [circa February] 1961), 14.

The 77-line version, with minor variants, was first published in a four-page leaflet by El Al Airlines, entitled "Dedication in verse composed by Robert Frost for the inauguration of President John F. Kennedy [...]," to honor "the Distinguished American Poet Robert Frost as Passenger on El Al Israel Airlines Intercontinental Jet Flight No. 228, New York to Tel Aviv, March 9, 1961." Line 67 was inadvertently dropped. The 77-line poem, with minor variants, now titled "Dedication for John F. Kennedy His Inauguration," was published in *The New York Times Magazine* (March 26, 1961, page 13), as part of Stewart L. Udall's article, "Frost's Unique 'Gift Outright.'" It was reprinted, with minor variants, as "Dedication," in an edition of eight hundred copies entitled, *Dedication. The Gift Outright. The Inaugural Address. Washington, D.C., January the Twentieth, 1961* (New York: Spiral Press, 1961).

l. 21. *written on the dollar bill*: the Latin phrases *"annuit cœptis"* and *"novus ordo seclorum"* appear on the back of the dollar bill. Frost translates these Virgilian phrases as "God nodded His approval" (*l.* 23) and "a new order of the age" (*l.* 19) respectively.

ll. 46–47. *the twain ... aeroplane*: the Wright brothers. Cf. "The Wrights' Biplane," "Kitty Hawk" and "Let Congress See To It."

ll. 49–50. *Some poor fool ... art*: during a 1957 interview with Cecil Day Lewis, Frost said of heroism: "I know of a book of history that says heroism is out of date. But it's in everything. It's in making a book, you know. And it takes a hero to make a poem" [78:34].

l. 56. *so close*: the votes cast for Kennedy were 34,227,096; the votes cast for Nixon were 34,107,646.

l. 60. *the book of profile tales*: Kennedy's *Profiles in Courage* (New York: Harper, 1956).

l. 71. *Augustan age*: interviewed after the Kennedy inauguration, Frost defined an Augustan age as "the joining of the arts and power. Make that poetry and power, just for alliteration" [51:254].

Accidentally on Purpose

First published in booklet form, being Frost's 1960 Christmas poem.

Title *Accidentally on Purpose*: during a reading, Frost reminisced that he was "brought up on that expression. When I did anything I shouldn't, I said I did it 'accidentally on purpose'" [25:190].

ll. 1–4. *The Universe is ... shiny*: Frost said,

> That's the universe. I haven't left anything out, have I? Only one line is all you need to describe the universe: just balls going round in rings. That gets us clear down to Adam. I haven't left anything out, far as I can see. The only thing left out, I might say is purpose. You see, that's another verse. Materially I have covered its purpose in another verse [103:393].

l. 9. *Darwin*: Charles Darwin (1808–1882), English naturalist, who put forth the theory of evolution and natural selection.

l. 24. *passionate preference*: during a 1960 interview Frost said:

> [...] talking to some scientists lately, I said to them, "Have we come up?"
>
> They said, "Yes," rather reluctantly. They did not know whether we had come up or not, but they said, "Yes."
>
> And I said, "What's brought us up?" And they thought it was more or less an accident, I guess.
>
> I said, "I think it's passionate preference." Passionate preference [51:226].

As he phrased it during a 1959 symposium on "The Future of Man":

> The chief guide in the world for us in the long way we've come is some more or less intelligent handling of that inexorable thing in us—Biblical thing, you know—passionate preference for something we can't help wishing were so, wishing were true.
>
> All your guidance in politics, religion, and love is something way at the middle of your heart that you can't help wishing was so. All the time [51:209].

A Never Naught Song

First published in *In the Clearing.*

ℓ **26.** *Yggdrasil*: a huge ash tree in Norse mythology that overspreads the world, binding together earth, heaven and hell.

Version

First published in an incomplete version in *In the Clearing*, the version in the later collections being corrected by E.C. Lathem from variant holographs. One holograph revision was first printed in 123:69. Frost joked about the incomplete and indecipherable version in *In the Clearing* by saying during a 1962 interview, "What modern editor would ask that a poem should mean anything, anyway? [...] I left it that way in order to be in fashion. It's never hard for me to write a poem that doesn't mean anything when I leave a part of it out" [51:276].

ℓ **9.** *the Phoenix pullet*: the Phoenix was a legendary bird which lives for five hundred years, cremates itself on a pyre, then rises from the ashes restored to youth to live another period. The Phoenix pullet would refer to its postresurrection phase as a young bird.

ℓ **10.** Μὴ ὄν: from Plato's *Sophist* (257b3), meaning "that which is not," or as Frost translates it (*ℓ* 8), "non-existence." Frost also used the Greek phrase in his essay, "On Emerson," when he wrote of Emerson as a Platonist who felt that evil "was a mere Τὸ μὴ ὄν that could be disposed of like the butt of a cigarette" [55:717].

A Concept Self-Conceived

First published in *In the Clearing.*

[Forgive, O Lord...]

First published as "The Preacher" in *A Remembrance Collection of New Poems* (New York, 1959). This poem was written at least as early as 1956 when he referred to it as a "prayer" [79:123]. Frost claims to have written the poem extempore when he was

> speaking about aids to the Arts. I was at the Waldorf with about a thousand people, five hundred of them poets, and five hundred of them foundation people from whom the poets have to beg. I had them all sitting there in front of me. There was a Bishop going to pray at the end, so I stole the show, with this couplet that I made right there [56:186].

Kitty Hawk
Back there in 1953 with the Huntington Cairnses (A skylark for them in three-beat phrases)

First published in a 128-line version with the subtitle "1894" in booklet form, being Frost's 1956 Christmas poem. A revised and expanded version of 432 lines was published in *The Atlantic Monthly*, November 1957. This version was reprinted with minor variants in *Anthology of Magazine Verse for 1958*, edited by W.S. Braithwaite and Margaret Carpenter (New York: Schulte's Book Store, 1959). The *Saturday Review* of March 21, 1959, contained a new 64 line poem, "The Great Event Is Science. The Great Misgiving, the Fear of God, Is That the Meaning of It Shall Be Lost," less than half of which consisted of excerpted lines from the expanded version. This 64 line poem was incorporated in its entirety into the final version as published in *In the Clearing.*

The poem was begun in 1953 after a visit to Kitty Hawk, North Carolina, with his friends, the Huntington Cairnses. "Kitty Hawk" was regarded by Frost as one of his most important poems [144:300]. It was dedicated to

Huntington Cairns [13:160]. During a 1959 interview with John Ciardi, Frost described the poem as

> a longish poem in two parts. Part One is a sort of personal story, an adventure of my boyhood. I was down there once when I was about nineteen. Alone, just wandering. Then I was invited back there sixty years later.
>
> That return after so long a time suggested the poem to me. I use my own story of the place to take off into the story of the airplane. I make a figure of speech of it: How I might have taken off from my experience of Kitty Hawk and written an immortal poem, but how, instead, the Wright brothers took off from there to commit an immortality. I knew one of the Wright brothers slightly: I had that little connection with them.
>
> Part Two goes into the thought of the on-penetration into matter and our great misgiving. [...] Part Two is the philosophical part [18:17–18].

During a 1959 reading at Bread Loaf, Frost said:

> And it begins with my visit when young [...] [to] Kitty Hawk, long before the Wright brothers were there. And it ends with its dawning on me that all science [...] is our hold on the planet. It's domestic, you see. It has been all the time. [...]
>
> But it dawned on me at the point that all, the whole, the great enterprise of life, of the world, the great enterprise of our race, is our penetration into matter, deeper and deeper; carrying the spirit deeper into matter. And though it looks like something different out into space, that's just deeper into matter, that's material penetration of the spirit—of the ethereal into the material. Put it that way. And that is our destiny—that is why science is our greatness. It's got to do with our penetration into the material [25:131].

l. 6. *When I came here young*: in November of 1894, although Frost did not actually reach Kitty Hawk.

l. 8. *Elizabeth City*: town in North Carolina.

ll. 50–51. *the Master / ... met*: Wilbur Wright. During a 1961 interview, Frost commented, "And I lived to know Wilbur Wright. Isn't it strange that I knew him well?" [71:8].

l. 53. *Alastor*: hero of poem by Percy Bysshe Shelley. Alastor, as explained by Shelley in his preface, "represents a youth of uncorrupted feelings and adventurous genius led forth by an imagination inflamed and purified through familiarity with all that is excellent and majestic to the contemplation of the universe. [...] He imagines to himself the Being whom he loves. [...] Blasted by his disappointment, he descends to an untimely grave" [135:32–33]. As Shelley wrote toward the end of the poem: "It is a woe 'too deep for tears,' when all / Is reft at once [...]" [135:43].

ll. 64–65. *the lie … first*: Louis Mertins noted "how greatly exercised Frost was over the fact that the encyclopedias were trying to take honor of the first heavier-than-air flight away from the Wright brothers":

> "Why," he sputtered, "when all this thing is written, that about Lindbergh and all, there will still remain only the Wright boys, the Columbuses of the air. Orville is eating his heart out over in Dayton because of what's being done and what is not being done. Shabby treatment."
>
> Asked if he thought Orville would be willing to bring his plane back from Europe to the Smithsonian Institution if Congress would give him the credit for making the first flight, he continued:
>
> "Of course he would. Why, they have a little insignificant contraption in the institute marked as the one which made the first flight, when all it was ever able to do was nose up and take a dive into the bay, and that without a pilot. I wanted to do all I could to help establish them in their rights. So I wrote a poem ["The Wrights' Biplane"] about our long having wheelwrights, wainwrights, and now we've got wingwrights. I want to print it and do what I can to help" [103:195–196].

See "The Wrights' Biplane" and "Let Congress See To It."

l. 70. *Herbert Hoover*: Herbert Clark Hoover (1874–1964), 31st president of the United States (1929–1933).

l. 88. *Hatteras*: cape in North Carolina, a long narrow sandbar.

l. 89. *Roanoke*: city in west-central Virginia.

l. 98. *Götterdämmerung*: twilight of the gods (German).

ll. 103–110. *Each and … Currituck*: during a 1961 interview Frost remembered, "And everybuddy had two demijohns of whiskey. And the men—and the men—from Norfolk or somewhere—had guns. It was duck-huntin' season, you see. […] And they went down there to hunt on the Currituck" [71:4].

ll. 139–166. *Then next … sound*: as Frost recalled:

> And then, about midnight, a fine-looking fellow, a sturdy figger walked in on us all, and—I wish I knew his name. He was a captain of a fishing crew on the coast, and his camp was down the coast somewhere, and he had seen this excitement, and he came up and he saw me there, and—a kid again—and he said, "You want to come out for a walk?" And I walked a long way with him up and down the beach. Fine man. We talked about many interesting things [71:5].

l. 147. *Theodosia Burr*: during Frost's November 1894 adventure, he fell in with a uniformed officer of the Life Saving Service patrolling the shore. When Frost asked him about the history of the Outer Banks, the man told him about the legend that Aaron Burr's daughter, Theodosia, was supposed to have been killed somewhere off the banks in this area [142:183].

l. **167.** *"And the moon was full,"*: from *l.* 60 of Tennyson's "Morte D'Arthur."

l. **175.** *Kitty Hawk, O Kitty*: repeat of opening line.

l. **199.** *aliquid*: somewhat (Latin).

ll. **217–218.** *that fall ... tree*: the Fall of Man. See Genesis 3:1–24.

ll. **219–224.** *But God's own ... substantiation*: during a 1959 reading, Frost said, "That's what our religion means. That's what the Christian religion means—God's own descent into flesh in substantiation" [25:131].

ll. **225–227.** *Westerners inherit ... into matter*: during a 1959 reading, Frost said:

> Sometimes in the by-product of science we lose the spirit entirely; but not in the act of scientific penetration—deeper, deeper, deeper, further, further, further [...] [see "Neither Out Far Nor In Deep"]. But—as far as we can and as deep as we can, as far out as we can—still we penetrate into matter, further into matter [25:131].

l. **229.** *a great misgiving*: during a 1959 interview, Frost said:

> I am not against science. I always dislike it when people assume that because I am a poet I must be against science. But in taking us deeper and deeper into matter, science has left all of us with this great misgiving, this fear that we won't be able to substantiate the spirit. [...]
>
> Flight is just one more penetration, no more than that. And so one more cause of the misgiving we must all risk [...] [18:17].

l. **236.** *West-Northwest*: on this idea of westward growth, Frost said, "Ours is a very ancient political growth, beginning at one end of the Mediterranean Sea and coming westward—tried in Athens, tried in Italy, tried in England, tried in France, coming westward all the way to us" [51:240].

l. **308.** *Earth is still our fate*: cf."Our Hold on the Planet" and "Birches" (*l.* 52), where Frost writes that "Earth's the right place for love."

l. **319.** *Pullman cars*: railroad passenger cars furnished for day and night travel.

l. **390.** *mens animi*: "the thoughts of my heart" (Latin) from Catullus 65, *l.* 4. Frost translates the phrase in the preceding two lines. Frost thought that everyone should "know what Catullus means by *mens animi*" [58:30].

l. **450.** *Action is the word*: this echoes passages in Emerson where action is placed in opposition to words. In "Discipline" from *Nature* Emerson wrote: "Words are finite organs of the infinite mind. They cannot cover the dimensions of what is in truth. They break, chop, and impoverish it. An action is the perfection and publication of thought" [30:30]. In "The Poet," Emerson wrote: "Words and deeds are quite different modes of the divine energy. Words are also actions, and actions are a kind of words" [30:450].

l. **470.** *Darius Green*: hero of John Townsend Trowbridge's popular 1869 poem, "Darius Green and His Flying Machine."

Auspex

First published in Elizabeth Shepley Sergeant's *Robert Frost: The Trial by Existence* (New York, 1960), the poem was written prior December 16, 1953, when it was inscribed in a copy of *Complete Poems* (1949) [120:89]. Alternate manuscript titles were "Auspices" [120:91] and "Limitations" [163].

l. **1.** *Once*: in the early 1950s Frost referred to this poem as "another memory of those events of seventy years ago" [120:92], placing the date of the subject of the poem in the early 1880s while Frost was living in San Francisco.

The Draft Horse

First published in *In the Clearing*, this poem was written about 1920, according to Frost [143:673]. An alternate manuscript title was "Percheron Horse" [120:92]. Frost inscribed in a copy of *Complete Poems* (1949) a fair copy of "The Draft Horse" without *ll.* 9–12, below which he wrote: "This belongs with 'The Lockless Door' and was written at about the same time" [120:92].

Ends

First published in *In the Clearing*.

ll. **11–12.** *And some will ... say*: as Frost wrote to Bernard DeVoto in April 1938, "I suppose love must always deceive" [66:470].

Peril of Hope

An incidental publication of a holograph draft of this poem appeared in *The Agnes Scott News* (Agnes Scott College, Decatur, Georgia) February 8, 1961. The poem is found in manuscript with "The Matchmaker" and "The Couplet," dating it as early 1950s. Frost referred to it during a reading as "another little singsongy one" [25:190].

Questioning Faces

First published as "Of a Winter Evening" in *The Saturday Review*, April 12, 1958, the poem was dated by Frost as of about "New Year 1958" [97:61]. The poem was apparently inspired by an incident which took place sometime before 1940 when Frost told Daniel Smythe:

> Once sitting in the kitchen in the last of a sunset, a great owl darkened the room. For a minute in the last sunlight, he showed the whole underside—the quills clear. The sight of that bird right close to you is just like a favor, something you did not expect—as if someone were on your side. [...] You feel flattered when something is vouchsafed you like that [136:57].

Does No One at All Ever Feel This Way in the Least?

First published as "Does No One But Me at All Ever Feel This Way in the Least?" in booklet form, being Frost's 1952 Christmas poem.

l. 24. *salt*: first publication through *In the Clearing* has note: "At this writing it seems pretty well accepted that any rivers added can only make the sea saltier."

l. 31. *spoken to before*: first publication through *In the Clearing* has note: "By King Canute and Lord Byron among others."

The Bad Island—Easter (Perhaps so called because it may have risen once)

First published in *The Times Literary Supplement*, September 17, 1954. A fair copy of this poem inscribed in *Collected Poems* (1949) in the early

1950s has the variant title, "The Bad Island—Easter So Called Because It Hasn't Risen (On a Head from Easter Island in the Portico of the British Museum)" [120:92].

Title *Easter*: island in South Pacific Ocean with gigantic statues of unknown origin.

l. 55. *kultur*: culture (German), with an emphasis on practical efficiency and individual subordination to the state.

Our Doom to Bloom

"Shine, perishing republic."
Robinson Jeffers

First published without the quotation from Robinson Jeffers as "Doom to Bloom" in booklet form, being Frost's 1950 Christmas poem. This poem was referred to as "Doomed to Bloom" in a letter to Louis Henry and Margueritte Cohn in September 14, 1950 [66:546].

Legend *"Shine, perishing ... Jeffers*: title and *l.* 12 of poem by Robinson Jeffers (1887–1962), published in his *Roan Stallion, Tamar, and Other Poems* (New York: Boni and Liveright, 1925).

The Objection to Being Stepped On

First published as "My Objection to Being Stepped On" in booklet form, being Frost's 1957 Christmas poem. It may have been inspired by an incident which happened in 1927 when Elinor broke her nose from stepping on a rake which hit her in the face [93:128]. Frost was thinking of the play between tools and weapons at least as early as 1942 when he wrote, "My favorite implements (after the pen) are the axe and the scythe, both of which besides being tools of peace have also been weapons of war. The Hungarian peasantry under Kossuth carried the scythe into battle [...]" [140:278].

Frost would certainly have been aware that the Latin word *arma* could be translated as either tool or weapon. During an interview in 1962, Frost remarked: "I often think about words now: weapon, tool. A tool can turn into a weapon. When the peasants rebelled, they turned their tools of labor into weapons" [51:285]. At a reading at Bread Loaf, Frost said of this poem:

> You have to be reminded that the Hungarian Revolution that occurred just

> before my time, that I heard a lot about when I was young, was all fought, nearly, with farm tools—the poor peasants—pitchforks and flails and anything they could lay hands on. Weapons go to tools and tools go to weapons—it's back and forth [25:132–133].

Cf. "From Iron."

A-Wishing Well

First published in booklet form, being Frost's 1959 Christmas poem.
ll. 41–42. *As Keats (or ... Caf)* from Keats' *Hyperion* (II.52–55):

> Nearest him
> Asia, born of most enormous Caf,
> Who cost her mother Tellus keener pangs,
> Though feminine, than any of her sons [95:205].

l. 49. *silphion*: silphium, genus of stout perennial resinous American herb, the gum-resin or juice of which was used anciently as a condiment or medicine.

l. 73. D*emiurge*: a Gnostic subordinate deity who is the creator of the material world. See "The Demiurge's Laugh."

l. 77. *Man's practically inexterminate*: for another example of Frost's belief in man's endurance, see "Our Hold on the Planet."

ll. 79–81. *Ararat*: according to Genesis 8:4, after the flood, Noah's ark rested upon the mountains of Ararat.

How Hard It Is to Keep from Being King When It's in You and in the Situation

First published in *Proceedings of the American Academy of Arts and Letters and the National Institute of Arts and Letters* (second series, number one, 1951), the poem was also published separately as "Hard Not to Be King" in 1951 by House of Books, Ltd., of New York in a signed limited edition of three hundred copies. This poem was written in early 1950 [144:194, 202] and first read as the Blashfield Address of the American Academy of Arts and Letters on May 25, 1950.

From a 1951 letter of Sidney Cox it is apparent that Frost spent much time thinking about this poem before it was completed: "It is fun to see (after the fact) a poem growing and then to see the poem. It's great to have evidence how much of living and how long thinking combines (in you, chiefly) with such frivolous-seeming jokes and sly innuendoes" [31:266].

During a reading at Bread Loaf, Frost commented that the source was "an old story in the *Arabian Nights* that you probably never read unless you've gone a long way in the *Arabian Nights*. I found it somewhere near the tail end of Burton" [25:191]. During an interview he confirmed he "lifted" the story from "one of the seldom-noted tales that has no sex in it" [18:18]. The poem's source which Frost referred to is found in volume 1 of Richard F. Burton's *Supplemental Nights to the Book of the Thousand Nights and a Night* (Printed by the Burton Club for Private Subscribers Only [1886?], 212–217). The tale, entitled "Tale of the King Who Kenned the Quintessence of Things" is tale C in section 12, "King Shah Bakht and His Wazir Al-Rahwan." Sources and analogues to this tale are found in volume 2 of the *Supplemental Nights* [320–328].

Title *How Hard It ... Situation*: during a 1959 interview, Frost referred to the title as "the kind of long title I sometimes like" [18:18].

***l.* 209.** *I'm not a free-verse singer*: as Frost often said, "I'd as soon play tennis with the net down as write free verse" [144:274]. Frost explained to Louis Mertins once:

> Because I have been, what some might call, careless about the so-called proper beat and rhythm of my lines, there have been those who think I write free verse. Now, I am not dead set against *vers libre*; but you know there is no idea you cannot express beautifully and satisfactorily in the iambic pentameter. Much of my verse is written in this form—blank, unrimed verse. I have always maintained that it takes form to properly perform, and free verse has no form, and so its performance is meager. These fellows, old Carl [Sandburg] and the rest, think they are being free, but they aren't. The greatest freedom poetry can attain is having form, a frame, to work in. Free verse is batting a ball into space and wondering why it doesn't return to the batter. Poetry written in form is like batting a ball against the side of a wall and feeling it return to the bat. A picture frame with its four simple lines is necessary to the showing of a picture. Try it and see. The frame thus becomes a part, even, of the picture [103:198].

As Frost said emphatically as early as 1923, "I do not write free verse; I write blank verse. I must have the pulse beat of rhythm, I like to hear it beating under the things I write" [51:52]. As he wrote in an unused preface to "The Death of the Hired Man, "By the way, it's in blank verse, not free verse" [120:241].

l. 218. *Tell them Iamb, Jehovah said*: pun on the name I AM for Jehovah, from Exodus 3:14, in which God said to Moses, "I AM THAT I AM" [131:73].

Lines Written in Dejection on the Eve of Great Success

First published, without the "Postscript" stanzas, in Frost's *A Remembrance Collection of New Poems* (New York, 1959). Frost remarked during a reading at Bread Loaf that this was a "joke about science [...] comic strip teasing [...]" [25:132].

ll. 1–5. *cow that jumped ... Goose*: refers to the Mother Goose rhyme which begins: "Hey diddle, diddle, / The cat and the fiddle, / The cow jumped over the moon."

l. 14. *A cow did ... it?"*: this is based on a true incident which Frost heard during his first Amherst period, 1917–1920, from Warren R. Brown [143:112].

l. 24. *papers'*: in a copy of the poem sent to Louis Untermeyer onJanuary 12, 1959, *Times'* was used instead of the general term "papers'" [151:378].

l. 25. *He answered her ... it?"*: in a copy of the poem sent to Louis Untermeyer on January 12, 1959, Frost had a slightly stronger variant. See 151:378.

The Milky Way Is a Cowpath

First published in *In the Clearing*.

l. 9. *Quidnuncs*: those who seek to learn all the latest news and gossip.

Some Science Fiction

First published, without the "Envoi" quatrain, in booklet form, being Frost's 1955 Christmas poem. The poem was originally dedicated to Edward Hyde Cox whom Frost met in Key West, Florida, in 1940.

Envoi *Hyde the Castaway of Crow Island*: Edward Hyde Cox. Crow

Island was Cox's home, off the coast of Manchester, Massachusetts.

Quandary

First published as "Somewhat Dietary" in *The Massachusetts Review*, fall 1959.

ll. 5–6. *It was by ... lasted*: first published as "The Old Pair" in *The New-England Galaxy* (summer 1960) and incidentally in an interview published in *The Paris Review* (summer-fall 1960) during which Frost introduced the couplet by saying: "One of them [the masques] turns on the thought that evil shows off to good and good shows off to evil. I made a couplet out of that for them in Kansas City, just the way I often do, off hand" [157:31]. During a July 1960 reading Frost said after reciting the couplet that it came out of his reading Emerson and how Emerson saw good and evil as, in Frost's words, "support[ing] each other just the same as two playing cards do, you know, when you stand them up just right" [25:145]. The passages in Emerson about which Frost had been thinking are from the poem "Uriel," in which Emerson wrote that "Evil will bless" and wrote of "the good of evil born."

Cf. *A Masque of Reason*

ll. 11–12. *To quote the ... thyself*: the phrase "Love thy neighbor as thyself" is attributed to the Greek philosopher, Thales (640?–546 B.C.).

A Reflex

First published in *In the Clearing*.

l. 8. *Qui vive*: literally, French for "long live who?", a sentinel's challenge, the response to which should be, "May the King live." The closest English translation would be what Frost uses in the next line, "Who goes there?"

Frost may have come across the phrase in James Fenimore Cooper's *The Last of the Mohicans* (considered by Frost one of his ten favorite books [57:355]:

> "Qui vive?" demanded a stern, quick voice, which sounded like a challenge from another world, issuing out of that solitary and solemn place.
>
> "What says it?" whispered the scout; "it speaks neither Indian or

English!"

"Qui vive?" repeated the same voice, which was quickly followed by the rattling of arms, and a menacing attitude.

In a Glass of Cider

First published in *In the Clearing.* Frost wrote to Bernard DeVoto on December 29, 1937:

> I said to Sidney Cox years ago that I was non-elatable. [...] After hearing all you said in my favor today, I tried it at the wistfullest I could command on Elinor. "What a lie," she answered. "You can't talk in public or private without getting elated. You never write but from elation" [66:452].

The image in this poem was used as early as August 1928 in a letter written by Frost to his daughter Lesley, in which he comments, "I notice the Giants rose to the surface like a dreg on a bubble got dropped by the bubble when it broke and are now going down to hitch onto another" [48:123].

From Iron
Tools and Weapons
To Ahmed S. Bokhari

First published, without subtitle and dedication, following incidental newspaper publication, as "The Sage" in Frost's *A Remembrance Collection of New Poems* (New York, 1959) with the preface, "This is to the memory of my great friend Ahmed Bokhari who had me down from Vermont to view his lump of purest iron ore at the United Nations in the room for meditation on Tools and Weapons."

Cf. "The Objection to Being Stepped On."

Apropos this poem, Frost has said:

> Up at the U.N. they have a meditation room. You'll have to go in pairs as they have only two chairs in the room. In the room, beside the chairs, is a lump of iron. The King of Sweden sent it to the U.N., and it's supposed to mean something. I take it that's why they had me down to see if I could tell 'em a metaphor for it. [...]
>
> That lump of iron is the basis of both tools and weapons. I'm on the weapon side. I sent that couplet to them. One very fine friend [Bokhari] [...] wants a poem, so I sent him that couplet, and when I met him again

he said, "Oh, you've written better poems than that." I don't know that I have. I've written a lot of couplets [103:360].

[...] this little couplet I made once from looking at a lump of iron that was supposed to be perfectly pure and meant to be the oneness that we could all attain—the purity. [...] The lump or iron—the purest iron—is at once tools and weapons as in that poem ["The Objection To Being-Stepped On"] that I told you about. It's tools and weapons right while you're looking at it. Everything's like that [25:134–135].

Dedication *Ahmed S. Bokhari*: an assistant secretary at the United Nations who invited Frost in August 1956 to write a poem for a Meditation Room in the U.N. in which was to be placed a lump of iron weighing many tons sent by the King of Sweden. Upon receiving the couplet, Bokhari rejected the poem, replying, "Mr. Frost, you have written better poems" [144:423].

[Four-room Shack...]

First published in *In the Clearing*.

[But Outer Space...]

First published as "The Astronomer" in *A Remembrance Collection of New Poems* (New York, 1959). In 1962, at the Bread Loaf Writers' Conference, Frost said, "It amuses me that some of my friends say I have got to face it—overpopulation" [44:53].

On Being Chosen the Poet of Vermont

First published, untitled, in newspapers following Frost's installation as Poet Laureate of Vermont on July 22, 1961. The Vermont State Legislature had passed a bill in late June designating Frost as the Poet Laureate of Vermont.

[We Vainly Wrestle...]

First published in *In the Clearing*, this poem was excerpted from an unpublished 1911 poem, "New Grief" (which see), where it stood as the final quatrain [162:HM 7237].

[It Takes All Sorts...]

First published, untitled, in *The Boston Sunday Globe*, December 30, 1956, it was also published as "The Poet" in *A Remembrance Collection of New Poems* (New York, 1959).

The couplet was perhaps conceived from remarks made at a 1955 reading, "On Taking Poetry," given at Bread Loaf, where Frost claimed that "a poem is a kind of fooling [...] poetry mounts somewhere into a kind of fooling" [25:76]. In a December 1956 interview on NBC's *Meet the Press*, Frost said: "I made up some lines the other day [...]. Poetry is a kind of fooling that you got to get the hang of, and I go around playing that. You cannot preach about it; you get in a little wisecrack and you read a poem and so on" [79:122].

In 1924, Frost wrote to Louis Untermeyer:

> I own any form of humor shows fear and inferiority. Irony is simply a kind of guardedness. [...] At bottom the world isn't a joke. We only joke about it to avoid an issue with someone to let someone know that we know he's there with his questions: to disarm him by seeming to have heard and done justice to his side of the standing argument. Humor is the most engaging cowardice [66:299–300].

He wrote Sidney Cox from England in 1914, "I am never so serious as when I am [joking]" [31:54].

l. 1. *in- and outdoor schooling*: Frost was often contrasting the merits of formal indoor schooling and informal experiential learning. Cf. "From Plane to Plane," *ll.* 1–6. Compare also Frost's statement in "The Death of the Hired Man" (*l.* 84) regarding Harold's "college-boy's assurance"—"Which showed how much good school had ever done him"—with his thoughts on outdoor schooling as expressed in "The Need of Being Versed in Country Things."

[In Winter in the Woods...]

First published by Frost in a holograph facsimile (Amherst College, 1962), this poem was written on January 12, 1962, while *In the Clearing* was going to press [13:161] for some of the people working at Amherst College on a documentary about Frost [123:69]. Frost said he "wrote it right off the reel" [25:192].

l. 12. *another blow*: Frost joked at a reading that this was "a threat to write another book. I didn't write it for that, but that's what it comes to" [25:192].

A Masque of Reason

First published in 1945 by Henry Holt. It was also issued in a limited, signed edition of eight hundred copies. The manuscript was completed in late 1943 [103:248; 35:11]. In 1945 the poet referred to this masque as a "comedy" and said that "All my poetry is a footnote to it" [26:355].

CHARACTERS	Job	God
	Job's Wife	Satan

Title *Reason*: in Job 13:3, Job says, "Surely I would speak to the Almighty, and I desire to reason with God" [131:577].

l. 4. *the Burning Bush*: in Exodus 3:2, "the angel of the Lord appeared unto him [Moses] in a flame of fire out of the midst of a bush; and he looked, and, behold, the bush burned with fire, and the bush was not consumed" [131:73].

l. 11. *the Emperor Alexius*: Alexius I Comnenus (1048–1118), Eastern Roman emperor (1081–1118). According to Lawrence Perrine, however, "It was actually the Emperor Theophilus (reigned 829–842) [...] who had the artificial birds made for his palace" [112:126].

l. 12. *Star of Bethlehem*: from Matthew 2:1–10, in which astrologers are aware of the birth of Jesus from having observed the rising of his star.

l. 18. *Blake's picture*: William Blake (1757–1827), English artist and poet, who published his *Illustrations of the Book of Job* in 1825, a set of twenty-one engravings, some of which contained an image of God. "Blake's picture" is again referred to in *l.* 85.

ll. 24–26. *Olympic tournament ... or Court of Law*: formal assemblies which were presided over by a judge or monarch.

l. 26. *Judgment Day*: the time when God or his Messiah will punish the wicked and redeem the righteous.

ll. 29–30. *Suffer yourself to ... says*: from "Go, lovely rose" by the English poet Edmund Waller (1606–1687) in which is found the following passage: "Bid her come forth, / Suffer herself to be desired, / And not blush so to be admired" [81:76].

l. 34. *my Patient*: pun on Job's patience and "patient" in a medical sense in that God cures Job of the boils with which Satan afflicted him.

l. 56. *One who in the beginning was the Word*: in John 1:1 it is stated, "In the beginning the Word already was. The Word was in God's presence, and what God was, the Word was."

l. 62. *essence of the trial*: cf. "The Trial by Existence."

l. 67. *Deuteronomist*: one who follows the laws expressed in the first five books of the Old Testament. As it relates to this passage, one who believes the tenets put forth in Deuteronomy 28:1–14, which begins:

> And it shall come to pass, if thou shalt hearken diligently unto the voice of the Lord thy God, to observe *and* to do all his commandments which I command thee this day, that the Lord thy God will set thee high above all nations on earth. And all these blessings shall come on thee, and overtake thee, if thou shalt hearken unto the voice of the Lord thy God [131:245].

and in Deuteronomy 28:15–68, which begins:

> But it shall come to pass, if thou wilt not hearken unto the voice of the Lord thy God, to observe to do all his commandments and his statutes which I command thee this day; that all these curses shall come upon thee, and overtake thee: Cursed *shalt* thou be in the city, and curst *shalt* thou be in the field [131:246].

l. **80.** *Thyatira*: Job's wife is unnamed in the Bible. Thyatira is a city mentioned in Revelation 1:11 and 2:18–19. The church of Thyatira was criticized for allowing a prophetess to teach.

l. **85.** *Blake's picture*: variant of line 18.

l. **89.** *women prophets ... witches*: in Exodus 22:18 it is stated, "Thou shalt not suffer a witch to live" [131:98].

l. **91.** *Except in their own country*: Jesus says in Matthew 13:57: "A prophet is not without honor, save in his own country, and in his own house" [131:1018].

l. **97.** *The Witch of Endor*: necromancer from the Canaanite city of Endor. See I Samuel 28:7–25. King Saul, on the eve of his fatal defeat by the Philistines at Gilboa, journeyed to Endor to direct its medium, the Witch of Endor, to raise up Samuel from the dead.

l. **99.** *Samuel*: prophet who ruled Israel at the end of the period of judges and who anointed the first two kings.

l. **103.** *my Note Book*: the Bible.

l. **112.** *Macbeth*: in Shakespeare's play (III.i.117-119), Macbeth says, arranging for the murder of Banquo: "and though I could / With barefac'd power sweep him from my sight, / And bid my will avouch it, yet I must not" [134:1324].

l. **114.** *Segub*: youngest son of a Bethelite named Hiel. He died when his father rebuilt the Jericho gates (1 Kings 16:34) fulfilling the word of Joshua (Joshua 6:26).

l. **118.** *What did you ... say?*: in Job 2:9 Job's wife says to her husband, "Dost thou still retain thine integrity? curse God, and die" [131:570].

l. **140.** *Plato*: Greek philosopher (427?–347 B.C.) who believed in a realm of universal idealized concepts. Life on earth was just an imperfect imitation of these concepts.

l. **160.** *time was found to be a space dimension*: reference to Einstein's theories of relativity.

l. **179.** *Kipling invokes You as Lord God of Hosts*: Rudyard Kipling (1865–1936), English author, in his 1897 poem "Recessional," refers to God as "Lord God of Hosts."

l. **186.** *Columbus-like*: cf. "America Is Hard to See" (*ll.* 43–44) in which Frost wrote of Columbus: "For these none-too-apparent gains / He got no more than dungeon chains."

l. **206.** *Wolsey*: Thomas Wolsey (1475?–1530), English cardinal and-statesman. In a manuscript dated May 26, 1944, Frost used Shakespeare instead of Wolsey. In *Henry VIII* (III.ii.440–441), Wolsey says, "Cromwell, I charge thee, fling away ambition! / By that sin fell the angels [...]" [134:1005].

l. **214.** *especially in war*: this masque was written during World War II.

l. **261.** *The artist in me cries out for design*: cf. "Pertinax," in which the poet exclaims, "I wait for form."

l. **284.** *Greeks*: the Greeks produced the world's first great philosophers in Plato, Aristotle, et al. It is being suggested here that there can be no new answers to life's questions.

ll. **285–288.** *We don't know ... misgivings*: this echoes the opening of Emerson's "Experience," which begins:

> Where do we find ourselves? In a series of which we do not know the extremes, and believe that it has none. [...] Ghostlike we glide through nature, and should not know our place again. [...] We do not know today whether we are busy or idle [30:471].

l. **303.** *Your kingdom come on earth*: from the *Lord's Prayer* in Matthew 6:10: "Thy kingdom come. Thy will be done in earth, as it is in heaven" [131:1002] and Luke 11:2: "Thy kingdom come. Thy will be done, as in heaven, so in earth" [131:1089].

l. **312.** *only four*: many times, following his January 6, 1941, speech before Congress, Franklin D. Roosevelt said that all men are entitled to four freedoms: freedom of speech and expression, freedom of every person to worship God in his own way, freedom from wants, and freedom from fear.

l. **314.** *twenty questions*: children's game in which the object is to identify something by asking no more than twenty yes-or-no questions.

ll. **316–322.** *Job says there's ... with*: this idea was expressed as early as 1935 when, in his "Letter to *The Amherst Student*," Frost wrote: "One can safely say [...] that the evident design is a situation here in which it will always be about equally hard to save your soul. Whatever progress may be taken to mean, it can't mean making the world any easier a place in which to save your soul [...]" [67:105–106]. This idea is also expressed in "The Lesson for Today" (*l.* 98–102).

l. 328. *Chapters One and Two*: in the first two chapters of Job, God accepts two challenges from Satan. The first challenge occurs in Job 1:8–12:

> And the Lord said unto Satan, Hast thou considered my servant Job, that there is none like him in the earth, a perfect and an upright man, one that feareth God, and escheweth evil?
>
> Then Satan answered the Lord, and said, Doth Job fear God for nought?
>
> Hast thou not made an hedge about him, and about his house, and about all that he hath, on every side? thou hast blessed the work of his hands, and his substance is increased in the land.
>
> But put forth thine hand now, and touch all that he hath, and he will curse thee to thy face.
>
> And the Lord said to Satan, Behold, all that he hath is in thy power; only upon himself put not forth thine hand [131:569].

The second challenge occurs in Job 2:3–6:

> And the Lord said to Satan, Hast thou considered my servant Job, that there is none like him in the earth, a perfect and an upright man, one that who feareth God, and escheweth evil? and still he holdeth fast his integrity, although thou movedst me against him, to destroy him without cause.
>
> And Satan answered the Lord, and said, Skin for skin, yea, and all that a man hath he will give for his life.
>
> But put forth thine hand now, and touch his bone and his flesh, and he will curse thee to thy face.
>
> And the Lord said unto Satan, Behold, he is in thine hand; but save his life [131:570].

l. 340. *serpent's tail ... throat*: a religious image symbolizing eternity, dating back to ancient Egypt, from the belief that at the end of a snake's life it devours itself, tail in mouth, and by feeding on itself is reborn.

ll. 343–344. *how rays return ... yet*: reference to Emerson's "Urie"' (*l.* 21–24):

> Line in nature is not found;
> Unit and universe are round;
> In vain produced, all rays return;
> Evil will bless, and ice will burn [1.2:264].

l. 364. *you must be wicked*: reference to "Childe Roland to the Dark Tower Came" (*l.* 84) by Robert Browning: "He must be wicked to deserve such pain" [11:282].

l. 365. *Browning and sheer Chapel Non-conformism*: the poet Robert Browning's beliefs were influenced by his early religious training in a chapel. "Chapel" was a word indicating a nonconformist sect while "church" referred to the Established Church.

l. 368. *Your comforters*: Eliphaz, Bildad and Zophar (see Job 2:11).

l. 373. *Deliver us from Committees*: echo of the Lord's Prayer, in which it is written, "Deliver us from evil."

l. 402. *Kodak*: camera.

ll. 416–417. *Like the one Milton ... blindness*: the "formula" Milton found is expressed in the sextet of his sonnet "On His Blindness":

> [...] God doth not need
> Either man's work, or His own gifts: who best
> Bear His mild yoke, they serve Him best: His state
>
> Is kingly; thousands at His bidding speed
> And post o'er land and ocean without rest:—
> They also serve who only stand and wait [81:62].

l. 418. *That strain ... it!*: quotation of two half-lines from Shakespeare's *Twelfth Night* (I.i.2, 4).

l. 421. *Lady Apple*: small red apple with a waxy skin. Also an allusion to the apple with which Satan tempted Eve.

l. 431. *business*: according to Luke 2:49, the twelve-year-old Jesus asks when found in the temple at Jerusalem: "How is it that ye sought me? wist ye not that I must be about my Father's business?" [131:1074].

ll. 435–437. *Stay, stay ... along*: from Robert Herrick's "To Daffodils" (*ll.* 5–10):

> Stay, stay
> Until the hasting day
> Has run
> But to the even-song;
> And, having pray'd together, we
> Will go along with you [81:91].

l. 458. *Burning Bush*: cf. note to *l.* 4.

l. 461. *Alexius Comnenus*: cf. note to *l.* 11.

l. 466. *Chapter Forty-three of Job*: the Book of Job contains forty-two chapters.

A Masque of Mercy

First published in 1947 by Henry Holt, the book was also issued in a signed, limited edition of seven hundred and fifty-one copies.

CHARACTERS	Jesse Bel	Keeper
	Paul	Jonah

l. 8. *Jesse Bel*: form of the name Jezebel, the idolatrous wife of King Ahab. See I Kings 16:29 and II Kings 9.

l. 9. *Paul*: St. Paul the Apostle was the author of the fourteen books of the New Testament from Romans through Hebrews.

l. 9. *Late, late ... now*: in Alfred Lord Tennyson's poem "Guinevere" from *Idylls of the King*, a novice in the convent at Almesbury sings a song to Guinevere which carries the burden: "Too late, too late! ye cannot enter now" [139:436].

l. 21. *Thompson's "Hound of Heaven"*: Francis Thompson (1859–1907) English poet, wrote "The Hound of Heaven" in 1890. Frost said about his discovery of this poem:

> I was seventeen, a bobbin-cart pusher in a mill in Lawrence. I rode a train to Boston, stopped at the Old Corner Bookstore, picked up *The Hound of Heaven*, and started to read. I kept on reading. I had only money enough for my railroad ticket. I used it all to pay for the book and walked the twenty-five miles to Lawrence, reading the poem over and over [13:20].

ll. 22–23. *"I fled Him ... years."*: first two lines of Thompson's "The Hound of Heaven."

l. 31. *We don't believe ... it*: the medieval church opposed the translation of the Bible into common tongues, believing that it was better interpreted by the clergy.

l. 36. *My Brother's Keeper*: when Cain in Genesis 4:9 is asked by God about Abel's whereabouts, he replies: "I know not. Am I my brother's keeper?"

l. 39. *the Brook Farm venture*: experimental communal society in Roxbury, Massachusetts, from 1841 to 1847. Hawthorne was a member. The society attracted the interest of Emerson and Margaret Fuller, although neither became a member.

ll. 48–49. *Moby Dick / By Rockwell Kent*: an edition of Melville's *Moby Dick* was published in 1930 by the Lakeside Press of Chicago and Random House of New York with illustrations by the American artist Rockwell Kent.

l. 55. *Jonas Dove*: the word Jonah in Hebrew means Dove (and see *ll.* 56–57). The story of Jonah is told in the Book of Jonah. Ordered by God to go to Nineveh to cry against its sins and wickedness, Jonah flees by sea. Thrown overboard by the sailors, he is swallowed by a great fish, commonly referred to as a whale, where he abides for three days. Spat up on dry land, he goes to Nineveh and prophesies its destruction in forty days. God repents, showing mercy to the city. This act displeases Jonah but God justifies himself to Jonah.

l. 64. *the city evil*: this noun-adjective inversion echoes other literary inversions such as the Siege Perilous from Malory's *Morte D'Arthur*, the House Beautiful from Bunyan's *Pilgrim's Progress* and the Forest Primeval from Longfellow's *Evangeline.*

l. 68. *agrarian*: reference to the antiurban group of American poets, including John Crow Ransom, Allen Tate and Robert Penn Warren, known as the Southern Agrarians. They published a magazine entitled *The Fugitive* (and see *l.* 137).

l. 77. *grapes we couldn't reach*: allusion to Aesop's fable of "The Fox and the Grapes."

ll. 108–109. *Mr. Flood ... will*: in E.A. Robinson's poem "Mr. Flood's Party" [*ll.* 15–16], Eben Flood offered himself a drink, "And answered huskily: "Well, Mr. Flood, / Since you propose it, I believe I will" [128:574].

l. 118. *You naughty ... pie*: quotation form the nursery rhyme, "The Three Little Kittens."

l. 126. *the Exegete*: St. Paul.

l. 133. *Wandering Jew*: according to legend, a Jew who was condemned to wander until the second coming of Christ.

l. 170. *Greenwich Village cocktail-party talk*: a district of New York City known as a gathering place for artists, writers, and Bohemians.

l. 172. *"I'm—bound—away!" (He quotes it to the tune.)*: from one of Frost's favorite folk songs, "Shenandoah," which has the chorus: "Ah ha I'm bound away, 'cross the wide Missouri" [1.1:807]. See "Away," *l.* 20.

l. 195. *every station*: Christ's Passion has traditionally been divided into fourteen episodes known as the Stations of the Cross.

l. 215. *beginning of all wisdom*: from Psalms 111:10: "The fear of the Lord is the beginning of wisdom" [131:655].

l. 228. *Funday Fault*: geologically, a fault is a crack in the earth's crust, a source of earthquakes. The Funday Fault under New York City is fictitious. Frost's Funday Fault plays with "all human fault" [*l.* 232] and the hedonistic, fun-filled, live-for-today attitude prevalent as part of city life.

l. 238. *as at Belshazzar's feast*: in Daniel 5, during a feast given by Belshazzar, king of Babylon, mysterious handwriting appears upon the wall.

l. 240. *Babel*: to punish men for attempting to construct a tower at Babel that would reach heaven, God confounded their languages, causing them to speak many languages instead of a common one. See Genesis 11:1–9.

ll. 242–243. *One to cap ... tongue-confusion*: possible allusion to James Joyce and his *Finnegans Wake*.

l. 274. *Like the one Joshua gave Jericho*: when the Israelites, under Joshua, marching against Jericho, blew their trumpets and shouted, the wall of Jericho fell. See Joshua 6.

l. 276. *The New Yorker*: weekly magazine begun in 1925.

l. 281. *A war is on*: this masque was written during World War II.

l. 288. *Great Books*: a program of adult education begun by Robert M. Hutchins and Mortimer J. Adler in the 1940s. In 1938, St. John's College in Annapolis, Maryland, had instituted an undergraduate curriculum advocated by Hutchins, then president to the University of Chicago. The purpose of this curriculum was to have the students read and discuss the approximately one hundred "Great Books" of the past [112:130–131].

l. 289. *a jealous God*: in the Old Testament, God is described as "a jealous God." See Exodus 20:5 and Deuteronomy 6:15.

l. 291. *How are the volumes fallen!*: echo of II Samuel 1:25, 27 in which David, lamenting the deaths of Saul and Jonathan, cried: "How are the mighty fallen [...]" [131:356].

l. 296. *My tongue ... True Thomas*: in the ballad "Thomas the Rhymer," when told he must hold his tongue in Elfin-land, True Thomas replied, "My tongue is my ain!" [4:4].

l. 297. *Bohning up on Thomism*: reference to the Bohn Library, a series of classic books issued from 1846 to 1921 by the English publisher Henry G. Bohn and his successors. Although there is no Bohn Library edition of the works of Thomas Aquinas, Thomism is discussed in a history of Christian thought which Bohn did publish [112:131].

l. 325. *Old Dana Lyle*: pun on Daniel.

ll. 332–340. *"The city's grotesque ... depth*: cf. Daniel 2:31–45.

l. 339. *The thought that ... height*: cf. Matthew 6:27: "Which of you by taking thought can add one cubit unto his stature?" [131:1002].

l. 375. *That book of yours*: relating to, not originating from, Jonah.

ll. 379–381. *After doing Justice ... shine*: cf. Milton's *Paradise Lost*, III, 80–134; Paul is quoting *l.* 134.

l. 441. *star-crossed lover*: in the Prologue to Shakespeare's *Romeo and Juliet*, Romeo and Juliet are referred to as "star-cross'd lovers."

l. 445. *Itzas*: a tribe of Mayan Indians which performed human sacrifices to their gods by throwing the victim into a cenote or sacred well.

l. 449. *butt of malmsey*: in Shakespeare's *Richard III* (I.iv) Richard's brother Clarence is stabbed by hired murderers and drowned in a butt, or large cask, of malmsey (wine).

ll. **460–461.** *The Andrew Jackson slogan ... out*: Andrew Jackson (1767–1845) was president of the United States, 1829–1837. The slogan *Vae Victus* is an ancient Roman slogan meaning, "Woe to the vanquished." The slogan "Turn the rascals out" was used by Horace Greeley in his campaign against Ulysses S. Grant in 1872.

ll. **462–468.** *Bel's favorite poet ... violence*: reference to William Butler Yeats (1865–1939) who in the closing poem of his play *Resurrection* (also the second poem in his "Two Songs from a Play") wrote:

> In pity for man's darkening thought
> He walked that room and issued thence
> In Galilean turbulence;
> The Babylonian starlight brought
> A fabulous, formless darkness in;
> Odour of blood when Christ was slain
> Made all Platonic tolerance vain
> And vain all Doric discipline [158:213].

The "doctrine of the Seven Poses" refers to Yeats' theory of masks as written in *Per Amica Silentia Lunae* and *A Vision*.

l. **473.** *Alexander Greeced the world*: Alexander the Great, by conquering most lands known to the West in the 4th century B.C., spread Greek culture and art throughout "the world."

l. **482.** *The Sermon on the Mount*: see Matthew 5:1–7:27.

ll. **517–518.** *approach to Christ ... Palestine*: the approach through Rome would refer to the Roman Church in which Christ was the Son of God, thus an approach, via St. Paul, that would be more theological and ecclesiastical; the approach through Palestine would refer to the Jewish idea of Christ as a man and prophet or philosopher, thus an approach, via Keeper, that would be more of a humanistic one.

l. **530.** *shining gate*: reference to John Bunyan's *The Pilgrim's Progress*, in which, near the beginning, Evangelist said,

> pointing with his finger over a very wide Field, Do you see yonder *Wicket-gate*? The Man said, No. Then said the other, Do you see yonder shining-light? He said, I think I do. Then said *Evangelist*, Keep that light in your eye, and go directly thereto, so shalt thou see the Gate [...] [12:147].

l. **557.** *Martin*: Martin Luther (1483–1546), German Augustinian friar who inaugurated the religious movement known as Protestantism.

l. **578.** *Karl Marx*: German political philosopher and socialist (1818–1883).

l. **591.** *many Gods to many men*: reference to I Corinthians 9:22, in which Christ says: "I am made all things to all men, that I might by all means save some" [131:1219].

l. **592.** *Roman Pantheon*: Roman temple for all the gods.

l. **604.** *Shadrach, Meshach, and Abednego*: Daniel's three companions in the fiery furnace. See Daniel 1:17.

l. **607.** *Jeffers and O'Neill*: Robinson Jeffers (1887–1962), American poet; Eugene O'Neill (1888–1953), American dramatist.

ll. **614–616.** *crucifix ... Aztec Indian*: as Frost would have learned from his readings in William H. Prescott's *The Conquest of Mexico*, the cross was a Mexican religious symbol predating the arrival of Cortez. Aztec Indian artwork includes many colorful painted murals.

l. **669.** *Who said*: Paul (see *l.* 9).

l. **684.** *the Presence*: Death.

ll. **717–725.** *We have to ... sight*: an echo of Psalms 19:14 in which it is written, "Let the words of my mouth, and the meditation of my heart, be acceptable in thy sight, O lord, my strength, and my redeemer" [131:607].

As Frost expressed it in a letter to G.R. Elliott in April 1947: "My fear of God has settled down into a deep inward fear that my best offering may not prove acceptable in his sight" [66:525].

PART TWO

A COMPANION TO THE UNCOLLECTED AND UNPUBLISHED POETRY

La Noche Triste

Considered by Frost to be his first poem, "La Noche Triste" was written when he was sixteen years old. The inspiration for this ballad came from a story he had read the summer before in Book IV of William Hickling Prescott's *History of the Conquest of Mexico*. The story told about the night when the Spaniards retreated under Cortes after the death of Montezuma. The Aztecs attacked the Spaniards as they retreated across a portable bridge which they used to cross over Lake Tezcuco from the island city of Tenochtitlan. About "La Noche Triste," Frost once said: "The first thing I ever wrote was a ballad. It was written hell for leather. It had a heroic sound. It was all heroes. It is heroic. Brave. That is the greatest emotion of all, to be brave. Brave" [44:54].

TENOCHTITLAN

Changed is the scene: the peace
And regal splendor which
Once that city knew are gone,
And war now reigns upon
That throng, who but
A week ago were all
Intent on joy supreme.
Cries of the wounded break
The stillness of the night,
Or challenge of the guard.
The Spaniard many days
Besieged within the place,
Where kings did rule of old,
Now pressed by hunger by
The all-relentless foe,
Looks for some channel of
Escape. The night is dark;
Black clouds obscure the sky—
A dead calm lies o'er all.
The heart of one is firm,
His mind is constant still,
To all, his word is law.
Cortes his plan hath made,
The time hath come. Each one
His chosen place now takes,
There waits the signal, that
Will start the long retreat.

THE FLIGHT

Anon the cry comes down the line,
The portals wide are swung,
A long dark line moves out the gate,
And now the flight's begun.

Aye, cautiously it moves at first,
As ship steered o'er the reef,
Looking for danger all unseen,
But which may bring to grief.

Straight for the causeway now they make,
The bridge is borne before,
'Tis ta'en and placed across the flood,
And all go trooping o'er.

Yet e'er the other side is reached,
Wafted along the wind,
The rolling of the snake-skin drum
Comes floating from behind.

And scarcely has its rolling ceased,
Than out upon the lake,
Where all was silence just before,
A conch the calm doth break.

What terror to each heart it bears,
That sound of ill portent,

Each gunner to escape now looks,
On safety all are bent.

Forward they press in wild despair,
On to the next canal,
Held on all sides by foe and sea,
Like deer within corral.

Now surging this way, now in that,
The mass sways to and fro,
The infidel around it sweeps—
Slowly the night doth go.

A war cry soundeth through the night,
The 'tzin! the 'tzin! is there,
His plume nods wildly o'er the scene,
Oh, Spaniard, now beware!

With gaping jaws the cannon stands,
Points it among the horde;
The valiant Leon waits beside,
Ready with match and sword.

The 'tzin quick springeth to his side,
His mace he hurls on high,
It crasheth through the Spanish steel,
And Leon prone doth lie.

Falling, he died beneath his gun,—
He died at duty's call,
And many falling on that night,
Dying, so died they all.

The faithful guarders at the bridge,
Have worked with might and main,
Nor can they move it from its place
Swollen by damp of rain.

On through the darkness comes the cry,
The cry that all is lost;
Then e'en Cortes takes up the shout,
And o'er the host 'tis tossed.

Some place their safety in the stream,
But sink beneath the tide,
E'en others crossing on the dead,
Thus reach the other side.

Surrounded and alone he sits,
Upon his faithful steed;
Here Alvarado clears a space,
But none might share the deed—

For darkness of that murky night
Hides deeds of brightest fame,
Which in the ages yet to come,
Would light the hero's name.

His faithful charger now hath fall'n,
Pierced to the very heart.
Quick steps he back, his war cry shouts,
Then onward doth he dart.

Runs he, and leaping high in air,
Fixed does he seem a space,
One instant and the deed is done,
He standeth face to face—

With those who on the other side
Their safety now have found.
The thirst for vengeance satisfied,
The Aztec wheels around.

So, as the sun climbs up the sky,
And shoots his dawning rays,
The foe, as parted by his dart,
Each go their sep'rate ways.

Upon the ground the dead men lie,
Trampled midst gold and gore,
The Aztec toward his temple goes,
For now the fight is o'er.
Follow we not the Spaniard more,
Wending o'er hill and plain,
Suffice to say he reached the coast,
Lost Fortune to regain.

The flame shines brightest e'er goes out,

Thus with the Aztec throne,
On that dark night before the end,
So o'er the fight it shone.

The Montezumas are no more,
Gone is their regal throne,
And freemen live, and rule, and die,

Date: March 1890. Length: 127 lines. Publication history: first published in the *Lawrence High School Bulletin* (April 1890), 1–2; reprinted in 46:17–22; 121:11–12; 103:427–431; 57:190–194.

God's Garden

"God's Garden" was written circa 1890 or earlier, according to Lawrance Thompson, and may possibly predate "La Noche Triste." Thompson also suggests that Frost's mother may have helped him with it [142:540–541]. At various times Frost denied the poem's authenticity. Although in 1938 Frost had acknowledged his authorship to Charles R. Green of the Jones Library in Amherst [142:540], and he had once scratched through four lines of the poem, initialling them "R.F.," in 1942 he told Green, "I don't write this way" [3:94].

This poem describes God's "beauteous garden" which has "But one straight, narrow pathway." If followed, it "leads you on to heaven." To reach heaven one must not be tempted by the gold flowers planted by "another master" which "hid the thorns of av'rice / That poison blood and bone."

Date: circa 1890. Length: 36 lines. Publication history: first published in *The Boston Evening Transcript* (June 23, 1898), 6; reprinted in 46:15–16; 142:540–541.

Song of the Wave

Except for the final two narrative lines, this poem is a soliloquy given by a wave as it goes on its way, prior to crashing on the rocks. This juvenile effort had been inspired by Frost's memories of his San Francisco childhood, particularly his experiences at the Cliff House watching the breakers crash into the rocks and ledges [121:12].

Date: May 1890. Length: 34 lines. Publication history: first published in the *Lawrence High School Bulletin* (May 1890), 3; reprinted in 46:22–24; 122:13.

The Sachem of the Clouds

"The Sachem of the Clouds" was first read as a Friday afternoon rhetorical exercise while Frost was attending Lawrence High School [110:26]. In this poem Frost shows his sympathy for the Native American races which were dying out, a theme he was further to explore in "Genealogical " and "The Vanishing Red."

When the sedge upon the meadows, crosses, falls and interweaves,
Spent, the brook lies wrapt in silence on its bed of autumn leaves;
When the barren fields are moaning, where the Autumn winds rush by,
And the leaves start up in eddies and are whirled athwart the sky;

On the lonely hillside, darkened by the over-hurrying clouds,
Ghostly, stand the withered corn-rows, in their waving moonlight shrouds,
Like the band of those departed, murmuring with discontent,
Come again to tell their sadness, hid in vengeance as they went.

Then the traveler, wending downward from the mountain's fading height,
Deep among the woody marshes, stretching back within the night,
Sees a hermit, grey and feeble, dwarfed beside a giant oak,
Sees the sachem of the storm-cloud, clad about with wreaths of smoke,

Piling high his pyre of hemlocks, weaving spell and crossing limb,
Till a hazy phosphorescence plays around the circle's rim;
All night long, 'mid incantations, hears the wizard's voice arise,
On the bleak wind wildly mingled with the forest's eerie cries.

And when far the flames up-reaching, lurid, gleam upon the vale,
Then the wizard's muttered croaking rises to a piercing wail:
"Come, O come, with storm, come darkness! Speed my clouds on Winter's
breath.
All my race is gone before me, all my race is low in death!

Ever, as I ruled a people, shall this smoke arise in cloud;
Ever shall it freight the tempest for the ocean of the proud.
'Thanks!' I hear their cities thanking that my race is low in death:
Come, O come, with storm, come darkness! Speed my clouds on Winter's
breath!"

Thus his voice keeps ringing, ringing, till appears the dreary dawn;
And the traveler, looking backward, see the ashes on the lawn,
Sees the smoke crowd to the hilltops, torn away, and hurried south;
Hears a shrieking answer speeded from the Winter's snowy mouth.

Date: 1891. Length: 28 lines. Publication history: first published in the *Lawrence Daily American* (November 2, 1891), 5, with the subtitle "A Thanksgiving legend."

A Dream of Julius Caesar

The poem begins with the narrator "In Nature's cradle lulled to calm repose." He is listening to the drowsy note of a thrush, watching the water of a brook, while thinking about times past. The pleasant scene is disturbed by an approaching storm. Between the darkening clouds, rays of light appear like long ladders between earth and heaven. The narrator sees a form approaching, a toga streaming in the wind. It is Caesar. Pointing toward a fallen tree trunk which serves as a bridge across the brook, Caesar tells the narrator to leave. Caesar has come, he is told, from Jupiter to rule with darkness and storm. He holds in his hand the lightning bolt of Jupiter. While the narrator hears the thunder of chariot wheels and legions fighting, Caesar vanishes. Blood falls in torrents from the sky, but instead of being sanguine, it falls in a "lighter hue" as rain, waking the narrator.

Date: 1891. Length: 67 lines. Publication history: first published in the *Lawrence High School Bulletin* (May 1891); reprinted in 46:24–26; 122:14; 57:195–197.

Caesar's Lost Transport Ships

"Caesar's Lost Transport Ships" is, in Frost's words, "some lines on the lost galleys of Caesar's which disappeared on the stormy passage of the channel when he first sought Britain" [120:160].

Date: spring 1891. Length: 12 lines. Publication history: first published in *The Independent* (January 14, 1897), 1; reprinted during Frost's lifetime in his *Three Poems* (Hanover, N.H.: Baker Library, 1935); reprinted in 46:26; 57:197.

[Where only some first cautious ghost might be...]

This fragment is found on the verso of the manuscript for "Caesar's Lost Transport Ships." It describes a level plain where "some first cautious ghost might be," far away from the "lorn city where the gold / Was sunken and the houses still."

Date: circa 1891. Length: 10 lines. Publication history: first printed in *Robert Frost: A Descriptive Catalogue of Books and Manuscripts in the Clifton Waller Barrett Library, University of Virginia,* compiled by Joan St. C. Crane (Charlottesville: University Press of Virginia, 1974), 160.

Clear and Colder—Boston Common

This poem describes the delight of a young man on Boston Common in early winter. It is written in a very formalized style in which, with only two minor variants, the first line and the closing three lines of each stanza remain constant. Only the second through fifth lines of each octet vary. Each stanza opens with "As I went down through the common," followed by four lines describing the scene which greets the poet, then closes with "As I went briskly down. / I felt my own quick step begin / The pace of the winter town."

Being shown this poem in November 1937 by his first biographer, Robert Newdick, Frost claimed that it was one he might still "approve of a little" [110:154].

Date: October 1891. Length: 32 lines. Publication history: first printed in Lawrance Thompson, *Robert Frost: The Early Years, 1874–1915* (New York: Holt, Rinehart and Winston, 1966), 110–111; reprinted in 57:199.

Evensong

Two quatrains are extant of what may possibly be a fragment, written out with no break between the stanzas. The first stanza has a traditional rhyme scheme (abab) while the second is unrhymed. The first two lines of each stanza offer a description of the wind, followed by two lines acting as a repeated chorus: "Someone has passed / That the stars are down."

Date: 1890s. Length: 8 lines. Publication history: first printed in *Robert Frost: A Descriptive Catalogue of Books and Manuscripts in the Clifton Waller*

Barrett Library, University of Virginia, compiled by Joan St. C. Crane (Charlottesville: University Press of Virginia, 1974), 159.

Class Hymn

Along with his future wife, Elinor White, Frost was co-valedictorian for the class of 1892 at the Lawrence, Massachusetts, High School. His "Class Hymn" was written for the graduation exercises and was related to thoughts and images expressed in his address, "A Monument to After-Thought Unveiled."

There is a nook among the alders
Still sleeping to the cat-bird's "Hush";
Below, a long stone-bridge is bending
Above a runnel's silent rush.

A dreamer hither often wanders
And gathers many a snow-white stone;
He weighs them, poised upon his fingers,
Divining each one's silvery tone.

He drops them! When the stream makes music,
Fair visions with its vault-voice swell:
And so, for us, the future rises,
As thought-stones stir our heart's "Farewell!"

Date: 1892. Length: 12 lines. Publication history: first published in the *Order of Exercises for the Forty-First Anniversary of the Lawrence High School, 1 July 1892* (Lawrence, Mass., June 1892); reprinted twice that year, in the *Lawrence High School Bulletin* for June 1892 and the *Report of the Superintendent of Schools to the School Committee*; reprinted in 46:29–30; 142:132; 121:21, 93; 151:172–173; 103:46; 120:illus. 3.

The Traitor

Frost described his ballad-like "The Traitor" as coming "right out of *Ossian*" [142:508]. The only part of this poem which does actually come directly out of James Macpherson's *Ossian* poems is the name Colla, from the poem "Dar-Thula." Otherwise, "The Traitor" appears to be original. The poem is a lament about Lorna, a traitor to the king, who, regretting his action, sacrifices himself for his people.

Date: 1892. Length: 30 lines. Publication history: first published in the *Phillips Andover Mirror* (June 1892), 24; reprinted once during Frost's lifetime in the *Phillips Andover Mirror* (February 1961); reprinted in 46:28–29; 142:508–509; 121:19; 57:198.

[Europe might sink...]

Written in the late 1880s ("after my leaving San Francisco in 1885" [97:44]), Frost's five-line fragment beginning "Europe might sink..." was written out after 1947 in a copy of *A Masque of Mercy* for William Meredith. The first three lines had previously been sent to John W. Haines on July 17, 1915, in a letter discussing World War I, about which Frost wrote, "We don't really care what happens over there. It doesn't touch us nearly enough. At least we can't see that it does" [66:183].

In this poem Frost writes that if Europe were to sink and the wave caused by her sinking were to reach our shores, we would not be affected. We should not be concerned with what happens in that direction, but only with what happens in the West, where our future is. The sentiments Frost expresses in this poem echo Thoreau's attitude in his essay "Walking": "Eastward I go only by force; but westward I go free. [...] We go eastward to realize history and study the works of art and literature, retracing the steps of the race; we go westward as into the future [...]" [145:176–177].

Date: 1885–1889. Length: 5 lines. Publication history: the three-line fragment first printed in *Selected Letters of Robert Frost*, edited by Lawrance Thompson (New York: Holt, Rinehart and Winston, 1964), 183. The five-line fragment first published in Elizabeth Shepley Sergeant, *The Trial by Existence* (New York: Holt, Rinehart and Winston, 1960), 31; reprinted in 97:44.

Poems from *Twilight*

In the fall of 1894, Frost took five of his poems to a job printer in Lawrence, Massachusetts, and had them printed as a book. *Twilight* was printed in an edition of two copies, on antique paper, and bound in leather. One copy was made for Elinor White; the second copy was kept for himself but was later destroyed. (For a detailed discussion of *Twilight*, see 142:chapter 16). The slender volume contained five poems: the title poem, "Twilight"; "My Butterfly," which was soon to be published in the November 8 issue of *The Independent*; "Summering," "The Falls," and "An Unhistoric Spot." Only "My Butterfly" was later collected by Frost in *A Boy's Will*. At the end of the volume, in Frost's hand, is a couplet beginning, "Save of trees chafing [...]" apparently excerpted from a poem which is no longer extant. It is unknown when this couplet was written out by Frost. *Twilight* has been reprinted in its entirety twice, in *Proof* 4 and in a limited facsimile reprint of 170 copies (Charlottesville, Va.: Reynolds Company for the Barrett Library, 1966). The couplet has been reprinted in 97:7; 35:5; 72; 73:22.

Twilight

This poem opens with the narrator questioning why he is being sadly regarded by Twilight personified. The spirits of the sorrowful twilight and the oppressed narrator pass in the air as "unmemoried consciousness," unable to meet.

Date: early 1890s. Length: 17 lines. Publication history: first published in *Twilight*; reprinted in 46: 30–31; 72; 73:15; 120:illus. 3.

Summering

The narrator in "Summering" describes the place he would go to sleep in "sleepy self-sufficiency." It is a place surrounded by forests, where the meadow is silent and the grasses deep, a place far away from commerce.

Date: early 1890s. Length: 12 lines. Publication history: first published in *Twilight*; reprinted in 46:31; 72; 73:19.

The Falls

"The Falls" describes a steep wooded area that once contained an Indian trail which is now too overgrown even for birds to alight.

Date: early 1890s. Length: 8 lines. Publication history: first published in *Twilight*; separately reprinted during Frost's lifetime in 1947 in sixty numbered copies by Earle J. Bernheimer at the Ward Ritchie Press in Los Angeles; reprinted in 46:31–32; 142:174; 72; 73:20.

An Unhistoric Spot

In this poem, Frost tells of how "passionate is rest" when he is yielding his body "in full length contact of sweet pain!" or when he leans "upon one grass-wrought hand." The poet has set himself apart from the rest of the world by the passion he feels as "every one that passes looks at me."

"An Unhistoric Spot" contains certain images which in part presage his 1923 poem "To Earthward" (which see).

Date: early 1890s. Length: 11 lines. Publication history: first published in *Twilight*; reprinted in 46:32; 72; 73:21.

Warning

"Warning" was originally a man's admonishment to his lover that she will soon forget him, but Frost admitted in 1962 to changing the pronouns to cover his autobiographical tracks [142:519] because of insecure feelings he was having during his courtship of Elinor White.

Date: circa 1895. Length: 18 lines. Publication history: first published in *The Independent* (September 9, 1897), 1; reprinted during Frost's lifetime in his 1935 *Three Poems*; reprinted in 46:33; 142:169; 57:200.

The Birds Do Thus

I slept all day,
  The birds do thus
That sing a while
  At eve for us.

To have you soon
  I gave away—
Well satisfied
  To give—a day.

Life's not so short
I care to keep
The unhappy days;
I choose to sleep.

Date: circa 1896. Length: 12 lines. Publication history: first published in *The Independent* (August 10, 1896), 1; reprinted in 46:32–33; 142:216.

A Summer's Garden

The narrator has made a garden so the birds and flowers he loves will be around him. He knows they would survive without him, but questions how well he would do without them. Although his small summer garden was not the untrimmed wild garden he had dreamt of having, it did lure the butterflies, bees and birds that he desired. As he thinks back on his garden, now withered, he wonders in a manner recalling medieval *ubi sunt* poems.

Date: circa 1896. Description: 20 lines in five quatrains (rhyming abab). Collection: unpublished manuscript in 162:HM 7653.

Greece

Turkey's declaration of war against Greece on April 17, 1897, prompted Frost to write "Greece." In the margin of a copy of "Greece" Robert Newdick sent him in 1936, Frost wrote, "Dreadful, dreadful. I was trying very hard to show sympathy with the people who made me learn Greek" [110:58].

They say, "Let there be no more war!"
And straightway, at the word,
Along the Mediterranean shore,
The call to arms is heard.

Greece could not let her glory fade!
Although peace be in sight,
The race the Persian wars arrayed
Must fight one more good fight.

Greece! Rise triumphant. Long ago
It was you proved to men

A few may countless hosts o'erthrow:
Now prove it once again!

Date: April 1897. Length: 12 lines. Publication history: first published in *The Boston Evening Transcript* for April 30, 1897, 6; reprinted once during Frost's lifetime in 1948 in an edition of forty-seven numbered copies by the Black Rose Press; reprinted in 46:16–17; 142:539.

Poems from *The Parachute*

"The Parachute" was a hand-stitched manuscript booklet Frost sent periodically to Carl Burell to give him the latest personal news. It occasionally contained snatches of verse, such as the following three poems: "Jewell Gets a Job," "In Memorium, R. Frost Exit" and "To Carl Burrell."

Jewell Gets a Job

"Jewell Gets a Job" celebrates the fact that Ernest Jewell, a friend of both Frost and Carl Burell, had become a teacher at Lawrence High School after graduating from Harvard. The poem was originally sent to Burell in an issue of "The Parachute" dated June 13, 1897.

Date: June 1897. Length: 8 lines. Publication history: first printed in Lawrance Thompson, *Robert Frost: The Early Years, 1874–1915* (New York: Holt, Rinehart and Winston, 1966), 544.

In Memorium, R. Frost Exit

An issue of "The Parachute" from autumn 1897, contains "In Memorium, R. Frost Exit" which is purportedly written by the printer's devil who edited the publication. It describes Frost as a man who wore a "long Scotch face / When things were going pore."

Date: autumn 1897. Length: sextet. Publication history: first printed in Lawrance Thompson, *Robert Frost: The Early Years, 1874–1915* (New York: Holt, Rinehart and Winston, 1966), 544.

To Carl Burell

Also in the autumn 1897 issue of "The Parachute" is "To Carl Burell." It is purportedly written by the same printer's devil who edited the "First Memorial Edition" of "The Parachute." It makes the claim that although the editors of "The Parachute" have their hands full "Mourning a dead man here worth two of you" the paper has not dropped its original mission: slander.

Date: autumn 1897. Length: 8 lines. Publication history: first printed in Lawrance Thompson, *Robert Frost: The Early Years, 1874–1915* (New York: Holt, Rinehart and Winston, 1966), 545.

Confusion

"Confusion" was written in 1897-1898 on the back endpaper of the 1889 Clarendon Press edition of Homer's *Odyssey*, one of Frost's Greek texts at Harvard. It claims that a decisive utterance or action creates at most two decisive factions, pro or con, while a doubtful speech creates twice as many.

Date: 1897-1898. Description: quatrain (rhyming aabb). Collection: unpublished manuscript in 164:Frost Y PA4022.A1 1889M.

[Perhaps you think I am going to wait...]

Written at Harvard in 1897-1898, this quatrain was directed, but never submitted to, Frost's English instructor, Alfred Dwight Shefield. Shefield insisted that all the submissions of students be treated merely as exercises, nothing more. Frost, addressing Sheffield as "You prig stick," makes the claim that he is not going to wait until he can write as well as a graduate before he writes any more poetry.

In 1917 Frost sent a copy of the quatrain to Charles Young with the explanation, "You see I was angry at the general disposition to take everything written by an undergraduate as an exercise. I never wrote exercises in my life" [142:539].

Date: 1897-1898, Harvard. Length: quatrain. Publication history: first printed in Lawrance Thompson, *Robert Frost: The Early Years, 1874–1915* (New York: Holt, Rinehart and Winston, 1966), 236.

The Rubaiyat of Carl Burell, His Misadventures and His Misfortunes

"The Rubaiyat..." is a series of five limericks sent to Burell in an eight-page stitched manuscript pamphlet on December 18, 1898.

Date: circa December 18, 1898. Length: 5 limericks. Publication history: first printed in Lawrance Thompson, *Robert Frost: The Early Years, 1874–1915* (New York: Holt, Rinehart and Winston, 1966), 545–46.

A Young Man from Podunk

This set of four limericks was sent to Carl Burell in a manuscript pamphlet in January 1900 with the lengthy title page, "A Young Man from Podunk, or, The Young Artist Goes to Seek His Fortune, or, An Overdose of Alcoholic Encouragement, or, The Foundations of Belief Unshaken."

Date: January 1900. Length: 4 limericks. Publication history: first printed in Lawrance Thompson, *Robert Frost: The Early Years, 1874–1915* (New York: Holt, Rinehart and Winston, 1966), 255–56.

[The reason of my perfect ease...]

This sestet explains that the reason the poet feels at ease "in the society of trees" is that their social class is too far below his for him to either care about or be afraid of them. Frost told Louis Untermeyer that it was one "that might have gone into my first book to show the mood I was in and gradually escaping from at the time" [151:381].

Date: 1890s. Length: sestet. Publication history: first printed in *Letters of Robert Frost to Louis Untermeyer* (New York: Holt, Rinehart and Winston, 1963), 381.

To Coebee

In 1902 or 1903 Carl Burell invited the Frosts to a flower convention. Frost sent their regrets in a rhymed letter in which he explained that the reason they could not attend was that Elinor Frost, "the Derry Gentian," was pregnant, or as he expressed it in the poem, they could not attend because of "the said flower's backward condition / And a hatch of eggs impending."

Date: 1902 or 1903. Length: 24 lines. Publication history: first printed in Lawrance Thompson, *Robert Frost: The Early Years, 1874–1915* (New York: Holt, Rinehart and Winston, 1966), 551; reprinted in 57:305–306.

My Old Uncle

"My Old Uncle" describes an elderly man rising from his after-dinner nap. After playing with the relationship between "gravity" and "grave," Frost determines that "Old age may not be kittenish / But it's not necessarily serious."

Date: circa 1903. Length: 26 lines. Publication history: first printed in *Robert Frost: A Descriptive Catalogue of Books and Manuscripts in the Clifton Waller Barrett Library, University of Virginia*, compiled by Joan St. C. Crane (Charlottesville: University Press of Virginia, 1974), 160–61. A 1916 version entitled "Old Age," with slight variants, was printed in *Letters of Robert Frost to Louis Untermeyer* (New York: Holt, Rinehart and Winston, 1963), 30–31.

Love Being All One

Formulaic in form, each stanza in this poem begins with "Could I forget thee, I should forget / (Love being all one)," going on to describe something the narrator has forgotten since falling in love. The final line of each stanza states that, if he forgot his love, he would "forget to forget" those things which he forgot in loving her: care, the gains which filled him with the pride of youth, and defeat.

Date: circa 1905. Description: 15 lines in three five-line stanzas (rhyming xabab). Collection: unpublished manuscript in 162:HM 7643.

Midsummer Birds

The first stanza of this poem states that if there is anything more hushed than the wings of midsummer birds, it is their voices; while the second stanza states that if there is anything more safe than the birds' hush, it is their nests. The final stanza describes the birds as being more still than the trees and grass in the field.

Date: circa 1905. Description: 15 lines in three five-line stanzas (rhyming xabba). Collection: unpublished manuscript in 162:HM 7644.

The Mill City

"The Mill City" was based on Frost's own observations during 1893-1894 when he worked in the mills of Lawrence, Massachusetts. The narrator describes the denizens of a dreary mill city: they pass by dreamlike in the morning under the unnatural bluish tint of an arc light, and pass again at night "like drowned men from the sea." The narrator supposes that he shares with the mill workers, as with all people, one hope. While "happier" people remain indoors fearing to confront the mill workers, he would go out among them, "resolute to cope" with the thoughts he would be compelled to think facing them.

Date: circa 1905. Description: sonnet. Collection: unpublished manuscript in 162:HM 7645.

What Thing a Bird Would Love

"What Thing a Bird Would Love" describes a slow homeward journey, interrupted by a lonely bird singing. The narrator pauses, turning to find the bird, and then realizes that had he not turned, he would have missed the sunset. Resuming his journey, he again turns to the singing bird, and contemplates the bird's insistent call, making the narrator realize that it must be something beyond the sunset which makes the bird sing so, leaving him in doubt whether he could know "what thing a bird would love."

The poem echoes Thomas Hardy's 1901 poem, "The Darkling Thrush," in which the "fervourless" narrator listens to a bird's "evensong / Of joy illimited" and realizes that "there trembled through / His happy good-night air / Some blessed Hope, whereof he knew / And I was unaware."

Date: circa 1905. Description: 24 lines in six quatrains rhyming (abxb). Collection: unpublished manuscript in 162:HM 7648.

A Winter's Night

"A Winter's Night" describes a small cottage in the winter, the icicles and snow of which are given to the moon for safe keeping. The image was used again a year later when Frost was writing "An Old Man's Winter Night" (*ll.* 21–22) in which the old man consigns to the moon "his snow upon the roof, / His icicles along the wall to keep."

Showing this poem to a friend in 1938, Frost said, "I use the best in lots of old poems and make it into something I'm willing to have published. Here, read this and see if you're familiar enough with my work to tell what it went into" [118:15].

Date: circa 1905. Description: 8 lines in two quatrains (rhyming abxb). Collection: unpublished manuscript in 162:HM 7650.

The Black Cottage (rhymed version)

Frost had written "two versions [of "The Black Cottage"], in and around 1905-1906, one in rhyme which I lost on purpose as a failure and the other that came down with some changes into *North of Boston*" [110:163].

The inspiration for the poem came from the cottage which stood between the Frost farm and Derry Village. It was inhabited by Sarah J. Upton, the widow of George R. Upton, the first volunteer from Derry to enlist in the Grand Army of the Republic near the start of the Civil War. He was killed in action [142:592].

Date: 1905-1906. Length: 40 lines (five octets rhyming aabcddbc). Publication history: first printed in Lawrance Thompson, *Robert Frost: The Early Years, 1874–1915* (New York: Holt, Rinehart and Winston, 1966), 592–93.

[There was a poor mortal believer...]

Frost's great suffering from hay fever caused him in October 1906 to write his own mock epitaph in limerick form.

Date: October 1906. Length: limerick. Publication history: first printed in Elizabeth Shepley Sergeant, *The Trial by Existence* (New York: Holt, Rinehart and Winston, 1960), 82; reprinted in 66:36.

Despair

In this sonnet the poet describes himself as a dead diver ensnared in weeds, who has dragged down some "White lily" in his struggles. The white lily represents his wife, Elinor White Frost, about whom Frost would sometimes feel guilty for having, as he wrote after her death, "dragged her through pretty much of a life for one as frail as she was" [143:511].

Date: circa 1900–1906. Length: sonnet. Publication history: first printed in Lawrance Thompson, *Robert Frost: The Early Years, 1874–1915* (New York: Holt, Rinehart and Winston, 1966), 267; reprinted in 57:226.

[When the speed comes a-creeping overhead...]

This sonnet was inspired by Frost's experiences in 1893 at the Arlington Woolen Mill in Lawrence, Massachusetts. It describes Frost's anger with the ways of the mills, where machines, being the law, turn human beings into automatons.

Date: circa 1906-1907. Length: sonnet. Publication history: first printed in Lawrance Thompson, *Robert Frost: The Early Years, 1874–1915* (New York: Holt, Rinehart and Winston, 1966), 158; reprinted in 57:226.

The Later Minstrel

This poem pays tribute to Henry Wadsworth Longfellow, the minstrel "With perfect songs to sing." Frost had always been an admirer of Longfellow, even when it was not popular to admit it. The title of Frost's first published book, *A Boy's Will*, was taken from Longfellow's poem, "My Lost Youth." As he wrote to Louis Untermeyer in 1930, "Longfellow was a true poet for anyone with the ears to judge poetry by the ear" [151:203].

Remember some departed day
When, bathed in autumn gold,
You wished for some sweet song and sighed
For minstrel days of old,

And that same autumn day
Perhaps the fates would bring
At eve, one knocking at your heart
With perfect songs to sing.

You knew that never bard on earth
Did wander wide as he
Who sang the long, long thoughts of Youth,
The Secret of the Sea.

You knew not when he might not come;
But while he made delays,
You wronged the wisdom that you had
And sighed for vanished days.

Song's times and seasons are its own,
Its ways past finding out,
But more and more it fills the earth
And triumphs over doubt.

Date: early 1907. Length: 20 lines. Publication history: first published in broadside form for the centennial of Henry Wadsworth Longfellow's birth, celebrated on February 27, 1907; reprinted during Frost's lifetime in *The Pinkerton Critic* (March 1909), 14; reprinted in 152:563; 110:167.

Lost Faith

This poem was written to be read at the February 29, 1907, meeting of the Men's League of the First Congregationalist Church. The poem was read by the Reverend Charles L. Merriam. Frost was unable at this stage of his career to read his poetry in front of an audience.

We shrine our fathers as their wars recede
With the heroic dead that die of old;
We shall strew flowers for them year after year;
They shall have flowers themselves more than they need!
But for the cause that was to them so dear,
Where shall it be so much as justly told
What that cause was?—which, as they lie in mould,
In our hearts dies as cold.
Have we for that no flowers, no mournful rhythm,
The soldiers dream, that, when they died, died with them?

No less a dream than of one law of love,
One equal people under God above!
But fallen to be a world of easy scorn.
See if it dies not—if it is not dead!
Who in our latter wisdom so unread
As not to know
Dark life too well for such a dream of morn,
What child so uninured to literal woe?
The Californian, by the western sea
Exults, and by the Gulf they laugh,
Saying, "How can all men be free,
How equal, when God made them wheat and chaff?"
They mock, that, in these recreant hearts of ours,
There should no lingering answer be,
And where it sprung the dream at last should fade
That did defy their powers.
Too strange it seems to men of the dull throng
That such belief can have been soldier's shroud
More glorious than his battle colors proud.
Yet how they do them wrong!

'Twere not enough to reckon the men brave,
'Twere not enough to reckon the men strong,
Not with the men themselves,—far more they crave
One tribute to the meaning of their strife
To which they gave youth, life.

It was the dream that woke them in this north,
And led the young man forth,
And pitched against the embittered foe their tent;
And fought their fight for them on many a field,
Their sword, their shield,
The still small voice that like a clarion pealed;
Strong as a dream and deathless as a dream,

As it did seem,
(Though destined to go down the way they went.)

The dream that, as it sent them on that way,
Gave Love the strength to stay
In these brave hills apart—
It, and naught else, for many a fireside heart!

Oh, such a dream as cannot have lost worth
Forever, for an unredeemed earth.
I cannot make it wholly dead to men.
Not late, but soon, it must return again—
In blood mayhap, with maddening fife and drum,
And reaping souls—I care not, so it come!
All beautiful and human as it was,
It could be terrible in its own cause;
As when it swept the skirts of Malvern Hill
And when it crouched in wait as deadly still
On Gettysburg's low height,
As the oncoming foe were swift and shrill.
Men knew us not until that wavering fight!
And keep not now the thought that moved in us!
How earthly death came ever near to touch
A dream so deathless, we to forget it thus,
I do not know; we saw it fade from sight,
Not while we slept, but while we strove too much
For things that were not beautiful and bright.

But fair it seems in passing as still day
In fainter gold behind the golden stars,
Or mists on water that the morning ray,
Without a seeming zephyr, moves away;
And truer in comparison of truth,
Than all the hopes the years abate from youth;
Truer than aught recovered from the vast
By souls that could not slumber, but must climb
The starlight in far suns to dwell a time—
So true in passing, if it must be past.

Date: February 1907. Length: 77 lines. Publication history: first published in *The Derry News* (March 1, 1907), 1, 4; reprinted in *The Derry News* (April 12, 1962), 7.

Genealogical

Major Charles Frost (1631–1697) was a well known fighter of New England Indians. A ruthless killer, he himself was murdered in ambush by a group of Indians. After his family buried him, the Indians exhumed his body and hung it from a stake at the top of Great Hill (now Frost's Hill) in Wells, Maine [66:600]. Robert Frost commemorates his ancestor in "Genealogical." In it Frost tells his gruesome family history with humor. He describes Major Frost as one who "aspired / To wipe out the whole of an Indian tribe to order" and who "was rather pointedly not instructed / To proceed in the matter with any particular / Regard to the laws of civilized warfare." Frost then describes the destruction of the Indian tribe, their vengeance, and the burial, exhumation; hanging and reburial of the body. He concludes with the biting witticism, "And I think he explains my lifelong liking for Indians."

Date: circa 1907. Length: 63 lines. Publication history: first printed in *Selected Letters of Robert Frost,* edited by Lawrance Thompson (New York: Holt, Rinehart and Winston, 1964), 604–6.

[It is an ancient friend of yours...]

This poem exists only in draft form. Actually a verse-letter, it opens with the "ancient friend" explaining that he is taking "a minute or two / To tell you how the business goes / And how the family do." They had entered a time of freezing cold and snow, when all the water froze and they had to wear fur caps just to think. Since that cold spell, Frost was left with a "strange power of speech / That makes me prose in verses [...]." The poem is written in the style of Coleridge's "Rime of the Ancient Mariner" complete with shoulder notes, such as "The ancient friend begins to explain why he hasn't written sooner" and "The sink regurgitates and the apples onions and potatoes go."

Date: 1907. Length: 47 lines. Publication history: first printed in Lawrance Thompson, *Robert Frost: The Early Years, 1874–1915* (New York: Holt, Rinehart and Winston, 1966), 337–38; reprinted in 57:306–308.

Across the Atlantic

Leaning, one speaks between surrounding hands,
With lashes lowered as deeming not to see,
And the tide smooths the beaches at her feet.
"Sister," she says, "I faintly hear thy word,
But hear thy word in heart-beats—speak again.
Darkness comes down upon you speaking there;
The waves go toward you standing under stars;
They come to me in sunlight further west;
Somewhere between they leap to the wind's love.
It is the old sea there, no man's abode,
Not time shall make less desert than it is,
And yet no more, no more the sundering sea.

"Once she held in the hollow of her wave
The little, tossing missive boat you sent.
Days, nights, she had it in her power to whelm,
But paltered with its fate and let it pass.
Time to come then between us for all time!
The ship, light-riding, came and went again,
Empty of India's jewels, to its port
To find before it there da Gama's fame
And nought to match against his prize in hand
But truth that lit the yards like Elmo's fire.
And the old sea was less the sundering sea.
She has strewn wrecks since then and ships from port
She has hurled back ashore and banked with sand.
Too many have come with sails, to sink them all;
And now they trample flat the waves they run.
Ever the sea is less the sundering sea.

"But demon-like she hides her secret thought;
She veils her face in mist and folds her hands;
She murmurs 'What have I to do with men?'
What had she ever, space made palpable,
What but keep aching heart from heart too long,
What but keep life too long from half the world?
But she has said it, little has she left
Could she but hear the word we pass today—
Perhaps she hears in the green moated gloom,
Or feels like leaden touch thru all her cold,
Like sea-stones smitten feebly under sea,
Like bell-stroke deadened downward from the keel.

I deem she hears. Could she but comprehend
And say if I speak less than truth to thee:—
It needs not shipping to come safely thru,
Sister; it needs not ropes of iron more
To hold, or she will part me from thy word:
Thy softest word shall reach me thru her storm.
Sister, dominion has past from her brow—
Forget the sea, no more the sundering sea."

Date: early 1908. Length: 48 lines. Publication history: first published in *The Independent* (March 26, 1908), 676.

An A No. 1 Sundown

Frost taught at the Pinkerton Academy in Derry, New Hampshire, from 1906 to 1911. One day during this period, Sylvia Clark, another teacher at the academy, witnessed a wonderful sunset from the chapel window. Calling to Frost and the school librarian to share her enthusiasm, she found that their joy did not quite equal her own and she emphatically told them so. The next morning Frost presented her with "An A No. 1 Sundown." Written in pencil on a sheet of yellow school paper, it describes the "sunset party" and Clark's subsequent anger.

Date: 1906–1911. Length: 16 lines. Publication history: first published in Sylvia Clark's "Robert Frost: The Derry Years" in *The New Hampshire Troubadour* (November 1946), 15; reprinted in 142:569–570.

Slipshod Rhymes

In 1909, while Frost was a teacher at Pinkerton Academy, the football team won a victorious match (score: 6–0) against their fiercest rival, Sanborn Seminary. At a celebration a few nights after the match (see below: "A Kitchen in School"), Frost wrote on the blackboard what he called "Slipshod Rhymes." They had been composed during class hours when his students were given theme work to keep them out of mischief. Consisting of seven short poems (one separately titled "Our Motto"), they are enthusiastic cheers and lines of praise commending the football team and commemorating their victory.

Our Motto

Said Mr. Brice to Mr. Potter:
Let's take this for our motter,
We've gotter—simply gotter.—and we did.

Said Potter, Now by kinter
Yon machine is for bucking inter;
You can't stop now for a splinter,
You can dig that out next winter.

How those subs upon the Second
Felt when Brice and Glory beckoned,
Can scarce in rhyme be reckoned.

I'll say this for little Cale,
He's no easy man to nail,
When he runs before the gale.

Even with such heavy men as Mills,
Mears, Page, Curtis, Grant, McClure, Haslam,
Hodsdon, Bartlett, Bartlett and Graham,
We didn't pretend to out *weigh* 'em,
So we simply had to out *play* 'em.

In the days of Captain John,
Sanborn Sem had nothing on,
    Pinkerton! Pinkerton!
"As it is in history," remarked Mr. Frost.

With Mr. Silver as principal,
Of course it would have been indefensible,
Not to have proven invincible.

Date: fall 1909. Description: seven short poems from three to five lines. Publication history: first published in *The Pinkerton Critic* (December 1909), 4–5; four of the poems are reprinted in 142:358.

A Kitchen in School, or, Goings On at a Staid Old New Hampshire Academy

In the fall of 1909, the Pinkerton Academy football team scored a triumphant victory over their rivals from Sanborn Academy. Before the match,

Ernest Silver, the principal of Pinkerton, announced that if the Pinkerton team won, he would cook them a celebratory dinner in the school's new domestic-science kitchen, with members of the faculty serving the food. On November 18, the dinner took place. In a lecture entitled, "How Much Is in Books," Frost said, "You know they set up places now, little model kitchens, model homes [...]. They have done that in colleges, I guess. They brought one to the country academy where I was, and I wrote a poem about it—I had forgotten that!" [50:3].

They added a kitchen to our school
With a cooking teacher from Simmons
To teach the girls how to boil water by rule,
And with all the rest of the trimmin's:
A brand new stove with hot water front,
That our Aggies have to chop wood for,
Kettles for every cooking stunt,
A real wet sink with open plumbing,
A five foot shelf of cook books—what?
(How much am I offered right now for the lot?)
And they told us what it all stood for,
Proclaimed it the EDUCATION A-COMING.
But all we fellows with minds of our own,
Whose time is devoted to Latin and Greek
And French and Geometry, not to speak
Of football and baseball, were not to be shown—
We couldn't see what it was good for;
At least we couldn't till here last fall,
On the eve of our final game of ball
With a school whose scalp we especially seek,
And, if memory serves me, not in vain,
(You have heard of it, Sanborn of Kingston Plain)—
Our principal told the football team
If we would agree to win that game,
We could all come up to the new school kitchen
And he would promise to pitch in
And cook us a regular three course dinner,
And, supposing the old school wasn't a winner,
We could come if we wanted to just the same,
And have the dinner, but sans ice cream.
We looked at each other, for then we saw
How a kitchen might play an important part
In a school intended by nature and art
To fit boys and girls for college.

Our principal, though no professional cook,
Would have to get practical knowledge
Of dietetics by hook or by crook
To know if his teacher were teaching this right;
And for folks to develop his cookery on
(And here his cunning began to dawn)
He could tell us off into poison squads
And cook for us wholesale, by jinks, he might,
When we did or didn't deserve it.
It added new terrors to football play,
Ye Gods!
But terrors to us I need not say
Were only so many additional charms
That made us prance and curvet;
Though for fear of causing needless alarms,
We didn't run home the nearest way
To tell our mothers what made us gay.
We held our peace till the fateful day.
Nor was it so terrible when it came.
The guests were assembled too many to name,
With a plastered eye and a cheek-bone raw
And a twisted nose and an arm in a sling
And many a less apparent thing
Like a broken rib or ankle,—
With everything but a broken jaw
(Which would have been barred that night by law);
But having survived our fate thus far,
And victors over our dearest foe,
With never a thought to rankle.
The oyster stew began to flow.
(Of course you know what stewed oysters are,
Though you never have been to Simmons).
We knew the principal made the stew,
For the dining room was the kitchen, too,
And we saw him hovering over the brew
In its mighty blue enamelled dish,
With a grace we had thought was women's;
As sanitary as you could wish
With a red cotton night-cap on his head—
I *think* 'twas a night-cap and *think* it was red.
There were sausages, then, and potaters.
The linked sausages, long drawn out,
In solid garlands and fat festoons,

The kind of potatoes you read about.
There were knives and forks and dishes and spoons.
The faculty were the waiters.
And I doubt if the faculty ever sped
To bring on food as fast for the mind,
But then this food was a different kind,
That they'd reason to know we wanted.
Sausages, potatoes, and more behind,
The ice cream due us and candy.
We ate till, when in the end undaunted,
We rose to toast our honored principal,
Whose promised dinner had made us invincible,
Our legs were visibly bandy.
But as one of our number sagely said,
There were worse things than being overfed,
And where football claimed its scores of dead,
Eating sent one to his trundle bed.
Our mood was properly thankful.
We allowed that a kitchen did come in handy,
And as for cooks, well, Bridget and Mandy
Were not the only ones, not by a bankful.
And a boy, with inspired and inspiring looks
Got up and proposed that we burn our books
In the kitchen range and all turn cooks.
"Although," he said, "it is true, too true,
That women always surpass their brothers
(Or could if they really wanted to,
And didn't happen to marry)
In the very tasks men elect to pursue,
Farming, the law, and others,
We must not forget on the other hand
Men always have shown superior worth
In the special tasks for women planned;
Men make the best milliners on the earth
(Just look at them over in Paris),
Best cooks, dressmakers, and—mothers."
And because he wasn't making merry,
But sincerely desired to be culinary,
The powers that day and night keep watch
To mark and encourage and never scotch
Each aspiration and impulse good,
The sympathized and understood
And offered a cooking course for boys,

Wherein we might taste again the joys
Of the good old days when dolls were toys.

The poem, when published, contained two footnotes, the first following "a boy" (line 99): "Jerome Mears," and the second following "Paris" (line 112): "Pronounced Paree, with the accent on the first syllable."

Date: between November 1909 and May 1910. Description: 122 lines (variant rhyme scheme). Publication history: first published in *The Pinkerton Critic* (May 1910), 4–5.

The Mother Died

The narrator in this poem is a woman who died, presumably of puerperal fever after childbirth. She is amazed at the simplicity of death. People had told her that she would live but she did not. Her baby girl, Ella, has written to her about the family Christmas tree. The mother questions how a letter could get to her from earth or how her baby could write it. She wonders in closing if the thought of Ella's writing to her could be another comforting lie like the thought that she would get well.

Date: 1900–1911. Description: 10 lines in two five-line stanzas (rhyming xabba). Collection: unpublished manuscript in 160:Frost # 001700.

My Giving

The poet asks in "My Giving," finished shortly before Christmas 1911, for no merrier a Christmas than that which "the hungry bereft and cold shall know." All that the poet can give as a good Christian at Christmastide is to be "thirsty with them that thirsts, / Hungry with them that are hungry and accurst." He cannot ask of the poor that they share his gladness. It is the right of the underprivileged that he should be sad with them.

Date: December 1911. Length: 20 lines. Publication history: first printed in Lawrance Thompson, *Robert Frost: The Early Years, 1874–1915* (New York: Holt, Rinehart and Winston, 1966), 380; reprinted in 57:227.

Poems from *"Susan Hayes Ward from Robert Frost, Christmas, 1911"*

In 1911 Frost put together a manuscript collection of seventeen poems which he sent to Susan Hayes Ward. Ward and her brother, William Ward, ran the New York magazine *The Independent*, which published Frost's first published poem in a paying market, "My Butterfly." This manuscript collection, stitched into a blue heavy-paper wrapper, was sent at Christmas as a token of appreciation for all of Ward's interest in Frost, and as a "peace offering" for his having been "such a laggard in letter writing [...]" [66:43].

Of the seventeen poems, nine were eventually published during Frost's lifetime, one waiting thirty years before making it into print. Following is a complete list of poems in the manuscript. An asterisk (*) before a title indicates a poem published during Frost's lifetime; a dagger (†) before a title indicates a posthumously published poem.

*Death [i.e., "The Rabbit Hunter"]
*The Little Things of War [i.e., "Range Finding"]
*Determent [i.e., "October"]
†My Giving
New Grief
†On the Sale Of My Farm
*Pan Desponds [i.e., "Pan with Us"]
Pursuit of the Word
Pussy-Willow Time
The Rain Bath
*Reluctance
*To a Moth Seen in Winter
*To the Loud Southwester
†Tutelary Elves
*Unchastened [i.e., "In Neglect"]
*Wind and Window Flower
Winter Winds

New Grief

A broken-hearted lover wanders alone "like a holy nun" where two had walked before. The lover, a woman, cannot indicate when love may return or when it departed. The poem explains that love does not die easily since it is difficult for anyone to believe that anything one cherishes "Can ever quite pass into utter grief, / Or wholly perish." The final four lines of this poem were published separately as "[We Vainly Wrestle...]" in 1962 in *In the Clearing.*

Date: 1911. Description: 18 lines in three sextets (rhyming aabcbc). Collection: unpublished manuscript in 162:7237.

Pursuit of the Word

Using pairs such as "Two Cinderella slippers" or "Two prettiest souls" to describe love, this sonnet asks for a single word to express the different pairs. The closing sestet laments that there is no word "that leaves the vision less than double."

Date: 1911. Description: sonnet. Collection: unpublished manuscript in 162:7237.

Pussy-Willow Time

Some aspects of pussy-willow time are described in this sestet. These six lines may possibly be the closing sestet of an unfinished sonnet.

Date: 1911. Description: sestet (rhyming aabccb). Collection: unpublished manuscript in 162:7237.

The Rain Bath

A group of young boys in a camp are awakened by a rain storm in the forest when the rain reaches them in their beds from a nearby open window. Laughing, they open the door, wait until the sky turns darkest and run naked through the storm for a rain bath.

Date: 1911. Description: sonnet. Collection: unpublished manuscript in 162:7237.

Winter Winds

This poem describes winter winds at midnight. During this frightening time people must, even if they are safely housed, sleep deeply so as not to be woken. This poem exhibits a type of escapist philosophy which Frost expressed in such poems as "Into My Own" and "The Lockless Door." It also gives expression to his fear of storms which he wrote about in "Storm Fear."

Date: 1911. Description: 16 lines in four quatrains (rhyming abxb). Collection: unpublished manuscript in 162:7237.

On the Sale of My Farm

In 1900, the Frosts moved into the Derry, New Hampshire, farm. In November 1911, when it became legally theirs, Frost sold the farm. This closing of an important period in the Frosts' life together inspired Frost to write a poem for his wife entitled, "On the Sale of My Farm." In it Frost describes how he cheerfully yields to the new owners the orchard, field, house, barn and shed, which he can "unlearn to love," provided it is understood that it will not be considered a trespass if he were to come back again some day "seeking ache of memory here."

Date: November 1911. Length: 16 lines. Publication history: first printed in Lawrance Thompson, *Robert Frost: The Early Years, 1874–1915* (New York: Holt, Rinehart and Winston, 1966), 368.

Tutelary Elves
Forest Flowers

The 1911 "Tutelary Elves" explains that some flowers live close to people, while others live by the road to watch people pass by. Although they have as strong an interest in mankind, forest flowers belong to neither group. They insist that people must humble themselves and come to them. The poem was revised for publication in 1917 as "Forest Flowers" with some major textual variants and the dropping of the final couplet:

Some flowers take station close to where we stay,
And some draw up on either side the way
To watch us, horse and foot, go trooping by,
And take our dust when summer winds are dry.
With neither of these the forest flowers belong,
Whose love for us perhaps is no less strong
Because they will that whoso touches stem
Of theirs must leave the world and come to them.

With minor variants, "Tutelary Elves" resurfaced in 1947 when Frost inscribed it in a copy of *Steeple Bush*.

Date: "Tutelary Elves" 1911; "Forest Flowers" 1917. Description: "Tutelary Elves" is ten lines (rhyming couplets); "Forest Flowers" is eight lines (rhyming couplets). Publication history: "Tutelary Elves" first printed in

Lawrance Thompson, *Robert Frost: The Early Years, 1874–1915* (New York: Holt, Rinehart and Winston, 1966), 557–58. "Forest Flowers" first published in *The Pinkerton Annual* (1917); reprinted in 49.

The Lure of the West

In 1912 the Frosts were contemplating a major move to either Canada or England. Their friends, John and Margaret Bartlett, had recently moved to Vancouver and had described the opportunities available there. Frost responded to Bartlett's enthusiasm with "The Lure of the West," in which he expresses his own interest in a place where one could discover "a new kind of grizzly bear [...] in sight / Of a busy municipal square!" He then warns the Bartletts that if they continue to tout this newly-developing land, he will hop a train, provided they send him the fare.

Date: summer 1912. Length: 28 lines. Publication history: first printed in Margaret Bartlett Anderson, *Robert Frost and John Bartlett: The Record of a Friendship* (New York: Holt, Rinehart and Winston, 1963), 29–30.

In England

Possibly Frost's first poem written in England, it was sent to Sidney Cox with a letter dated December 26, 1912, from Beaconsfield. Beginning with an image of sadness ("Alone in rain I sat today"), the narrator refers to four objects: a gate, a bird, a watery breeze, and a hill. These land-locked images are transformed when the poet reveals that the gate on which he leans is a ship's railing, the bird is a sea-bird, the watery breeze is not rain but ocean spray, and the hill is a wave. These images remind the narrator that England is surrounded by seas from which the breezes blow fresh, and that the English country life "is never far from sailing."

Date: December 1912. Description: 20 lines. Publication history: first published in *Fifty Years of Robert Frost* (Hanover, N.H.: Dartmouth College Library, 1944), 15; reprinted in 142:395–396; 31:23; 156:26.

Good Relief

"Good Relief" was inspired by a Christmas shopping trip Frost took to High Wycombe, in December 1912, while living in England. The poem describes two young children of striking colliers looking in a toyshop window. When asked what toys they would choose if they could have anything they wanted, one child takes his finger out of his mouth and points at a toy train. "And where he wet the window pane it froze." The solemnity of the scene makes Frost ask "why like the poor fathers on the curb / Must we be always partizan and grim?" The last seven lines of the poem lament that there is no "perfect cure for grief / In law or gospel or in root or herb." This conclusion was inspired by Frost's memory of a doctor he once spoke with in his Derry days. The doctor said that the most one could claim for any root or herb was not a cure, but merely "good relief."

Date: December 1912. Description: 31 lines. Publication history: first published in Lesley Frost's anthology *Come Christmas* (New York: Coward-McCann, 1929), 4–5; reprinted in 142:430–431; 57:362–363.

Poems from *A Boy's Will* (1913)

When *A Boy's Will* was originally published in 1913 by David Nutt, it contained three poems which were excluded from Frost's *Collected Poems* in 1930: "Asking for Roses," "In Equal Sacrifice," and "Spoils of the Dead." In 1934 only "Asking for Roses" was recollected. The 1939 edition of the *Collected Poems* and all subsequent editions omitted all three poems.

Asking for Roses

A house that lacks, seemingly, mistress and master,
With doors that none but the wind ever closes,
Its floor all littered with glass and with plaster;
It stands in a garden of old-fashioned roses.

I pass by that way in the gloaming with Mary;
"I wonder," I say, "who the owner of those is."
"Oh, no one you know," she answers me airy,
"But one we must ask if we want any roses."

So we must join hands in the dew coming coldly
There in the hush of the wood that reposes,
And turn and go up to the open door boldly,

And knock to the echoes as beggars for roses.

"Pray, are you within there, Mistress Who-were-you?"
'Tis Mary that speaks and our errand discloses.
"Pray, are you within there? Bestir you, bestir you!
'Tis summer again; there's two come for roses.

"A word with you, that of the singer recalling—
Old Herrick: a saying that every maid knows is
A flower unplucked is but left to the falling,
And nothing is gained by not gathering roses."

We do not loosen our hands' intertwining
(Not caring so very much what she supposes),
There when she comes on us mistily shining
And grants us by silence the boon of her roses.

Date: prior to 1913. Description: 36 lines. Publication history: first published in the 1913 edition of *A Boy's Will*, 27–28, excluded from the 1930 edition, recollected in the 1934 edition and excluded from all other editions; reprinted in 46:53–54.

In Equal Sacrifice

Thus of old the Douglas did:
He left his land as he was bid
With royal heart of Robert the Bruce
In a golden case with a golden lid,

To carry the same to the Holy Land;
By which we see and understand
That that was the place to carry a heart
At loyalty and love's command,

And that was the case to carry it in.
The Douglas had not far to win
Before he came to the land of Spain,
Where long a holy war had been

Against the too-victorious Moor;
And there his courage could not endure
Not to strike a blow for God
Before he made his errand sure.

And ever it was intended so,
That a man for God should strike a blow,
No matter the heart he has in charge
For the Holy Land where hearts should go.

But when in battle the foe were met,
The Douglas found him sore beset,
With only strength of the fighting arm
For one more battle passage yet—

And that as vain to save the day
As bring his body safe away—
Only a signal deed to do
And a last sounding word to say.

The heart he wore in a golden chain
He swung and flung forth into the plain,
And followed it crying "Heart or death!"
And fighting over it perished fain.

So may another do of right,
Give a heart to the hopeless fight,
The more of right the more he loves;
So may another redouble might

For a few swift gleams of the angry brand,
Scorning greatly not to demand
In equal sacrifice with his
The heart he bore to the Holy Land.

Date: begun in early 1890s in Lawrence, Mass. [142:577], but probably not put in its final form until after 1911 or 1912 when an early draft entitled "A Heart in Charge" was sent to John Bartlett. Description: 40 lines. Publication history: first published in the 1913 edition of *A Boy's Will*, 44–46, but omitted from all subsequent editions; reprinted in 46:63–64. "A Heart in Charge" was first printed in Lawrance Thompson, *Robert Frost: The Early Years, 1874–1915* (New York: Holt, Rinehart and Winston, 1966), 577–78.

Spoils of the Dead

Two fairies it was
On a still summer day
Came forth in the woods
With the flowers to play.

The flowers they plucked
They cast on the ground
For others, and those
For still others they found.

Flower-guided it was
That they came as they ran
On something that lay
In the shape of a man.

The snow must have made
The feathery bed
When this one fell
On the sleep of the dead.

But the snow was gone
A long time ago,
And the body he wore
Nigh gone with the snow.

The fairies drew near
And keenly espied
A ring on his hand
And a chain at his side.

They knelt in the leaves
And eerily played
With the glittering things,
And were not afraid.

And when they went home
To hide in their burrow,
They took them along
To play with to-morrow.

When *you* came on death,
Did you not come flower-guided
Like the elves in the wood?
I remember that I did.

But I recognized death
With sorrow and dread,
And I hated and hate
The spoils of the dead.

Date: prior to 1913. Description: 40 lines. Publication history: first published in the 1913 edition of *A Boy's Will*, 50–51, but omitted from all subsequent editions; reprinted in 46:67–68; 142:558–59.

Fragment Written in England in 1914 or 13

This fragment, inscribed "For Katherine Cowles," describes in the first stanza the different kind of "foot-printer" the poet is in England as compared with back home in America: in England he leaves black footprints in mud; in America, white footprints in snow. The second stanza expresses his hesitation at going for walks when his companion does not wish to join him.

Date: 1913-1914. Description: 13 lines. Publication history: first printed as "A Remembrance" in 1974 in a limited edition of 500 copies (Amherst, Mass.: Friends of the Amherst College Library, 1974).

[Nothing ever so sincere...]

This quatrain appears in one of Frost's notebooks. It states that no matter how sincere someone is in the telling of something, it may be boring to hear about unless it comes from something mischievous or queer.

Date: 1912–1914? Length: quatrain. Publication history: first printed in William H. Pritchard's *Frost: A Literary Life Reconsidered* (New York: Oxford, 1984), 128.

Flower Guidance

This poem was found in an untitled pocket notebook which Frost kept from 1912 to 1915 while in England. The narrator is flower-guided, led "from flower to flower" until he is ultimately led to some picked flowers, lying dead. The poet purports that anyone who picks flowers, leaving them dead, will find themselves "In an evil hour."

Date: circa 1912–1915. Description: 10 lines. Publication history: first printed in Lawrance Thompson, *Robert Frost: The Early Years, 1874–1915* (New York: Holt, Rinehart and Winston, 1966), 584.

Poets Are Made Not Born

This poem was written during a time when Frost was becoming aware of how his poetic temperament differed from Ezra Pound's. Pound wanted to adopt Frost into his school of poetry. Despite Frost's refusal to be a disciple of Pound, he found himself feeling jealous over Pound's attention to the newly married imagist poets, Hilda Doolittle and Richard Aldington. Frost wrote this free verse parody in which he admits that his "nose is out of joint" because his "father-in-letters [...] Has been brought to bed of another poet" and has given birth to twins "prodigiously united in wedlock." The twins had written their first poems in free verse and sold them to Pound. Frost concludes that "it is a cinch that twins so well born will be able to sell almost anything they write."

Date: circa July 6, 1913. Description: 20 lines. Publication history: first printed in Lawrance Thompson, *Robert Frost: The Early Years, 1874–1915* (New York: Holt, Rinehart and Winston, 1966), 420; reprinted in 5:87.

[I am a Mede and Persian...]

Although Ezra Pound had done much for Frost in England, including reviewing *A Boy's Will*, Frost often felt that Pound was making too many demands. As he wrote to Thomas Mosher on July 17, 1913, "You will be amused to hear that Pound has taken to bullying me on the strength of what he did for me by his review in *Poetry*. [...] He says I must write something much more like *vers libre* or he will let me perish of neglect. He really threatens" [66:84]. Frost gave in to his anger by writing a parody of free verse. In this poem, Frost admits that he was afraid of Pound's power in the literary world.

> I was willing to take anything you said from you
> If I might be permitted to hug the illusion
> That you liked my poetry [...].

Frost was grateful, he writes, for Pound's review, although he suspects that Pound was less concerned with Frost's merits as a poet than with his own demonstration that he could "thrust anything upon the world [...]." All Frost wanted from Pound, he explained, was for Pound to consider him a poet.

Intending to send this poem to Pound, Frost first sent it to his friend F.S. Flint. Flint was able to convince Frost that although the poem would annoy Pound, Pound's "bark is much worse than his bite," and that even though Pound irritates, "we mustn't allow ourselves to be irritated, don't you think? Don't you feel it as a weakness?" [66:87]. The poem was never sent to Pound.

Date: circa July 20, 1913. Description: 46 lines. Publication history: first printed in *Selected Letters of Robert Frost*, edited by Lawrance Thompson (New York: Holt, Rinehart and Winston, 1964), 85–86; reprinted in 142: 421–423; 5:165–167.

[Hail First President of the...]

Amy Lowell was elected president of the New England Poetry Club in 1915. Unable to attend the May 18 meeting announcing the newly elected officers, Frost sent her a congratulatory five-line jingle on May 21. In a sly effort at praise—Frost did not like Lowell's work—he states that *if* he admired her poetry before, he would like it even more now that she has been so honored.

Date: May 1915. Description: 5 lines. Publication history: first printed in *Selected Letters of Robert Frost*, edited by Lawrance Thompson (New York: Holt, Rinehart and Winston, 1964), 175; reprinted in 143:529.

Any Sun

Inscribed into a copy of *Mountain Interval* shortly after its publication in 1916, this quatrain explains that even though we have no knowledge about what keeps the sun burning, it wouldn't be of any use to expect its burning out.

Date: 1916. Description: quatrain. Publication history: first printed in the *Dartmouth College Library Bulletin* (April 1988), 75.

[To voyses ah there, won is of the see...]

This couplet appeared in a letter to Louis Untermeyer, dated July 17, 1916, in which Frost wrote, "Well there may be seven arts; but there are only two voices" [151:39]. The poem contains some typically Frostian, humorous spellings.

Date: July 17, 1916. Description: couplet. Publication history: first printed in *Letters of Robert Frost to Louis Untermeyer* (New York: Holt, Rinehart and Winston, 1963), 39.

On Talk of Peace at This Time

Addressed to France during World War I, when there was talk of an early armistice, this sonnet urges the country to keep fighting. Even though Frost knows it is wrong of him to ask such a thing "as watcher from a quiet place apart...," he expresses his belief that the war should not end until what "might have been distorted / Is made secure for us and Hell is thwarted." Frost referred to the poem as "some impulsive lines" which "should have aged a little in my notebook before I ventured into public with them" when he inscribed them on December 6, 1916, in a copy of *Mountain Interval* [97:22]. The next day he sent another copy of the poem to Edward Thomas, whose unit was being shipped off to France [156:264]. This poem may have been influenced by Wordsworth's "Poems Dedicated to National Independence and Liberty," and "Sonnets Dedicated to Liberty and Order."

Date: early December 1916. Description: sonnet. Publication history: first printed in *Robert Frost 100*, 21; reprinted in 28:77; reprinted with minor variants as "Suggested by Talk of Peace at This Time" in *Poetry Wales* (vol. 22, no. 4, 1987) and 156:210.

One Favored Acorn

This poem opens with a reference to the millions of fallen acorns which end up as squirrel feed. They can find themselves carried far by a gale or plummeting straight down from the tree, or perhaps bounced down a hill. Some lay in heaps. Some, aided by autumn's dampness, have put out a slender root in a "toothlike gleam / which might have been a fuse [...]." All must perish unless the poet intervenes and chooses one which he might plant "to alter a village scene / And be of long regard." Whether he picks it with "faithfully shut / Or intelligently open eyes," the poet wishes to choose an acorn which would appreciate its having been chosen to live.

Date: late 1910s? Description: 30 lines. Publication history: first printed in David A. Sohn and Richard Tyre, *Frost: The Poet and His Poetry* (New York: Holt, 1967), 26–27; reprinted separately in booklet form (New York: Spiral Press, 1969).

[Winter has beaten summer in fright...]

This poem opens with the image of Winter having beaten Summer away, having found an open gate and no resistance. Summer has fled, first having hurried away the birds and the flowers. Summer's "royal fault," pride, was being punished, and Winter is going to sow salt in the ruined city. Throughout the poem Frost employs the male pronoun for the overpowering Winter and the female pronoun for the defeated Summer. This poem was given to Stark Young when both he and Frost and were young teachers at Amherst College. It was written into a first edition of Frost's *North of Boston* [94:39].

Date: circa 1917–1920. Description: 16 lines in four quatrains (rhyming xaxa). Collection: unpublished manuscript in 161.

The Seven Arts

In the spring of 1916 a group of young writers launched a new magazine, *The Seven Arts*, which was to have a cultural and national viewpoint rather than a socialistic or sociological one. On the advisory board were Frost, Louis Untermeyer, Van Wyck Brooks and others. *The Seven Arts* first published Frost's "The Bonfire" and "A Way Out." Although they attempted to keep politics out of it, the war could not be avoided. The magazine, offending the government and also its sponsors, ceased publication with its twelfth issue [151:35].

On November 3, 1917, Frost sent Untermeyer a short letter containing this limerick. Its purpose was to remind Untermeyer that when the magazine was first founded, Frost had warned him that there were six Arts. Punning on the name of Randolph Bourne—whose articles, many believed, sped up the magazine's demise—Frost ended with the statement that if you add politics to the six Arts, "the Seven will all die a-Bourneing."

Date: circa November 3, 1917. Description: limerick. Publication history: first printed in *Letters of Robert Frost to Louis Untermeyer* (New York: Holt, Rinehart and Winston, 1963), 60; reprinted in 143:113.

For Allan, Who Wanted to See How I Wrote a Poem

William Neilson, then president of Smith College, had a son, Allan, who showed an interest in how Frost wrote poetry. Shortly after Christmas 1917, Frost sent to the young boy the short poem "For Allan, Who Wanted to See How I Wrote a Poem," on a card that also held a sketch of a field and a grove of trees by Frost's daughter, Lesley.

The poet describes living on his farm among mountains on which grow a thousand Christmas trees [cf. "Christmas Trees"]. Frost writes that he would like to send Allan one of the trees but he cannot; he can only send such things as

A book, a useful knife, a toy,
Or even a rhyme like this by me
(I wrote it just like this you see). [57:308].

Date: circa Christmas 1917. Description: 11 lines. Publication history: first printed in Robert Frost, *Poetry and Prose*, edited by Edward Connery Lathem and Lawrance Thompson (New York: Holt, Rinehart and Winston, 1972), 308–9.

John L. Sullivan Enters Heaven

The poet Vachel Lindsay once suggested to Frost, Sara Teasdale and Louis Untermeyer that each of the four should write a poem on one theme and then collectively publish them in *Poetry*. The subject of the poem proposed by Lindsay was pugilist John L. Sullivan. Although the idea was joked away, Lindsay was serious, eventually writing the poem, "John L. Sullivan, the Strong Boy of Boston," dedicated "To Louis Untermeyer and Robert Frost." With a letter sent to Untermeyer dated February 18, 1918, Frost enclosed a parody of Lindsay's work, "John L. Sullivan Enters Heaven." A note under the title reads, "To be sung to the tune of 'Heaven Overarches You and Me'" [151:65; 150:139–143].

This narrative poem begins with Sullivan's arrival in the lowest level of Heaven "which is sometimes mistaken for the very highest Hell," the realm of "barkeeps, pugilists, jockeys, and gamblers [...]." The gatekeeper tells him that many "fighting characters" have been waiting for him to "see if they can lick you [...]." Among them is Hercules. Sullivan is told by the gatekeeper that the best way to win is to rush the fighters: he still weighs something while the longer occupants of Heaven weigh nothing. Sullivan rushes into Heaven. Devils watch through holes in the fences of Hell as he drives the "angels pell-mell."

Date: early 1918 (before February 18). Description: 42 lines. Publication history: first partially (*ll.* 1–24, 37–42) published in Louis Untermeyer's *From Another World* (New York: Harcourt, Brace, 1939), 141–42; the complete poem was printed in *Letters of Robert Frost to Louis Untermeyer* (New York: Holt, Rinehart and Winston, 1963), 65–66; reprinted in 5:167–168.

The Cow's in the Corn

This verse-play was based on Frost's observations while staying in the house of John and Mary Lynch in Bethlehem, New Hampshire. The Frosts had stayed with the Lynches in the summers of 1906 to 1908 and 1911 and February of 1915.

John Lynch was a voracious reader of newspapers and Mary Lynch had many stories about her inability to get his attention once he was absorbed in reading. Her favorite story forms the basis for Frost's poem: Mary tells her husband that their cow has got into the corn. Without lifting his eyes from the newspaper, he asks, "Who's corn's she in?" On his wife's replying that it was their own, he instructs her to drive the cow into someone else's corn.

Date: circa November 5, 1918 [120:201]. Description: 16 lines. Publication history: first published in *The Dearborn Independent* (June 18, 1927); reprinted during Frost's lifetime in limited edition booklet with the subtitle "A One-Act Play in Rhyme" (Gaylordsville, Conn.: Slide Mountain Press, 1929); reprinted in 142:566; 151:197–198; 5:164–165.

Fish-Leap Fall

To make it easier to catch water, the narrator has made a "fall" in the brook which runs on his farm. He notes that although it may be good for the people on the farm, it was not so for the fish because if the trout did not meet the fall just right, they would die on the grass. Despite the narrator's cavalier attitude toward one dead fish he finds ("if he didn't like the death, / He'd better not have been a trout."), the poem ends with his saving one landed trout by putting it back in the water beyond the fall.

Date: 1919 (before June 30). Description: 20 lines. Publication history: first printed in *Letters of Robert Frost to Louis Untermeyer* (New York: Holt, Rinehart and Winston, 1963), 90–91; reprinted in 143:50; 35:28.

On the Inflation of the Currency, 1919

This poem deals with the pain of inflation regardless of whether we feel it more intellectually or emotionally.

Date: 1919. Description: 8 lines. Publication history: first published in limited edition booklet (privately printed for Earle J. Bernheimer, 1948).

The Parlor Joke

Inspired by labor troubles in Lawrence, Massachusetts, during 1909 and 1910, this poem describes the creation of a modern industrial city, designed by the rich who filled it with immigrants from Ellis Island and then withdrew to their homes on the hill above the city. Feeling threatened by their creation, they

> [...] fortified their windows
> With a screen of potted plants,
> And armed themselves from somewhere
> With a manner and a glance.

It might have ended there in a "feeble parlor joke" but that the workers in the city had a vision: "Out of stench and steam and smoke, / Out of vapor of sweat and breathing" they saw a mass form, ready for rebellion. It spoke of "how you may pull the world down / If you know the prop to pull." The poem concludes with the narrator's exasperation at the "wisdom" which could invoke such a rebellious spirit, tempting the nation's well-being, just to "reduce the labor-rate!"

Date: between 1910 and 1920. Description: 78 lines. Publication history: first published in *A Miscellany of American Poetry 1920* (New York: Harcourt, Brace and Howe, 1920), 25–28; reprinted in 57:283–285.

A Correction

The narrator explains that his attempt to guess the temperature outside was made while he was dressing by the kitchen stove inside. His guess had to be adjusted after making a "sortie."

Date: winter 1920. Description: 8 lines. Publication history: first in David McCord's anthology *What Cheer* (New York: Coward-McCann, 1945); reprinted in 57:286.

The Return of the Pilgrims

In 1920, George P. Baker wrote and produced a pageant in celebration of the tercentenary of the Pilgrims' landing at Plymouth. Frost wrote "The Return of the Pilgrims" for this pageant, although at least two of the stanzas, the fourth and sixth, were written as early as the 1890s [3:77–78].

When landing weary from the narrow deck,
You stumbled up the rugged beach and fell,
Here still afraid of God, though safe from wreck,
You spoke a vow that was a prayer as well.
And first it was like fire in grass and trees,
Across the open, up a wooded slope;
And then like sunlight, over both of these—
A vow that was a prayer, that was a hope.

[Your hope of landing was your gift to men.
As freely of it as was yours to give
You gave it to us to be ours to hope again,
And hope forever to be free and live.]

[Your faith entrusted it to multitude,
To enter change, and not be lost
While races by new places were renewed
And by each other, overlapped and crossed.]

No ship at all that under sail or steam
Have gathered races to us more and more
But, Pilgrim-manned, the Mayflower in a dream
Has been their anxious convoy to the shore.

[When losers come around us like the dark
To lose us to ourselves in peace and war
By moving bounds or rubbing out a mark
Your help has helped us cling to what we are.]

Come in a Second Coming to the West,
Coming in a Second Coming to the land
Where once you left the print of feet impressed
As deep in rock as others have in sand.
Come seeing fresh again from wind and wave.
Say for us we have held the meaning fast;
We are good keepers of the gift you gave,
Confirm us keepers of it to the last.

Date: 1890s (*ll.* 17–20, 25–32) –1920. Description: 32 lines. Publication history: first in George P. Baker's *The Pilgrim Spirit* (Boston: Marshall Jones Co., 1921), 134–36. Frost excerpted one quatrain (*ll.* 17–20) and published it in *West-Running Brook* (1928) as "Immigrants."

[It would take a first class believer...]

A rhymed couplet, written between the two wars, referring to the need to be a "first class believer" to have any faith in what was being done in Geneva.

Date: circa 1920s–1930s. Description: couplet. Publication history: first printed in Elizabeth Shepley Sergeant, *The Trial by Existence* (New York: Holt, Rinehart and Winston, 1960), 389.

[To prayer I think I go...]

Three versions of Frost's poem beginning "To prayer I think I go" were sent to Louis Untermeyer over a twenty-year period. The first version was sent to Untermeyer on July 7, 1921, and the second, with minor variants, was sent on September 26, 1921. They deal with Frost's apparent reluctance to be religious. As he wrote in the July 7 letter, "I shouldn't wonder if my last end would be religious [...]" [151:131] and similarly in the September 26 letter, "I cannot make up my mind to go now where I must go sooner or later" [151:136]. The final version, sent twenty years later on January 14, 1942, expresses Frost's belief that he may approach religion at the end, as "an unconsoled / And utter loss" unless he is spoken to before it is too late. As he confesses in an accompanying letter, "I believe I am safely secular till the last go down [...]. I can't myself say how serious the crisis was and how near I came to giving in" [151:331].

Date: 1921–1942 (version I, July 7, 1921; version II, September 26, 1921; version III, January 14, 1942). Description: versions I and II, 9 lines; version III, 16 lines. Publication history: all three versions were first printed in *Letters of Robert Frost to Louis Untermeyer* (New York: Holt, Rinehart and Winston, 1963), 130–31, 136; 331, version III reprinted in 57:342.

The Nose Ring

On February 1, 1922, Frost sent to Louis Untermeyer "The Nose Ring," stating that the poem "is for you, not particularly for anyone else" [151:143]. This private poem expresses Frost's occasional indignation with honor, which is like a nose ring by which the poet is led, making his "sensitive nose more sensitive." The ring causes him to "wince" when he tries to use his nose as a plow to go "below the surface." In the final couplet the poet expresses his willingness to dispense with his honor if he could regain his ability to "get down again to the roots of things."

Lawrance Thompson assumed that the poem which Frost told Untermeyer was "for you, not particularly for anyone else" was about Untermeyer. Thompson interprets the poem as a "dramatic monologue, couplet-rhymed, which permitted the Untermeyer-like speaker in the poem to indulge some insinuatively erotic wordplay" about his [Untermeyer's] extramarital relationships [143:346]. Thompson failed to see Frost's statement as a simple reminder to his friend that his poem dealt with a particularly private feeling, Frost's occasional dismay with fame, which the poet did not wish to be made public.

Date: early 1922. Description: 9 lines. Publication history: first printed in *Letters of Robert Frost to Louis Untermeyer* (New York: Holt, Rinehart and Winston, 1963), 143; reprinted in 143:346.

Gone Astray

"Gone Astray," written in the first person, is the lament of a man who feels lost in a place not his own: "This field was not my field, / Nor was this town my town [...]." The opening imagery presages Frost's style in "Directive," in which he writes of "a farm that is no more a farm / And in a town that is no more a town." Here he finds himself weary of having to say who he is to have men treat him well. He concludes by realizing that he should have kept some place where he could have found rest for more than just his body. This poem expresses Frost's apparent exasperation with the way he was sometimes treated as a celebrity as compared with the more honest treatment he sometimes received when he was writing in neglect on the farm in Derry, New Hampshire. It continues the theme expressed in the closing couplet of "The Nose Ring," in which he writes, "But let me get down again to the roots of things / And I will dispense with my honor in rings."

Date: circa 1923. Description: 16 lines in four quatrains (axxa). Collection: unpublished manuscript in 165.

The Road That Lost Its Reason

This fragment describes a road in a wooded area which seems to have lost its reason for existing. It mentions such things as the maple and spruce trees which were not the road's reason. From these extant lines it is not possible to determine how Frost would have completed the poem.

Date: possibly written in the mid–1920s, based on Frost's handwriting [3:96] and the poem's thematic association with another fragment, "The Mountain Road," although it is attributed to the 1890s in 120:161. Description: fragment (10 lines). Publication history: first printed in *Robert Frost: A Descriptive Catalogue of Books and Manuscripts in the Clifton Waller Barrett Library, University of Virginia*, compiled by Joan St. C. Crane (Charlottesville: University Press of Virginia, 1974), 161.

The Mountain Road [So steep one bag made as heavy a load...]

A group of fragments, not necessarily related to each other, relate to many different Frost poems. The fragments are found on the verso of a manuscript of "A Minor Bird [circa 1924–1926]. These fragments, totalling 13 lines, were arranged by the collector Paul C. Richards, given the title "The Mountain Road" and printed in *Robert Frost Memorial Service: An Observance of the Poet's 101st Birthday*, a brochure for the service held at the First Parish Unitarian Church of East Bridgewater, Massachusetts, on March 23, 1975. Lines 3–7 of the manuscript (*ll.* 9–13 of the Richards' version) are a variant of "The Times Table" from *West-Running Brook*. Lines 8–13 (Richards' *ll.* 1–6) are thematically related to the fragment "The Road That Lost Its Reason." Line 12 (Richards' line 5) is a variant of line 46 of "Directive" from *Steeple Bush*.

Date: circa 1924–1926. Description: fragment (13 lines). Collection/publication history: unpublished manuscript in 164. "The Mountain Road" first printed in *Robert Frost Memorial Service: An Observance of the Poet's 101st Birthday* (East Bridgewater, Mass.: First Parish Unitarian Church, 1975).

[Oh thou that spinnest the wheel...]

On January 4, 1925, Frost sent to Leonidas Payne two versions of a parody of free verse beginning, "Oh thou that spinnest the wheel...." He prefaced the two versions with: "And yet speed is a thing I can see the beauty of and intend to write a poem in free verse on if ever I am tempted to write anything in free verse. Let's see how do you write the stuff [...]." They are followed by: "But I desist for want of knowing where to cut off my lines unhocuspocusly" [66:306].

Version I asks of "thou that spinnest the wheel" such speed in going from point A to point B that point A will not be forgotten at one's arrival at point B so that the two images, appearing simultaneously, will invite comparison and metaphor. Version II asks for such speed that curves which pull one from left to right unperceptibly may be felt.

Date: January 1925. Description: version I, 10 lines; version II, 11 lines. Publication history: first printed in *Selected Letters of Robert Frost*, edited by Lawrance Thompson (New York: Holt, Rinehart and Winston, 1964), 306.

The Pans

A voice bids the narrator to shut his eyes and hold out his hands, in which are to be placed the scale-pans of Justice. The narrator cringes, flinching from the duty entrusted to him, and the pans fall.

Date: circa 1926. Description: sonnet. Publication history: first printed in *Robert Frost: A Descriptive Catalogue of Books and Manuscripts in the Clifton Waller Barrett Library, University of Virginia*, compiled by Joan St. C. Crane (Charlottesville: University Press of Virginia, 1974), 167–168.

The Middletown Murder

Jack, a lumberman, returns home to his wife, Kate, from a journey which should have lasted a week. Gun in hand, he confronts her about his friend, Walt, who is inside the house with her. Walt makes a run for it out the back door and Jack shoots, purposefully missing the first four times, but shooting him through the heart with the fifth bullet. At the end, the sheriff comes to take Jack to jail, and Kate is left alone.

Frost uses a slightly less-refined language than is usually found in the poems he allowed to be published: "you goddam snide [...]. The joke's on me for trusting a whore [...] the galloping bastard." Obviously he was having fun with the poem, as shown in the couplet when Jack confronts Walt ("You have been my friend; you have eaten my salt; / But this was eating my sugar, Walt."); or when he describes Kate as hating "to be the death of two. / But what was a woman going to do?"; or the greatly understated concern after the murder, "But my, the sheriff would probably scold."

Frost referred to this ballad in a letter to his daughter Lesley as "my vindictive poem" [48:121].

Date: early–mid 1928. Description: 93 lines. Publication history: first published in *The Saturday Review of Literature* (October 13, 1928), 216; reprinted in 57:286–289.

[The fact sat tight...]

This short poem describes how "the fact" sat inside a rock while listening to our "foolish talk." The idea expressed would find its way into Frost's "The Secret Sits" a few years later.

Date: circa 1928. Description: quatrain (rhyming aabb). Collection: unpublished manuscript in 165.

[Lowes took the obvious position...]

During the summer of 1930 Frost attended a dinner party in Cambridge to celebrate the dedication of the Amy Lowell Poetry Room at Harvard's Widener Library. Present was John Livingston Lowes, author of a study of Coleridge, *The Road to Xanadu,* in which Lowes introduced the scientific method to literary criticism. During the course of Frost and Lowes' conversation, Lowes commented that poetry is all one texture of quotations that the poet writes out of all the books he has ever read; that it is the critic's job to come after the poet and trace his sources [143:381–382]. Frost took offense at such a remark because in 1919 William Heinemann hesitated to bring out an English edition of Frost's selected poems, largely because of what he considered Frost's unacknowledged borrowing from other poets [143:649]; Heinemann did, however, publish them in 1923.

Frost vented his anger at Lowes in this poem which begins, "Lowes took the obvious position / That all of art is recognition [...]." He defends himself by writing,

> A poet need make no apology
> Because his works are one anthology
> Of other poets best creations [...].

Frost refers to the play between the critics and poets as being like the game of Hare and Hounds.

Date: 1930. Description: 15 lines. Publication history: first printed in Lawrance Thompson, *Robert Frost: The Years of Triumph, 1915–1938* (New York: Holt, Rinehart and Winston, 1970), 382.

Trouble Rhyming

In 1930 Burgess Johnson, author of light verse, asked Louis Untermeyer and Frost to each write a sonnet with each line ending in words selected by Johnson. The lines should end preserving the order of the words: whole, sweet, greet, goal, roll, feet, neat, soul, sleep, pass, know, deep, alas, go. Frost sent his sonnet to Untermeyer on October 1, 1930. He completely burlesqued the idea of predetermined rhymes by his uncontrollable punning, such as using the mark of transposition on the "oa" of goal to make the British spelling of jail and using alas to mean a lass.

Date: circa September 1930. Description: sonnet. Publication history: first printed in *Letters of Robert Frost to Louis Untermeyer* (New York: Holt, Rinehart and Winston, 1963), 206.

[If all those stars...]

This poem expresses Frost's belief in the claim of astronomers that the stars are both vast and far away. The poem states in a simple way the fact that these two theories are mutually dependant on each other.

Date: sestet, post–1930; octet, post–1945. Description: two versions—one sestet, one octet. Publication history: sestet first printed in *Robert Frost: A Descriptive Catalogue of Books and Manuscripts in the Clifton Waller Barrett Library, University of Virginia*, compiled by Joan St. C. Crane (Charlottesville: University Press of Virginia, 1974), 44; octet first printed in *Robert Frost at Agnes Scott College* compiled by Edna Hanley Byers (Decatur, Ga.: McCain Library, Agnes Scott College, 1963), 4.

[The telescope has come...]

Knowing Frost's interest in astronomy, Louis Untermeyer sent him a telescope and tripod in 1931. On October 26, 1931, Frost sent his friend a rhymed letter thanking him for the gift. Frost could not help playfully stating in his letter that even with the help of such a glass, "I can't see Hoover as the Lord's anointed; / I can't see E.A. Robinson's last book." He concludes the letter with a playful echo of Shakespeare's Sonnet 29: "I had—I had the other fellow's scope. / I need nobody else's art, I hope."

Date: October 26, 1931. Description: 22 lines. Publication history: first printed in *Letters of Robert Frost to Louis Untermeyer* (New York: Holt, Rinehart and Winston, 1963), 215–16; reprinted in 57:309.

Let Congress See to It

In a letter postmarked August 22, 1932, Frost sent to Louis Untermeyer two quatrains about the Wright Brothers. The first, "The Biplane of Wilbur and Orville Wright" was collected as "The Wrights' Biplane" (which see) in *A Further Range*. The second, "Let Congress See to It," refers to Frost's belief that the Wrights had not been properly honored. Cf. "Kitty Hawk," *ll.* 64–65.

Date: August 1932. Description: quatrain. Publication history: first printed in *Letters of Robert Frost to Louis Untermeyer* (New York: Holt, Rinehart and Winston, 1963), 229.

The Offer

The narrator of "The Offer," out in a snowstorm, finds he must "narrow eyes and double night" to avoid the hard and dry flakes which "smite" him. He wants to know what more the flakes wish him to do beside blink. Is he to think that the flakes have been comparing themselves to him for years because they both might be considered "hard and dry"? Should he, or the flakes, or both melt? He concludes with the question, "If I supply the sorrow felt, / Will they supply the tears?" A similar image was later used in "The Wind and the Rain" in which the poet wrote, "Rain was the tears adopted by my eyes [...]."

While Frost was gathering poems for *A Further Range* in 1935, he asked Louis Untermeyer for a copy of this short poem which had been originally sent to Untermeyer on August 20, 1932. Frost referred to the poem as the one about "proposing to supply the sorrow felt if the storm will supply the tears" [151:265]. Frost ultimately decided not to include "The Offer" in *A Further Range* or in any later collection.

Date: 1932. Description: 10 lines. Publication history: first printed in *Letters of Robert Frost to Louis Untermeyer* (New York: Holt, Rinehart and Winston, 1963), 228; reprinted in 57:342; 35:29, 138:29.

[A man is as tall as his height...]

Frost met Thomas Hornsby Ferril in Denver in 1931 and developed a liking for the young poet. In 1932 Frost inscribed into Ferril's copy of Frost's *Collected Poems* this sestet of praise for the Denverite:

A man is as tall as his height
Plus the height of his home town.
I know a Denverite
Who measured from sea to crown
Is one mile five foot ten
And he swings a commensurate pen.

Date: 1932. Description: sestet. Publication history: first published in 1934 when used by Yale University Press to advertise Ferril's book of poetry, *Westering*; reprinted in 143:655.

A Restoration

This humorous poem was inspired by Robert Hillyer's *The Coming Forth by Day*, which was itself based on *The Book of the Dead*. A basic concept in Hillyer's book is that it was necessary to retain one's name to achieve immortality in ancient Egypt. Frost sent Hillyer "A Restoration" on September 28, 1932, in part as a note of thanks for Hillyer's defense of Frost in his essay "Robert Frost 'Lacks Power'" which appeared in the April 1932 issue of *The New England Quarterly*. "A Restoration" opens with Frost having lost his name and coming to the realization that without it he was "simply nobodee." He calls upon the gods, who cannot help him. So at last the "Ra Rah Rah King summoned Robert Hillyer" to help "restore" Frost's name, which Hillyer did. Frost concludes happily with an expression of gratitude: "Oh what a friend to have for my familiar."

Date: 1932. Description: 25 lines. Publication history: first printed in Robert Frost, *Poetry and Prose*, edited by Edward Connery Lathem and Lawrance Thompson (New York: Holt, Rinehart and Winston, 1972), 310–11; reprinted in 120:233–234.

A Little Kingdom

The king in this little kingdom has outlawed the mentioning of war or slaughter during times of peace, even if the danger were imminent.

He wanted his people
To love and increase
And be peaceful minded
In time of peace.

Date: circa 1932. Description: 24 lines. Publication history: first printed in *The Robert Frost Collection in The Watkinson Library*, compiled by Marian G.M. Clarke (Hartford: Watkinson Library, Trinity College, 1974), 23.

Winter Ownership

Reminiscent of the man in "Stopping by Woods on a Snowy Evening" who watches the "woods fill up with snow"—or Thoreau as "self-appointed inspector of snow-storms" [148:337]—the man in this poem has been inspecting the first snowfalls of winter for fifty years. He is out to assure himself of his "winter ownership" of land hidden by snow.

The snow falls with a "sandy hiss," recalling the "song [...] of hissing" the first snow makes in "The Onset." The man is "charged with both possessing and being possessed," a phrase which anticipates "The Gift Outright" in which Frost wrote of "Possessing what we still were unpossessed by, / Possessed by what we now no more possessed."

Date: 1934. Description: 24 lines. Publication history: first published in the *New York Herald Tribune Magazine* (March 4, 1934), 12; reprinted in 57:363–364.

Pride of Ancestry

Edward Morgan Lewis, president of the University of New Hampshire, asked the young poet Shirley Barker to send Frost a copy of her 1934 book, *The Dark Hills Under*, because of what he believed were similarities between the two poets. Frost was not impressed. One poem, "Portrait," Frost mistakenly interpreted as Barker's romantic and sentimental belief that she had received her poetic gifts through her descent from the illegitimate offspring of the ancestor described in her poem. Frost's "Pride of Ancestry" satirizes Barker's poem, describing a Deacon's wife who, being "a bit desirish [...] lay with one of the shanty Irish [...]." From this union the Deacon's child was conceived. The Deacon's wife knew the child was not really her husband's because with him she had "restricted her calisthenics / To the sterile arc of her lunar rhythm." A portrait of this woman inspires "a family of nobodies" to attribute to her "their genius and love of drink."

Date: circa August 1934–1937. Description: 24 lines. Publication history: first printed in Lawrance Thompson, *Robert Frost: The Years of Triumph, 1915–1938* (New York: Holt, Rinehart and Winston, 1970), 473; reprinted in 57:434.

[I only go...]

About a 1939 lecture at which Frost was to share the platform with other speakers, Frost said, "Not my kind of affair. I like a one-man show" [2:196]. Frost composed this couplet to express his preference for the "one-man show."

Date: circa 1935. Description: couplet. Publication history: first printed in Lawrance Thompson, *Robert Frost: The Years of Triumph, 1915–1938* (New York: Holt, Rinehart and Winston, 1970), 424.

[Unless I call it a pewter tray...]

The artist Charles J. Connick had designed a small medallion of Sandwich glass symbolizing Frost's "Stopping by Woods on a Snowy Evening." Frost wrote this short poem to thank Connick for his "stained glass wonder gift."

Date: 1936? Description: 11 lines. Publication history: first published in Charles J. Connick's *Adventures in Light and Color: An Introduction to the Stained Glass Craft* (New York: Random House, 1937), 92.

[Dear Leonard Bacon...]

Leonard Bacon published his *Rhyme and Punishment* in 1926 with a dedication to Robert Frost. Frost wrote Bacon a rhymed letter of thanks in January 1937. In it Frost uses the hyperdithyrambic meter of Ogden Nash, which he refers to as a "trick of rhyme without much obvious metre." After his opening thanks and a brief discussion of politics and religion, he closes with his acceptance of the fact that "there's nothing that we can do for the present except write poems and farm / And meet in some quiet place like Franconia for a talk next summer—that couldn't do any harm."

Date: January 24, 1937. Description: 30 lines. Publication history: first printed in *Selected Letters of Robert Frost,* edited by Lawrance Thompson (New York: Holt, Rinehart and Winston, 1964), 439–40; reprinted in 57:311–312.

Loyalty in a Time Like This

This incomplete poem describes a debate between a king, his vizier and a jester at a banquet. The vizier begins with a statement that loyalty might possibly be a different thing in the present time than it was in the past. The king goads the vizier to elaborate, who then explains nervously that he does not know who started the argument but that a person should not be considered "false-hearted" simply because he changes his mind. The king challenges, "Who is it now you are planning to forsake[?]" The jester interrupts with a joke about loyalty being something a man invokes to a woman whose passion is dwindling. The king again challenges the vizier to continue his argument who then explains that at certain times values change. At this point in the manuscript it becomes unclear who is speaking, but the basic declaration is that even in the present time they all agree that a crime is still a crime and that treason is still a crime against the king as in past times when talk against the king could lead a traitor straight to the block, without a trial. The poem breaks off at this point.

During a 1959 interview, Frost made the following statement, which has some bearing on this incomplete poem:

> I keep seeing articles by people who talk about "Loyalty in Times Like These." But loyalty doesn't change with the times. If you decide to be disloyal *for good and sufficient reasons*—perhaps because new loyalties demand it of you—you do so at your own risk. Past, present or future, disloyalty is always the same as far as the necessary group is concerned. Disloyalty is that for which your gang will take you out and shoot you if they catch you at it [18:54].

As he reiterated in "On Emerson," "Loyalty is that for the lack of which your gang will shoot you without benefit of trial by jury" [55:717].

Date: circa 1930s. Description: 64 lines in 16 quatrains (rhyming aabb). Collection/publication history: unpublished manuscript in 160:Frost #001885; a portion of the manuscript was printed in facsimile in 157:8.

On Tiring of Someone's Lines

This fragment deals with the conflict between nature, represented as "land," and machine, represented as "Chicago."

Date: circa 1940. Description: fragment, approximately 33 lines with variant rhyme scheme. Collection: unpublished manuscript in 160:Frost # 001888.

[I'd rather there had been no war at all...]

In August 1944, Frost found that his thirty-year friendship with Louis Untermeyer was in trouble. Untermeyer had joined the Office of War Information as senior editor of publications and was working with other writers against fascism. He tried to get Frost to participate in some way with the efforts to defeat Nazi Germany. Frost was one, however, who would not join causes, or write on demand. Despite his opposition to Hitler and his sympathy with the fate of European Jews, he held firmly to his separatist attitude. He would not write propaganda, no matter how important the cause.

Untermeyer was both outraged and hurt: outraged by Frost's determination to remain above the battle; hurt by his apparent indifference to the fate of Untermeyer's fellow Jews. As Untermeyer wrote,

> Although I knew that Robert refused to be drawn into anything political, I counted on his peculiar ordinariness, his combination of humanism and indignation, to help the war effort. [...]
>
> Perhaps I counted on Robert too much; it was a great grief to me when I found that he could not be counted on during the war. [...] I was offended when he insisted on staying "above the battle"; the issues involved seemed so catastrophic that they would prevent anyone from remaining aloof. I should have remembered how much Robert prided himself on being a "separatist," a disdainer of all parties and platitudes, especially the patriotic ones. I should have respected his private isolationism. When I forgot and urged him to do something, he wrote me a sad, intimate, rueful, and deeply touching letter-poem. [...]
>
> But until the war was over there was a coolness, a rift, that made us both unhappy [149:144–146].

The epistle begins with Frost dealing with what he believed was the central issue for Untermeyer: "the war is more or less / About the Jews and as such you believe / I ought to want to take some part in it." He explains that he is not fit to serve in the army and "hero at the rear I will not be." As he wrote during the first World War, in "On Talk of Peace at This Time":

> But God forbid that I should be more brave
> As watcher from a quiet place apart
> Than you are fighting in an open grave.

Frost writes of the good of paternal protectivism of the greater nations ("John Bull and we two other Bullies") over the smaller. He also deals with his never having thought of the Jewish people as a "race apart" but instead had treated them as a race "lost in ours": "And even the part that is a race apart / I sympathize with. Give them back I say / All Palestine. No race without a country / Can be a nation." In closing he pleads with Untermeyer to "come on off your cosmic politics." Their disagreements start Frost thinking about all the different kinds of friend he has found in Untermeyer and he feels he is in Untermeyer's debt "so far beyond my power / To pay I can but turn up now and then / And by acknowledging the debt renew it."

Date: August 12, 1944. Description: 184 lines. Publication history: first printed in *Letters of Robert Frost to Louis Untermeyer* (New York: Holt, Rinehart and Winston, 1963), 335–40.

Ten-Thirty A.M.

"Ten-Thirty A.M." describes a rainstorm which rages outside of the poet's house, but leaves the inside and its occupant unaffected.

Date: circa 1944. Description: sestet. Publication history: first printed in *Robert Frost: A Descriptive Catalogue of Books and Manuscripts in the Clifton Waller Barrett Library, University of Virginia*, compiled by Joan St. C. Crane (Charlottesville: University Press of Virginia, 1974), 183.

A Bed in the Barn

This sonnet describes a tramp who, given a bed of hay in a barn for the night, offers the owner his pipe and matches to keep things safe. The owner is treated to a lengthy boast: "a rigmarole / Of self respect to shame the soul [...]." He reaches the conclusion that a man should stay "Where other people can tell his praise" because "you're sadly apt to overdo / Your praise when wholly left to you."

Date: circa 1944–1947. Description: sonnet. Publication history: first printed in *Robert Frost: A Descriptive Catalogue of Books and Manuscripts in the Clifton Waller Barrett Library, University of Virginia*, compiled by Joan St. C. Crane (Charlottesville: University Press of Virginia, 1974), 188–89.

[High-brow, low-brow...]

This couplet was from a 1948 talk, "Speaking of Loyalty." It evolved from a questionnaire the poet had received from an editor asking him his opinion on the state of middle-brow literature in America. Never having heard the term "middle-brow" before, Frost said, "But right away I thought of a way to use it, not here but in verse, in writing" [57:408].

Date: 1948. Description: couplet. Publication history: first published in Frost's "Speaking of Loyalty" in the *Amherst Graduates' Quarterly* (August 1948); reprinted in 57:408.

[She had no brow but a mind of her own...]

This quatrain is an offhand opening for a poem Frost was contemplating writing. He said it was "about the girl Hanno and his sailors captured on the [...] coast of Africa, down the Gold Coast, outside the Gates. Its one of those old Polybius stories" [57:409].

Date: 1948. Description: quatrain. Publication history: first published in Frost's "Speaking of Loyalty" in the *Amherst Graduates' Quarterly* (August 1948); reprinted in 57:409.

[Aires Taurus...]

This quatrain was originally inscribed into a copy of Frost's 1949 *Complete Poems*. Only ten words in total, it has four signs of the Zodiac asking in chorus for "the answer."

Date: post–1949. Description: quatrain. Publication history: first printed in *Robert Frost: A Descriptive Catalogue of Books and Manuscripts in the Clifton Waller Barrett Library, University of Virginia*, compiled by Joan St. C. Crane (Charlottesville: University Press of Virginia, 1974), 93; a variant version was first published as *ll.* 36–39 of Frost's 1956 poem "Kitty Hawk."

[Life is a stream...]

This short poem describes life as a stream which, before it has travelled far, has been split apart on islands. It meets itself further on, estranged, yet having learned enough to see through all masks.

Date: 1940s? Description: 7 lines (rhyming abbaccc). Collection: unpublished manuscript in 160:Frost # 001896.

Tendencies Cancel

This fragment describes the process in which tendencies cancel themselves out by pairing and that these pairs collide in space to produce a sun. "That's where the one comes in," Frost wrote, and this "one" lets the action, presumably the action which creates life, begin. This idea of life beginning where opposite tendencies meet found expression as the central theme in Frost's "West-Running Brook." It may have stemmed from a statement Frost wrote in 1936; "A philosopher may worry about a tendency that, if run out to its logical conclusion, might ruin all; but he worries only till he can make out in the confusion the particular counter tendency that is going to collide with it to the cancellation of both" [19:xii]. This fragment is not to be confused with Frost's 1936 poem "Tendencies Cancel," collected as "Evil Tendencies Cancel," in *A Further Range.*

Date: circa 1940s? but possibly as early as 1920s. Description: 14 line fragment. Alternate title: "That's Where the One Comes In." Publication history: first in the Washington *Post* (March 27, 1947); reprinted in 144:388.

[Above yon ebon peak...]

A star-rise above a black mountain is giving off too weak a light to be considered dawn-like. An incomplete second stanza confirms that even this weak star-rise has its priests. The final quatrain explains that there is nothing we can as yet "do" to the stars and that any plan we may design would be nothing but an idle threat.

Date: 1940s? Description: 11 lines in three quatrains (rhyming abab) of which the second is incomplete. Collection: unpublished manuscript in 160:Frost # 001896.

Cocktail Bar in 45th Street

This poem opens with the narrator overhearing some "babble" in a bar where the people "sound as if they had the authority / To send one down to hell for being wrong." The narrator sits in a dark corner, sipping ginger-ale, wondering if they are aware of him. He comments that there are many things he can be sent to Hell for that he cannot be sent to jail for. He feels that if the people in the bar are going to judge and punish him, they should burn him for his heresies now while there is still flesh to burn, not wait till after his death when he is merely soul. How could these people know if he was wrong? "They'd just been to a play / About it all." They talked about the necessity of sinning more so as to have more about which to repent. One person thought you should sin fast and get it over with; another that you could sin until you were forty before you needed to bother about repentance.

The narrator wonders if he should speak up, but does not. It is closing time and the people are leaving. Before he leaves, the narrator decides to give his opinion to the bartender: Sin is not anything one commits, it comes of being born, when our first outcry calls selfishly for the attention someone else might better deserve. There is no way for man after birth but to be selfish. What one man has, someone else is kept from having. It is all the sin of selfishness.

Date: July 1952. Description: 98 lines (blank verse). Collection: unpublished manuscript in 160:Frost # 951490.

On the Question of an Old Man's Feelings

The Amherst poet Robert Francis published his poem "Apple Peeler" in 1953:

> Why the unbroken spiral, Virtuoso,
> Like a trick sonnet in one long, versatile sentence?
>
> Is it a pastime merely, this perfection,
> For an old man, sharp knife, long night, long winter?
>
> Or do your careful fingers move at the stir
> Of unadmitted immemorial magic?
>
> Solitaire. The ticking clock. The apple
> Turning, turning as the round earth turns [38:11].

Francis tells the following story about Frost's reaction to this poem:

> When he came to [...] "Apple Peeler," something remarkable happened. I was still sitting beside him. *Oh*, he exclaimed with a mischievous smile and looking round at me as if he had caught me in the act, *this poem*. At first I hadn't the faintest idea what he was getting at. But he kept smiling

> at me and making hints, and at last I caught on. He thought I was taking a dig at him in the poem, possibly that the whole poem was really about him. He supposed that his sonnet "The Silken Tent" was the only sonnet in one sentence in the English language. He suspected, therefore, that he was the "virtuoso" turning out "trick" poems after his real inspiration had been exhausted. What a thought! I hardly knew what to say to disabuse him. I didn't deny that I knew about his sonnet and that it might have been in my mind when writing the poem. But I insisted that I had not been thinking of him in particular, certainly not trying to disparage him, or that I had used the word "trick" in a disparaging sense even as applied to the actual apple peeler. I could see he was not entirely convinced. *Mr.Frost,* I said, *your poem "The Silken Tent" is as beautiful as anything you ever did, and there is no trick about it. As for sonnets in one sentence, David Morton does them all the time.*
>
> *He does, does he?* asked F with the trace of mischief in his smile. *Then that makes it all right* [37:37–38].

Around this time Frost wrote "On the Question of an Old Man's Feelings" about Francis; it begins:

> He found fault with an aging friend for reeling
> A sonnet off with skill for lack of feeling
> In one unbroken length like apple peeling.

Date: circa 1953. Description: 12 lines. Publication history: first printed in Lawrance Thompson and R.H. Winnick, *Robert Frost: The Later Years, 1938–1963* (New York: Holt, Rinehart and Winston, 1976), 206.

Poems from *A Remembrance Collection of New Poems*

In 1959 a celebration in honor of Frost's eighty-fifth birthday was held at the Waldorf-Astoria Hotel in New York. For it, Holt, Rinehart and Winston published a booklet of eight new poems in a limited edition of one hundred and fifty copies. Five of the poems were later collected in *In the Clearing*:

"The Preacher" as "[Forgive, O Lord...]"
"Lines Written in Dejection on the Eve of Great Success"
"The Sage" [as "From Iron"]
"The Astronomer" as "[But Outer Space...]"
"The Poet" as "[It Takes All Sorts...]"

Three poems ("The Prophet," "The Philosopher," and "Marx and Engels") remained uncollected.

The Prophet

Frost writes in this tercet of the difference between truth freeing one as opposed to truth enslaving one to the revelator. The enslavement may be, Frost sums up, just what one wants. In his 1959 essay "On Emerson," Frost wrote :

> Never mind how and where Emerson disabused me of my notion I may have been brought up to that the truth would make me free. My truth will bind you slave to me. [...] We may not want freedom [55:715].

Date: the first two lines were written at least as early as May 1936 when Frost inscribed them into a copy of *A Further Range* [39.3:149]. Description: tercet. Publication history: first published in Frost's *A Remembrance Collection of New Poems*; reprinted in 39.3:149.

The Philosopher

"The Philosopher" invites one to look through a telescope as far as possible to realize the "lavish waste it took / Of the sidereal principle" to create the "puny human race."

This quatrain was originally written as *ll.* 15–18 of an unpublished fragment, owned by the Dartmouth College Library, beginning "Returning to the figure of the pod [...]." The poem deals with waste and man's "tendency to squander." The excerpted quatrain forms the central idea about the amount of waste it takes for anything to be accomplished.

Date: 1950s? Description: quatrain. Publication history: first published in Frost's *A Remembrance Collection of New Poems.*

Marx and Engels

This poem discusses the role Karl Marx and Friedrich Engels played in wishing to "homogenize" mankind, and their dream of such a one as Stalin rising supreme. A version lacking the final tercet was read at Bread Loaf on

July 3, 1961. Frost called it a "terrible one" which "I'd never print but I'd say it confidentially" [25:182]. Frost had apparently forgotten that the poem had been published in 1959.

Date: 1950s? Description: 11 lines. Publication history: first published in Frost's *A Remembrance Collection of New Poems*; an eight line, untitled version was printed in 25:182.

[At eve the rain blurred windows...]

It is autumn and the narrator is looking at "rain-dimmed mountains" through "rain blurred windows." He observes that the only thing that keeps autumn from being winter is that it is raining, not snowing.

Date: circa 1950–1955. Description: 16 lines in four quatrains (rhyming abxb). Collection: unpublished manuscript in 160:Frost # 001979.

[You know what we do when we fear...]

The first quatrain of this poem asks: What do the narrator and his family do when a new snow spreads such a clean white sheet over the ground that it could not stay unmarked by prowlers? The second quatrain answers: they "rumple up the snow" by playing fox-and-geese, hoping to be unaware of the footprints of an intruder. This poem is based on Frost's lifelong fear of tramps and prowlers. This same fear formed the basis for his poems "The Fear," "House Fear," and "The Lockless Door."

Date: circa 1950–1955. Description: 8 lines in two quatrains (rhyming abab). Collection: unpublished manuscript in 160:Frost # 001979.

[For his desire was towards her...]

This seven-line poem is composed of one sentence. It describes a woman who is being desired by a man. His passion is so strong that the woman's thoughts are swept by them back to herself so that she sees herself through his eyes: as one mounted on a pedestal or a mountain. In a prose note following this poem, Frost questions whether a woman looks at a man. What she sees in her imagination is how the man sees her [160:Frost # 001729].

Date: circa 1950–1955. Description: 7 lines (blank verse). Collection: unpublished manuscript in 160:Frost # 001729.

The Couplet

The first quatrain of this poem explains that "bees are only go-betweens" bringing messages from flower to flower with pollen dust. Four different versions of the second quatrain exist in the same notebook. The premise is that the poet links, or couples, thoughts together, locking them with a rhyme.

Date: circa 1950–1955. Description: 8 lines in two quatrains (rhyming abba). Alternate title: "Matchmakers." Collection: unpublished manuscript in 160:Frost # 001979, Frost # 001894.

Let's Not Think

"Let's Not Think" is a poem which plays on the word "reflection." It describes small pools, formed by a rainstorm, which appear to be made for reflection. A drying west wind blurs them, keeping them from reflecting. The poet, addressing the wind, states that if it is "against the rules" to reflect, then he will also refrain from reflection.

Date: 1951? Length: 15 lines. Alternate title: "No Reflections" from variant manuscript in 160:Frost # 002323. Publication history: first published in the *Harvard Class of 1901, Twelfth Report, Fiftieth Anniversary, June 1951,* facing page 54.

Pares Continuas Fututiones

Harvard president James Bryant Conant's early research into oral contraception prompted Frost in September 1951 to write a limerick in which he states that even if we cannot keep the poor from copulating, we can at least keep them from conceiving. The title translates as "Preparations Bordering on Copulation." The limerick was originally sent in a letter to Louis Cohn in which Frost explains that

> Conant has undertaken [...] to make the planet less uncomfortably crowded with a new kind of manna (manna from Hell not Heaven, a religious friend Al Edwards calls it), a contraceptive to be taken at the mouth so we can stop breeding without having to stop futution. I made a five line poem on the event entitled '*Pares Continuas Fututiones*' (Catullus XXXII) [66:549].

Frost's reference to Catullus is to the only known use of the Latin word *fututiones*. In Catullus XXXII is found *sed domi maneas paresque nobis / novem continuas fututiones* (*ll.* 7–8), which translates as "but stay at home and have ready for me nine consecutive copulations" [16:38–39].

Date: September 1951. Description: limerick. Publication history: first printed in *Selected Letters of Robert Frost*, edited by Lawrance Thompson (New York: Holt, Rinehart and Winston, 1964), 549.

[Mary had a little lamb...] [Consider now the number ten...]

When Louis Untermeyer compiled his *Treasury of Ribaldry*, Frost, to show him that he not only was not "too pure to read it" but that "I could have given you material for it" [151:374], recited three ribald quatrains. The first, beginning "Mary had a little lamb," refers to Mary's lamb as Jesus, with God being the ram. The second recited a quatrain Untermeyer referred to as "not only blasphemous and bawdy but unprintable" [151:374]. The third, beginning "Consider now the number ten," says that the number of times 1 (man) goes into 0 (woman) can prove a man either a "laggard or a hero."

Date: in or prior to October 1957. Description: three quatrains. Publication history: first and third quatrains were first printed in *Letters of Robert Frost to Louis Untermeyer* (New York: Holt, Rinehart and Winston, 1963), 374; the second was never printed and may not be extant.

Poems from the Bryn Mawr Manuscript

On March 22, 1960, Kay Morrison, Frost's secretary, presented the Bryn Mawr College Library with a manuscript of Frost poems. The manuscript dates from the fifties: probably prior to 1958 when one poem, "[What're You Back Here For?...]," was recited; definitely prior to 1959, when some of the poems in the manuscript were published. The poems from this manuscript published during Frost's lifetime are:

"Peril of Hope"
"A Never Naught Song"
"[Forgive, O Lord...]"
"Lines Written in Dejection on the Eve of a Great Success"
"Version"
"A Reflex"
"The Milky Way Is a Cowpath"
"Quandary" (*ll.* 6-7)
"Kitty Hawk" (*ll.* 95–116)

The manuscript contains one posthumously published poem, "[What're You Back Here For?...]," and four unpublished poems:

"[No Matter How Straight Forth...]"
"Soldiers"
"[First Came the Rise of Heroes...]"
"[Thermometer Joe]"

[What're you back here for?...]

Frost's couplet tries to answer the question of why adults go back to school. The reason is that one returns to school if one went to school as a youth without any result. Frost said that he was "going to write more on education, but I got lost in the couplet" [103:360].

Date: circa 1950s. Description: couplet. Publication history: first printed in Louis Mertins, *Robert Frost, Life and Talks-Walking* (Norman: University of Oklahoma Press, 1965), 360.

[No matter how straight forth...]

This quatrain suggests that regardless of how forthright one's reasoning is, one always ends up looking back at where one has started from. People's reasoning is circular because of the shape of their brain pan. A variant of the same quatrain beginning "The reason why you think you're getting on [...]" appears in the same manuscript. Thematically this poem is related to *ll.* 201–2 of "Build Soil."

Date: 1950s. Description: quatrain (rhyming abab). Collection: unpublished manuscript in 159.

Soldiers

Two types of peace-keepers are described in this quatrain: the soldiers who make peace during wartime and the policemen who make peace during peacetime. Soldiers fight anytime, but policemen are found to be most active at night.

Date: 1950s. Description: quatrain (rhyming aabb). Collection: unpublished manuscript in 159.

[First come the rise of heroes...]

Different historical periods are traced in this poem: first when heroes founded kingdoms; next when the "ascendancy of Number One" was handed down from son to son; then came the period when the ruling scepter was a sword; until at last the middle class rose to the summit of power, when there has never been such a diffusion of rights.

Date: 1950s. Description: 12 lines in four tercets. Collection: unpublished manuscript in 159.

[Thermometer Joe]

Thermometer Joe was a man who liked to watch his thermometer drop. The coldest period he ever recorded was minus 63 degrees. His biggest boast was the night in Franconia, New Hampshire, when the bottom blew out of his thermometer.

Date: Frost dated this one as "very very old." Description: 7 lines (rhyming aaaabbb). Collection: unpublished manuscript in 159.

Entree

This sestet, which has strongly bawdy overtones, is an amusing boast to a new acquaintance.

Date: circa 1950s? Description: sestet (rhyming aabbcc). Collection: unpublished manuscript in 160.

[For travelers going sidereal...]

This limerick was added at the page-proof stage of *In the Clearing* in 1962, but deleted before publication. It plays on the "bacterial" dangers of going "sidereal."

Date: circa 1950–1955. Description: limerick. Publication history: first printed in 57:434.

A Poem About the Lemming

In this limerick Frost admits that it is "not much to quote" but he had written it to pay a debt to Mr. Flemming.

Date: circa 1950–1955. Description: limerick. Collection: unpublished manuscript in 160:Frost # 001728.

[At least it's a sort of a feeler...]

This limerick is about the nonpayment of debts.

Date: circa 1950–1955. Description: limerick. Collection: unpublished manuscript in 160:Frost # 001728.

Old Gold for Christmas

This incomplete narrative poem begins with the narrator's meeting an elderly man named Rice on the street at night. Rice has just slipped on the ice and asks to be allowed to lean on the narrator for a minute until he can get his thoughts straight. Rice then explains that he needs to get home, if the narrator is willing to take him there. He needs to think of what he will tell his daughter-in-law who will have been waiting up. The narrator must think of what he will do with the man. Feeling he was doing Rice some good just to let him lean on him, he has not forced Rice to let go. They go to the house of Rice's friend, where his son is called to bring him home.

Rice's story, pieced together during the poem, is as follows: He was known as the Gold for Christmas Man because the company where he had stoked the furnace for forty years paid him in gold the week of Christmas. He was paid twenty dollars each year. His wife wanted him to stand up for himself and demand more money. She brought up their children to the idea that their father had robbed them of what he did not earn, depriving them because he would not demand more. Rice could not ask for more because he felt that there is one art to work, another art to getting compensated for it. He would not ask for a raise because it involved self-praise, which was a poor substitute for the praise of others. If he was worthy of more pay it was not for him to say so. A similar commentary on self-praise occurs in Frost's "A Bed in the Barn," in which he states that "you're sadly apt to overdo / Your praise when wholly left to you."

Date: circa 1950s? Description: three versions exist, somewhat fragmented, between 100 and 200 lines. Alternate title: Gold for Christmas. Collection: unpublished manuscript in two unpublished manuscripts in 160:Frost # 001275; one unpublished manuscript in Agnes Scott College [122:64].

[Unless I get as nuclear...]

Originally delivered at the Cambridge School Commencement in June, 1955, this quatrain was written down at the request of someone present. In it, Frost says he won't be "pushed off this star" even though he has not become as "nuclear" as everyone else is.

Date: June 1955. Description: quatrain (rhyming aaaa). Collection: unpublished manuscript in 164.

[It was nothing to nothing...]

In 1956 Frost was invited to write a piece for *Sports Illustrated* on one of his favorite sports, baseball. In the essay, "A Perfect Day—A Day of Prowess," Frost mentions one of his "unfulfilled promises"—to write "an epic poem some day about a ball batted so hard by Babe Ruth that it never came back, but got to going round and round the world like a satellite" [67:89]. Frost then offered this introductory couplet to the unwritten poem.

Date: 1956. Description: couplet. Publication history: first published in Frost's "Perfect Day—A Day of Prowess" in *Sports Illustrated* (July 23, 1956); reprinted in 67:89.

[People keep saying...]

This untitled quatrain states that although people keep saying it is not a good idea to learn things by heart, it is sometimes nice to have some "pretty things," such as poems, in your head.

Date: 1959. Description: quatrain. Publication history: first published in *Look* (March 31, 1959); reprinted the same year on the dust jacket for Frost's *You Come Too* (New York: Henry Holt and Co., 1959); reprinted in 120:102.

[The purpose of the universal plan...]

In this couplet Frost plays with the idea that the design or plan of the universe leaves room for smaller plans made by man.

Date: circa 1961. Description: couplet. Publication history: first published in Frost's "Remarks on the Occasion of the Tagore Centenary" in *Poetry* (November 1961).

Homology

This unfinished poem, originally planned for *In the Clearing*, discusses the homological relationship between infants and adults. This communication in which eye corresponds to eye, smile corresponds to smile, shows that it is not so much what we say as how we say it that is of significance. Frost first wrote of this correspondence in his introduction to Edwin Arlington Robinson's *King Jasper*: "We began in infancy by establishing correspondence of eyes with eyes. We recognized that they were the same feature and we could do the same things with them. We went on to the visible motion of the lips—smile answered smile [...]" [129:vi]. It was also touched upon in "All Revelation" (*ℓ* 16).

Date: circa 1962. Description: 40 lines, variant rhyme scheme. Collection: unpublished manuscript in 160:Frost # 002311.

[Up here where late I face the end...]

The poet is writing from the vantage point of the end of a long life, "Up here where late I face the end / A broken will [...]." No longer a farmer or breeder of dairy cows—one who represses nature into controlled forms—he tends a wild garden now. Even though there are some who want to have their say in the world's outcome, by controlling nature, the poet admonishes: "respect the variant / And let the force of nature vary." The draft manuscript of this poem is written below a prose variant of Frost's dedication to *In the Clearing*. The poem itself may have been intended as a dedicatory poem to his final volume.

Date: circa 1962. Description: 16 lines in four quatrains (rhyming abab). Collection: unpublished manuscript in 160:Frost # 001980.

The Prophets Really Prophesy as Mystics, The Commentators Merely by Statistics

This was the last poem Frost was to complete and publish. It deals with science's attempt to break the "Divine Safe's combination lock." Yet this "Promethean defiance" is still defied. Tired of the "routine and monotony" we experience on earth, what does all this scientific knowledge avail us if Earth cannot break out of its orbit and go for a ride through space? The difficulty mankind faces is whether to "seek a scientific sky / Or wait and go to Heaven when they die [...]." The poem concludes with Frost's expressing his belief that our world is such a "charming earnest world" that "It seems too bad to steer it off by force."

Date: 1962. Description: 36 lines. Publication history: first published in *Poetry* (October/November 1962); reprinted during Frost's lifetime as his 1962 Christmas poem; reprinted in *Life* (February 8, 1963), 46, as "His Last Poem"; 57:460–461; 144:339–340.

[The King said to his court...]

Frost dictated these fragments to Anne Morrison Gentry about a week before his death. Incomplete, with lines of varying length, this final effort opens with a king summoning prophets not only to interpret a dream, but to actually tell what the dream was without hearing it. The prophets plead that they cannot both tell and interpret the dream. The king dismisses them as "common commentators [...] false mystics" and orders their execution. The king is left alone with his dream. A "wastrel" appears who the king challenges to tell the dream. The final two lines of the main fragment are given in quotation marks as if spoken by the king. Within the context of the poem, the lines must be split between the two characters: the first part being the king's challenge ("If you're a prophet not just a commentator on the news") and the second line being the vagabond's response ("You dream the only dream there is to dream.") Further notes made by Anne Gentry from Frost's discussion about the direction he wanted the poem to take explain that the "only dream" compares the difference "between mercy and discipline—like Christ who died for it." They also indicate that the king proclaims the vagabond a real prophet. The prophet's name is Daniel [144:442].

Date: January 1963. Description: approximately 20 lines. Publication history: first printed in Lawrance Thompson and R.H. Winnick, *Robert Frost: The Later Years, 1938–1963* (New York: Holt, Rinehart and Winston, 1976), 341.

"[I met you on a cloudy...]"

First published ten years after Frost's death, this short poem is written to Janet Forbes, a nurse who substituted for two days as Frost's private nurse at the Peter Bent Brigham Hospital in January 1963. On her second and last day, according to Forbes, "Mr. Frost asked for a scrap of paper, borrowed my pen and wrote down a few words and then gave it to me. I didn't realize what he was writing until I left the room" [*The Brigham Bulletin* (September 1973) 8]. The second stanza is a variation of Frost's "Dust of Snow."

Date: January 9, 1963. Description: 10 lines, unrhymed. Publication history: first published in the *Boston Herald American* (September 29, 1973), 3; reprinted in *The Brigham Bulletin* (September 1973), 8.

APPENDIX: SPURIOUS AND DOUBTFUL POEMS

Dream-Land
Down the Brook—And Back
Parting

Three poems were published in 1891 in the *Lawrence High School Bulletin*: "Dream-Land" in April, and "Down the Brook—And Back" and "Parting" in December. They have been attributed to Frost by Lawrance Thompson in 142:506, 510–11, although Thompson did not attribute them to Frost when he coedited 121 with Edward Connery Lathem. The poems did not carry Frost's name or initials when published in the *Bulletin* and have not been acknowledged by Frost. These three poems were not listed in *Robert Frost: A Bibliography* by W.B. Shubrick Clymer and Charles R. Green (Amherst, Mass.: Jones Library, 1937), which does list other contributions to the *High School Bulletin*.

Although there is no corroborating evidence, it is possible to assign both "Down the Brook—And Back" and "Parting" to Frost based on his claim that, as editor of the *High School Bulletin*, having received little or no copy for the December 1891 issue, he "got mad. And I went down to the printer's office, and in the little cubby hole down there I wrote the whole number. I wrote a story; I wrote an essay; I wrote editorials; I wrote a poem—the poem, even then" [121:16]. "Parting" had no attribution, but "Down the Brook—And Back" was signed Amnessel, an anagram for Nameless. If this nameless poet was Frost, then by association the poem "Dream-Land," which was also signed Amnessel in the April 1891 issue, was his.

All three poems were published in the *Lawrence High School Bulletin*.

"Down the Brook—And Back" is reprinted in 46:27 and 121:69. "Parting" is reprinted in 46:28; 142:116; and 121:71.

I Had a Love Once
Sea Dream

Lawrance Thompson attributed both these poems to Frost, dating them in the mid-nineties. Frost repudiated them in a letter to Robert Newdick on December 28, 1937, stating, "It is of course preposterous to ascribe either 'Sea Dream' or 'I Had a Love Once' to me. They are not in my handwriting, they are not in my wife's handwriting, I didn't sign them, she didn't sign them and I deny having written them" [110:160]. In the spring of 1975, Frost's daughter Lesley, at the request of Andrew Angyal, examined photoreproductions of both manuscripts and felt certain that the handwriting was neither her father's nor her mother's [3:96]. Both poems were printed by Thompson in 142:531.

Corn Stalks

An unidentified poem, possibly titled "Corn Stalks," is mentioned in the research findings of Robert Newdick. The first reference is in his notes for August 30, 1935: "Also Corn Stalks about 1900, in a place where he [Frost] forgets," followed by a corrected date of "1891!" [110:271]. A second reference appears in his notes for October 1938: "Poem about corn shocks or shooks in Bost. Transcript about Christmas time, 1891 or 1892" [110:374]. Newdick attempted to locate the poem by searching the September, November and December issues of the *Boston Transcript* for the years 1891 and 1892 and, on reporting his lack of success to Frost, the poet recollected that "The corn shocks poem was in a Lawrence paper of late '91" [110:123]. This poem, if it really existed and was not simply a misremembering on Frost's part, has not yet been found.

Date: 1890s? Length: unknown. Publication history: unknown.

Young Sure and Twenty

Frost recalled this undiscovered poem in a 1951 letter to Louis Untermeyer when he wrote, "I remember years ago trying to laugh off the annoyance college boys gave me in a piece of blank verse I sent you and you didn't quite like called 'Young Sure and Twenty'" [151:366].

Date: unknown. Length: unknown (blank verse). Publication history: unpublished.

BIBLIOGRAPHY

1. *American Poetry: The Nineteenth Century* (New York: Library of America, 1994).

2. Anderson, Margaret Bartlett. *Robert Frost and John Bartlett: The Record of a Friendship* (New York: Holt, Rinehart and Winston, 1963).

3. Angyal, Andrew J. "Robert Frost's Poetry Before 1913, A Checklist" (*Proof 5, The Yearbook of American Bibliographical and Textual Studies,* 1977).

4. *The Ballad Book: A Selection of the Choicest British Ballads,* edited by William Allingham (Freeport, N.Y.: Books for Libraries Press, 1969).

5. Barry, Elaine. *Robert Frost on Writing* (New Brunswick, N.J.: Rutgers University Press, 1973).

6. Basler, Roy P. "Yankee Vergil—Robert Frost in Washington" (*Voyages,* spring 1969).

7. Beddoes, Thomas Lovell. *Selected Poems,* edited by Judith Higgens (Manchester, England: Fyfield Books/Carcanet Press, 1976).

8. *Bread Loaf Anthology* (Middlebury, Vt.: Middlebury College Press, 1939).

9. Brooks, Cleanth, and Robert Penn Warren. *Understanding Poetry* (New York: Holt, Rinehart and Winston, 1976).

10. Brower, Reuben. *The Poetry of Robert Frost: Constellations of Intention* (New York: Oxford University Press, 1963).

11. Browning, Robert. *The Poetical Works of Robert Browning* (Boston: Houghton Mifflin, 1974).

12. Bunyan, John. *Grace Abounding to the Chief of Sinners, and, The Pilgrim's Progress from This World to That Which Is to Come,* edited with an introduction by Roger Sharrock (London: Oxford University Press, 1966).

13. Burnshaw, Stanley. *Robert Frost Himself* (New York: G. Braziller, 1986).

14. Burroughs, John. *Accepting the Universe: Essays in Naturalism* (Boston: Houghton Mifflin, 1920).

15. ____. *The Gospel of Nature* (Chester, Conn.: Applewood Books, n.d.].

16. *Catullus, Tibullus, Pervigilium Veneris* (Cambridge, Mass.: Harvard University Press, 1988).

17. Chaucer, Geoffrey. *The Complete Poetry and Prose of Geoffrey Chaucer,* edited by John H. Fisher (New York: Holt, Rinehart and Winston, 1989).

18. Ciardi, John. "Robert Frost: Master Conversationalist at Work" (*Saturday Review*, March 21, 1959).

19. Cleghorn, Sarah N. *Threescore: The Autobiography of Sarah N. Cleghorn*, with an introduction by Robert Frost (New York: Harrison Smith & Robert Haas, 1936).

20. Clemens, Cyril. *A Chat with Robert Frost* (Webster Groves, Mo.: International Mark Twain Society, 1940).

21. *Come Christmas: A Selection of Christmas Poetry, Song, Drama and Prose*, edited by Lesley Frost (New York: Coward-McCann, 1929).

22. Connick, Charles J. *Adventures in Light and Color: An Introduction to the Stained Glass Craft* (New York: Random House, 1937).

23. Cook, Reginald L. *The Dimension of Robert Frost* (New York: New York: Rinehart, 1958).

24. ____. "Frost on Frost: The Making of Poems" (*American Literature*, March 1956).

25. ____. *Robert Frost: A Living Voice* (Amherst: University of Massachusetts Press, 1974).

26. ____. "Robert Frost's Asides on his Poetry" (*American Literature*, January 1948).

27. Cox, Sidney. *A Swinger of Birches* (New York: Collier Books, 1961).

28. Cronenwett, Philip N. "Frost Drafts Inscribed in Presentation Volumes" (*Dartmouth College Library Bulletin*, April 1988).

29. Dante Alighieri. *The Divine Comedy; The John Ciardi Translation* (New York: Norton, 1977).

30. Emerson, Ralph Waldo. *Essays and Lectures* (New York: Literary Classics of the United States, 1983).

31. Evans, William R. *Robert Frost and Sidney Cox: Forty Years of Friendship* (Hanover, N.H.: University Press of New England, 1981).

32. Fabre, J. Henri. *The Hunting Wasps* (New York: Dodd, Mead, 1915).

33. Feld, Rose C. "Robert Frost Relieves His Mind" (*New York Times Book Review*, October 21, 1923).

34. *Fifty Poets: An American Auto-anthology*, edited by William Rose Benet (New York: Duffield and Green, 1933).

35. *Fifty Years of Robert Frost: A Catalogue of the Exhibition Held in Baker Library in the Autumn of 1943*, edited by Ray Nash (Hanover, N.H.: Dartmouth College Library, 1944).

36. Francis, Lesley Lee. *The Frost Family's Adventure in Poetry: Sheer Morning Gladness at the Brim* (Columbia: University of Missouri Press, 1994).

37. Francis, Robert. *Frost—A Time to Talk: Conversations & Indiscretions*, recorded by Robert Francis (Amherst: University of Massachusetts Press, 1972).

38. ____. *The Orb Weaver* (Middletown, Conn.: Wesleyan University Press, 1960).

39. *Frost: Centennial Essays*, compiled by the Committee on the Frost Centennial of the University of Southern Mississippi (Jackson: University Press of Mississippi, 1974–1978).

40. Frost, Lesley. *New Hampshire's Child: The Derry Journals of Lesley Frost*, with notes and index by Lawrance Thompson and Arnold Grade (Albany: State University of New York Press, 1969).

41. Frost, Robert. "Address of Robert Frost to the Conference on the Poet and Reality, October 7, 1950—Kenyon College" (unpublished typescript in Amherst College Library).

42. ____. *Aforesaid* (New York: Henry Holt, 1954).

43. ____. "Before the Beginning and After the End of a Poem" (*Carrell* 6, 1965).

44. ____. "Between Prose and Verse" (*Atlantic Monthly,* January 1962).

45. ____. "The Constant Symbol" (*Atlantic Monthly,* October 1946).

46. ____. *Early Poems* (New York: Avenel Books, 1981).

47. ——. "Education by Poetry" (*Amherst Graduates' Quarterly*, February 1931).

48. ____. *Family Letters of Robert and Elinor Frost*, edited by Arnold Grade (Albany: State University of New York Press, 1972).

49. ____. *Forest Flowers, An Early Poem Recovered* (Amherst, Mass.: Friends of the Amherst College Library, 1978).

50. ____. "How Much Is in Books[?]" (unpublished typescript in Amherst College Library).

51. ____. *Interviews with Robert Frost,* edited by Edward Connery Lathem (New York: Holt, Rinehart and Winston, 1966).

52. ____. "'Last' Frost Poem Turns Up in Hub" (*Boston Herald American*, September 29, 1973).

53. ____. "Letter to *The Amherst Student*" (*The Amherst Student*, March 25, 1935).

54. ____. *A Masque of Reason* (London: Jonathan Cape, 1948).

55. ____. "On Emerson" (*Daedalus,* fall 1959).

56. ____. "Playful Talk" (*Proceedings of the American Academy of Arts and Letters and the National Institute of Arts and Letters*, 1962).

57. ____. *Poetry and Prose*, edited by Edward Connery Lathem and Lawrance Thompson (New York: Holt, Rinehart and Winston, 1972).

58. ____. "Poetry and School" (*Atlantic Monthly*, June 1951).

59. ____. *The Poetry of Robert Frost*, edited by Edward Connery Lathem (New York: Holt, Rinehart and Winston, 1969).

60. ____. "Poverty and Rural Life: An Interview with Robert Frost" (*Rural America*, June 1931).

61. ____. *Prose Jottings of Robert Frost: Selections from His Notebooks and Miscellaneous Manuscripts*, edited by Edward Connery Lathem and Hyde Cox (Lunenburg, Vt.: Northeast-Kingdom Publishers, 1982).

62. ____. "[Remarks of Robert Frost Dedication of Chalmers Library, October 28, 1962]" (Kenyon College, *Alumni Bulletin,* January-March 1963).

63. ____. "Remarks on the Occasion of the Tagore Centenary" (*Poetry*, November 1961).

64. ____. *Robert Frost: Farm-Poultryman*, edited by Edward Connery Lathem & Lawrance Thompson (Hanover, N.H.: Dartmouth Publications, 1963).

65. ____. "Robert Frost's Speech at Denison University" (unpublished typescript in Amherst College Library).

66. ____. *Selected Letters of Robert Frost*, edited by Lawrance Thompson (New York: Holt, Rinehart and Winston, 1964).

67. ____. *Selected Prose of Robert Frost*, edited by Hyde Cox and Edward Connery Lathem (New York: Holt, Rinehart and Winston, 1966).

68. ____. "Speaking of Loyalty" (*Amherst Graduates' Quarterly*, August 1948).

69. ____. *Stories for Lesley* (Charlottesville: University Press of Virginia, 1984).

70. ____. *Three Poems* (Hanover, N.H.: Baker Library Press, 1935).

71. ____. "A Trip to Currituck, Elizabeth City, and Kitty Hawk (1894): Arthur Palmer Hudson's Transcription of a Tape-Recorded Conversation, March 3, 1961" (*North Carolina Folklore*, May 1968).

72. ____. *Twilight* (Charlottesville, Va.: Reynolds Company for the Barrett Library, 1966).

73. ____. *Twilight* (*Proof 4, The Yearbook of American Bibliographical and Textual Studies*, 1975).

74. ____. "Two Lectures by Robert Frost" (*Biblia*, February 1938).

75. ____. "A Walk with Robert Frost" (*Reader's Digest*, April 1960).

76. ____. "What Became of New England?" (Oberlin *Alumni Magazine*, May 1938).

77. ____. *You Come Too* (New York: Henry Holt, 1959).

78. ____, and C. Day Lewis. "It Takes a Hero to Make a Poem: A Conversation Broadcast, 13th of September, 1957 in the Third Programme of the BBC" (*Claremont Quarterly*, vol. 5, no. 3).

79. Gerber, Philip L. *Critical Essays on Robert Frost* (Boston: G.K. Hall, 1982).

80. ____. *Robert Frost* (New York: Twayne Publishers, 1967).

81. *The Golden Treasury of the Best Songs and Lyrical Poems in the English Language*, selected and arranged by Francis Turner Palgrave, with a fifth book selected by John Press (London: Oxford University Press, 1964).

82. *The Goliard Poets*, edited and translated by George F. Whicher (Norfolk, Conn.: New Directions, 1949).

83. Greiner, Donald J. *Robert Frost* (Chicago: American Library Association, 1974).

84. Hakluyt, Richard. *The Principal Navigations, Voyages, Traffiques and Discoveries of the English Nation* (London: Dent, 1907).

85. Hall, Dorothy Judd. *Robert Frost: Contours of Belief* (Athens: Ohio University Press, 1984).

86. Hawthorne, Nathaniel. *Novels* (New York: Literary Classics of the United States, 1983).

87. Holden, Raymond. *Reminiscences of Robert Frost* (unpublished typescript in Dartmouth College Library).

88. Holmes, John. "Close-Up of an American Poet" (*New York Times Magazine*, March 26, 1950).

89. Horace. *The Odes and Epodes*, with an English translation by C.E. Bennett (Cambridge, Mass.: Harvard University Press, 1988).

90. Hurd, John, Jr. "Poets and Writers Flock to Bowdoin for the Round Table of Literature" (Boston *Globe*, May 10, 1925).

91. James, William. *Writings, 1878–1899* (New York: Library of America, 1992).

92. ____. *Writings, 1902–1910* (New York: Literary Classics of the United States, 1987).

93. Katz, Sandra Lee. *Elinor Frost: A Poet's Wife* (Westfield: Institute for Massachusetts Studies, Westfield State College, 1988).

94. Kazin, Alfred. *New York Jew* (New York: Alfred A. Knopf, 1978).

95. Keats, John. *The Poetical Works of Keats* (Boston: Houghton Mifflin, 1975).

96. Lathem, Edward Connery, compiler. *A Concordance to the Poetry of Robert Frost* (New York: Holt Information Systems, 1971).

97. ____. *Robert Frost 100* (Boston: David R. Godine, 1974).

98. Lentricchia, Frank. *Robert Frost: Modern Poetics and the Landscapes of Self* (Durham, N.C.: Duke University Press, 1975).

99. ____, and Melissa Christensen Lentricchia. *Robert Frost: A Bibliography, 1913–1974* (Metuchen, N.J.: Scarecrow Press, 1976).

100. Longfellow, Henry Wadsworth. *Outre-Mer and Drift-Wood* (Boston: Houghton Mifflin, 1886).

101. Lucretius. *The Nature of Things*, translated by Frank O. Copley (New York: W.W. Norton, 1977).

102. Marcus, Mordecai. *The Poems of Robert Frost: An Explication* (Boston: G.K. Hall, 1991).

103. Mertins, Louis. *Robert Frost: Life and Talks-Walking* (Norman: University of Oklahoma Press, 1965).

104. ____, and Esther Mertins. *Intervals of Robert Frost: A Critical Bibliography* (Berkeley: University of California Press, 1947).

105. Monteiro, George. *Robert Frost & the New England Renaissance* (Lexington: University Press of Kentucky, 1988).

106. Morrison, Kathleen. *Robert Frost: A Pictorial Chronicle* (New York: Holt, Rinehart and Winston, 1974).

107. Morrison, Theodore. "The Agitated Heart" (*Atlantic Monthly*, July 1967).

108. *The New-England Primer: A History of Its Origin and Development*, edited by Paul Leicester Ford (New York: Teachers College, Columbia University, 1962).

109. *New Poets of England and America*, edited by Donald Hall, Robert Pack and Louis Simpson (Cleveland: World, 1957).

110. Newdick, Robert. *Newdick's Season of Frost: An Interrupted Biography of Robert Frost*, edited by William A. Sutton (Albany: State University of New York Press, 1976).

111. Orton, Vrest. *Vermont Afternoons with Robert Frost* (Rutland, Vt.: Tuttle, 1971).

112. Perrine, Laurence. "A Set of Notes for Frost's Two Masques" (*Resources for American Literary Study* VII, 1978).

113. *The Pilgrim Spirit: A Pageant in Celebration of the Tercentenary of the Landing of the Pilgrims at Plymouth, Massachusetts, December 21, 1620*, edited by George Pierce Baker (Boston: Marshall Jones, 1921).

114. Poirier, Richard. *Robert Frost: The Work of Knowing* (New York: Oxford University Press, 1977).

115. Pritchard, William H. *Robert Frost: A Literary Life Reconsidered* (New York: Oxford University Press, 1984).

116. Reeve, F.D. *Robert Frost in Russia* (Boston: Little, Brown, 1964).

117. Richards, E.A. "Two Memoirs of Frost" (*Touchstone*, March 1945).

118. Robbins, J. Albert. *An Interlude with Robert Frost: Being a Brief Correspondence with the Poet and Recollections* (Bloomington, Ind.: The Private Press of Frederic Brewer, 1982).

119. *Robert Frost: A Bibliography*, compiled by W.B. Shubrick Clymer and Charles R. Green (Amherst, Mass.: Jones Library, 1937).

120. *Robert Frost: A Descriptive Catalogue of Books and Manuscripts in the Clifton Waller Barrett Library, University of Virginia*, compiled by Joan St. C. Crane (Charlottesville: University Press of Virginia, 1974).

121. *Robert Frost and the Lawrence, Massachusetts, "High School Bulletin,"* edited by Edward Connery Lathem and Lawrance Thompson (New York: Grolier Club, 1966).

122. *Robert Frost at Agnes Scott College*, compiled by Edna Hanley Byers (Decatur, Ga.: McCain Library, Agnes Scott College, 1963).

123. *The Robert Frost Collection in the Watkinson Library*, compiled by Marian G.M. Clarke (Hartford, Conn.: Watkinson Library, Trinity College, 1974).

124. *The Robert Frost Library, Dedication, October 24, 1965.*

125. *Robert Frost Memorial Service: An Observance of the Poet's 101st Birthday* (East Bridgewater, Mass.: First Parish Unitarian Church, 1975).

126. *The Robert Frost Review* (Rock Hill, S.C.: Department of English, Winthrop College, 1991–).

127. Robinson, Clara Weaver. *Poems by Clara Weaver Robinson; Sonnets and Other Verses by Ethel Robinson Murphy* (Schenectady, N.Y.: Ernest L. Robinson, 1970).

128. Robinson, E.A. *Collected Poems of Edwin Arlington Robinson* (New York: Macmillan, 1961).

129. ____. *King Jasper* (New York: Macmillan, 1935).

130. Rodman, Selden. *Tongues of Fallen Angels: Conversations with Jorge Luis Borges, Robert Frost [et al.]* (New York: New Directions, 1974).

131. *The Schofield Reference Bible*, edited by C.I. Schofield (New York: Oxford University Press, 1945).

132. Sergeant, Elizabeth Shepley. *Fire Under the Andes: A Group of North American Portraits* (Port Washington, N.Y.: Kennikat Press, 1966).

133. ____. *The Trial by Existence* (New York: Holt, Rinehart and Winston, 1960).

134. Shakespeare, William. *The Riverside Shakespeare* (Boston: Houghton Mifflin, 1974).

135. Shelley, Perce Bysshe. *The Poetical Works of Shelley* (Boston: Houghton Mifflin, 1974).

136. Smythe, Daniel. *Robert Frost Speaks* (New York: Twayne Publishers, 1964).

137. Snow, Wilbur. "The Robert Frost I Knew" (*Texas Quarterly*, autumn 1968).

138. Sohn, David A., and Richard Tyre. *Frost: The Poet and His Poetry* (New York: Holt, Rinehart and Winston, 1967).

139. Tennyson, Alfred Lord. *The Poetical Works of Tennyson*, edited by W.J. Rolfe (Boston: Houghton Mifflin, 1974).

140. *This Is My Best,* edited by Whit Burnett (New York: Dial Press, 1942).

141. Thomas, Edward. *The Collected Poems of Edward Thomas* (Oxford: Oxford University Press, 1981).

142. Thompson, Lawrance. *Robert Frost: The Early Years, 1874–1915* (New York: Holt, Rinehart and Winston, 1966).

143. ____. *Robert Frost: The Years of Triumph, 1915–1938* (New York: Holt, Rinehart and Winston, 1970).

144. ____, and R.H. Winnick. *Robert Frost: The Later Years, 1938–1963* (New York: Holt, Rinehart and Winston, 1976).

145. Thoreau, Henry David. *Excursions* (Gloucester, Mass.: Peter Smith, 1975).

146. ____. *Journal* (New York: Dover Publications, 1962).

147. ____. *Reform Papers* (Princeton, N.J.: Princeton University Press, 1973).

148. ____. *A Week on the Concord and Merrimack Rivers; Walden, or, Life in the Woods; The Maine Woods; Cape Cod* (New York: Literary Classics of the United States, 1985).

149. Untermeyer, Louis. *Bygones: The Recollections of Louis Untermeyer* (New York: Harcourt, Brace & World, 1965).

150. ____. *From Another World: The Autobiography of Louis Untermeyer* (New York: Harcourt, Brace, 1939).

151. ____. *Letters of Robert Frost to Louis Untermeyer* (New York: Holt, Rinehart and Winston, 1963).

152. Van Dore, Wade. *Robert Frost and Wade Van Dore: The Life of the Hired Man*, revised and edited by Thomas H. Wetmore (Dayton, Ohio: Wright State University, 1986).

153. Van Egmond, Peter. *The Critical Reception of Robert Frost* (Boston: G.K. Hall, 1974).

154. *The Viking Book of Folk Ballads of the English-Speaking World*, edited by Albert B. Friedman (New York: Penguin Books, 1976).

155. Virgil. *The Aeneid*, translated by Robert Fitzgerald (New York: Random House, 1983).

156. Walsh, John Evangelist. *Into My Own: The English Years of Robert Frost, 1912–1915* (New York: Grove Press, 1988).

157. *Writers at Work: The Paris Review Interviews, Second Series* (New York: Viking Press, 1963).

158. Yeats, W.B. *The Poems* (New York: Macmillan, 1989).

Library Collections

159. Canaday Library, Bryn Mawr College, Bryn Mawr, Pa. 19010.

160. Dartmouth College Library, Hanover, N.H. 03755.

161. Henry W. and Albert A. Berg Collection, New York Public Library, 5th Avenue and 42nd Street, New York, N.Y. 10018.

162. Huntington Library, 1151 Oxford Road, San Marino, Calif. 91108.

163. The Jones Library, 43 Amity Street, Amherst, Mass. 01002.

164. Mugar Library, Boston University, 771 Commonwealth Avenue, Boston, Mass. 02215.

165. Robert Frost Memorial Library, Amherst College, Amherst, Mass. 01002.

INDEX